Further praise for *Daughter of Dust*

'I read Leila's story with infinite gratitude. She shares with those of us from her world that human choice: cheer; resilience and strength can overcome hardship. *Daughter of Dust* is a unique story of leadership by example. I hope that many more Leilas will emerge out of that world to tell their story. Bravo Leila'
Ayaan Hirsi Ali

'This story of a woman born into misery who has had the guts and resilience to change her destiny provides a refreshing glimpse into a country often reported on, but rarely truly explored'
Time Out

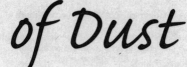

Daughter of Dust

Growing up an Outcast in the Desert of Sudan

WENDY WALLACE

POCKET
BOOKS

LONDON · SYDNEY · NEW YORK · TORONTO

First published in Great Britain by Simon & Schuster UK Ltd, 2009
This edition published by Pocket Books, 2010
An imprint of Simon & Schuster UK Ltd
A CBS COMPANY

This is a work of non-fiction. While all major events of Leila's life
are true, names and details have been changed. Some minor characters
are composites and some childhood events are reconstructions.

1 3 5 7 9 10 8 6 4 2

Simon & Schuster UK Ltd
1st Floor
222 Gray's Inn Road
London WC1X 8HB

www.simonandschuster.co.uk

Simon & Schuster Australia
Sydney

A CIP catalogue record for this book is available
from the British Library.

ISBN: 978-1-84739-635-8

Typeset in Palatino by M Rules
Printed by CPI Cox & Wyman, Reading, Berkshire RG1 8EX

For the abandoned everywhere

Contents

Prologue

The room is always different, always the same. The light is dim, the concrete floor covered in fine, red dust. The cots are still there, their bars dented, the paint worn away. The air is thick with the smell of urine, sickness and grief. The sound of crying bounces from the walls, echoes inside me.

I move from one cot to the other, picking up the children one by one. I hug them, kiss them, laugh with them. As I hold them, they grow calm. As soon as I put down one child, another begins to scream. I move from child to child, trying to give them what they need.

The smallest lie two to a cot, bottles propped in their mouths. In one cot is a bundle, wrapped in white cloth. It is stiff. Silent. Two more arrive under a nanny's arm, wriggling in a torn towel. She lays them on a mattress, naked and screaming.

I step outside, into the brilliant, relentless light. The veranda where we used to play lies empty; a plastic swing hangs motionless. A breeze rises and the seeds of the Beard of the Pasha tree shiver and rattle in the silence.

I know only one thing. It is my responsibility to help these children.

Chapter 1

ABANDONED

I wake to the thump of my own heart, my cheek stuck to the rubber mattress. Flies crawl around my eyes and into the corners of my open mouth. I smell the milky sourness that comes from a roomful of children, sense the warm air on my limbs. For a minute, I lie without moving, absorbed in these sensations that tell me I exist. I am alive.

Then, I'm all yearning.

I wait for a voice that doesn't come. A familiar smell, of bitter oil mixed with perfume. Arms that encircle me. A face I know. But there's nothing. I'm hungry. I begin to yell. I hear my own crying and scream more loudly; the roar fills my head, pierces my ears, until there is nothing in the world but my screaming.

My fingers find the cool bars; as I grip them, my crying slows. Crying is useless. Crying brings nothing. I pull myself

---

3

up, still searching for the face that doesn't come. I bang my head against the metal. Feel the judder that runs through the bars and back into my hands. The jarring of my head against the cot tells me there is something there. Bang, bang, bang.

I can hear other kids doing the same. Banging. Rocking. Thumping.

It's during these days, these months, before I can speak or think, that the 'unfuture' closes around me. The unfuture is a state of emptiness, of waiting, that never ends. Of wanting, that dwindles to hopelessness.

Milk keeps me alive. I clench the bottle between my hands, sucking hard on the teat. I swallow every drop and when it's finished I scream for more. I chuck the empty bottle over the bars; it clatters on the floor. I pause, and look at the way it rolls, empty. Then I begin to yell again, this time banging my head on the wall.

This is my life, given to me by God's will. I won't let it go.

*

A year later, or maybe two, I emerge from Mygoma orphanage, alive. Three of us leave together in a car: me, Amal and Wagir. I am on the seat next to the window, Amal is in the middle and Wagir bounces on the lap of a nanny. No one comes out to see us off. The taxi bumps and lurches over the potholes as it pulls away into the ordinary day. We sit in the back, startled by the light, the noises, the smells.

Amal and I wear the same new cotton dresses, in a pattern of squares with a bobbly texture. The shoulders hang down on our elbows; the hems droop to our ankles. For the first time, I have shoes on my feet. White plastic sandals, strapped tight. I am using one shoe to try and prise off the other when the nanny reaches over and slaps my calf. She wipes away the snot coming out of Amal's nose.

'God protect us,' she mutters, pulling her *tobe* further forwards over her face. 'What is to become of such children?'

I look at her. I don't understand words. Only voices.

The air smells of dust and exhaust fumes, of bean patties frying at stands by the side of the road and the morning's bread, carried in baskets on women's heads. Schoolchildren wait in crowds for buses; goats stand on their hind legs, biting at the leaves on the branches of trees. Lines of cars queue at petrol stations; men exit from the mosque, pulling on their shoes.

The taxi driver winds down his window and calls out to people for directions. He stops in front of a high wall with wrought-iron gates set into it. He leans on his horn and a man emerges and drags open the gates. He sees me staring at him and brings his hand up to his forehead in a sharp salute. The car rolls up a sandy drive edged with bushes, to where a woman stands waiting on the steps of a big house with shuttered windows.

I don't want to leave this car. I get down on the floor, behind the driver, grabbing hold of the bottom of the seat. The nanny drags me out by my arm. A crowd of children gathers, all taller and older than me. They surround us, staring at us. In front of me is a girl with a round, dark face. She has two plaits, small teeth, quick eyes. She steps forwards, grabs me under my armpits and lifts me up. She holds me against her chest, staggers, then slides me on to her hip. I recognize the pressure of her arms, the strength of her body. She is part of a dream I once had. The circle of children, the smell of blossom, fall away as I grope after something out of reach, below the surface of memory.

The girl hugs me hard and, without warning, drops me on to the sandy ground. She walks off. The children laugh and suck their fingers. The nanny climbs back into the battered yellow taxi and it slides down the path to disappear through the open gates.

*

'What are you waiting for?' A woman stands over my bed. She twitches the sheet off me with one hand and with the other lifts me by my arm on to the floor. I feel the chill of the tiles under my feet, see the dizzying pattern of leaves stretched over her belly at the height of my head.

'What's your name?'

I stare at her face.

'Copy the others,' she says, leading me towards the door. 'And you'll be all right.'

So begin my days at the Institute for the Protected. This bed is the centre of my new world. I wake up in it, dizzy from the lack of bars. I wriggle against the wall, press my spine against the plaster, for something solid to tell me where I end and the world begins. The room is full of birdsong; light forces its way around the shuttered window, and falls in stripes and diamonds across the walls. The sheet underneath me is made of rough blue cotton. Below the bed is a brown tiled floor, measured out in squares. A curled shape rests under another sheet on the far side of the room. I know without thinking about it that it is Amal.

A clanging metal bell makes me jump. Two other girls rise immediately from their beds, their eyes still shut. They fold their sheets, holding the corners in their teeth. I slide off the bed and cross the squared floor to where Amal is resting. I can swing open the door of the cupboard and climb up to the third shelf for my dress. There are beads on the next shelf to play with. Beyond this room lie other worlds: the bathroom, where mosquitoes hover and whine in the gloom. Amal and I stick close together in there. The smell – carbolic soap, stagnant water – carries danger. Then there is the big girls' bedroom, next to ours, and the dining room, with chairs crowded around its long table. Behind the house is a sandy garden where we play, and at the end of it a clump of lime trees by the wall, so far away from the house that they are in another country.

This bigger space that stretches from my bed all the way to the trees opens up something inside me. Released from the cot, my movements grow larger. Away from the constant noise of crying, I hear the sound of my own voice. In the mornings, braced against the wall, I experiment with this voice, singing and chatting with the birds until the bell rings.

Whenever I can, I watch the girl. I stare at her quick feet as she plays hopscotch in front of the house. I study her small hands as she eats her breakfast and examine her plaits, the long twists of hair. The nannies call her Zulima. I feel her looking at me. Our eyes meet and glance off each other. Sometimes she grabs me, swinging me on to her lap. 'Say "hello",' she says, leaning her face in close to mine. 'Say "goodbye". Say "Zulima".'

I gaze at her face, her tongue, the movement of her lips. Her breath smells like water.

'What's the matter with you?' she asks, fiercely. 'Don't you remember anything?'

She walks away.

*

The nannies are bad-tempered before the visitors come. From when they arrive, we're not allowed to play inside in case we make a noise. If we do, the nannies slap at us. Some children get hit more than others. Ahmed trips over other kids; he drops things and forgets what he's meant to be doing. He's always in trouble. The nannies call him *Shaitan*. Devil.

The ladies who come for meetings never hit us. They are tall and slim. They wear high-heeled mules, carry handbags. The Director comes out of her office to greet them. Their drivers sit under the trees till they are ready to leave again. Sometimes they let the boys sit in the cars. On their way out, the ladies call us to come and see them. They ask how old we are and what our names are and they talk in bright voices then smile sadly over our heads. I can smell their scent in the air after they've gone. The nannies throw off their shoes and laugh a lot, once the gate closes again.

Every day after lunch we have to lie down and rest. I fidget, waiting for the time to pass. I'm not allowed to talk to Amal, to sing or to sit up. The nannies lie on beds in the hallway, chatting. It's during these afternoons that I learn the words that will cling to my ears all my life: *Awlad Haram. Bint Haram.* Forbidden children. Daughter of shame. Sometimes they talk about one child, sometimes about all of us. Ahmed's name is always on their lips. I hear him coughing, from the boys' bedroom.

Sometimes I hide. I cram myself into a cupboard, crouch behind the door to the big girls' room, press myself behind the trunk of one of the lime trees. I know that when I am found, I might be in trouble. But I like hearing the nannies calling my name, knowing they're searching for me.

What I hate most is when they shove my head into a bowl of water. They rub soap over my head with strong fingers, sloshing more water over me so the soap goes in my eyes. Afterwards I stand between the nanny's knees, my head back, while she drags a comb through my hair. I scream throughout, unless it's Nanny Samia. Nanny Samia is younger than the others; her body is soft and her face round, with three long curving scars down each cheek. I run my fingertips down them as she dries my hair with a towel. She laughs. When she hugs me I feel happy. It reminds me of something.

Amal and I share the room with three other girls. The oldest, Nahid, keeps her clothes on the shelf above mine. Her face is hard and fierce when she looks down at me; she catches hold of my hand and bends it back towards my wrist until it makes a cracking noise. She grabs my biscuit at breakfast and sticks out her tongue when she looks at me. One day she tears the sandal off her foot and attacks me with it, hitting and slapping me all over. She says I've broken her necklace.

*

Amal and I start to go to a special room in the garden of the Institute. Nanny Souad says we have to go because we are *five*. Children who don't live at the Institute come there. They stare at us and we stare at them. All the children have to sit on the floor and a woman stands in front of us. She is not a nanny. She is something else. I don't listen to what she says except when she sings to us. I like hearing her voice, singing.

Amal and I always sit together. When it's time to go back to the Institute for lunch, I hide by a tree outside. I watch the other children going home. There is one girl called Lublubah. The same woman comes every day to meet her. The woman is young and pretty. She wears a pink *tobe* and she has gold bangles on her arms and dark patterns on her hands and feet. She comes up the path, smiling, and when she sees Lublubah she opens her arms. Lublubah runs towards her and the woman lifts her up in the air, kissing her face. I watch every day, I never get tired of seeing it. One day, I ask Lublubah what that nanny's name is and she says she is not a nanny. She says that is her *mother*.

The nannies sleep at the Institute, but the Director arrives in the mornings dressed in a white *tobe*. Her name is Madame. She bends down to shake our hands and sometimes she calls one of the nannies and asks: why haven't they washed our faces, or cut our nails? The nannies always say 'yes' to her and they never say 'no'.

At lunchtime, after I've watched Lublubah go out of the gates, I go and sit on the steps of the Institute until the Director comes out, with her handbag on her arm.

'You here again?' she says, when she sees me on the steps.

I look at her.

'Are you settling in all right?' she asks, in a kind voice.

And then she answers her own question.

'As well as can be expected,' she says.

Musa, the guard, salutes her when she leaves, like he salutes me. I start to salute her too when I see her. It makes her laugh. I feel happy when I hear her laugh. It means she has noticed Leila, and not just a girl with a dirty face.

Chapter 2

GIFT OF ORANGE

Nanny Souad pulls me by the wrist down the path, past the sharp-leaved bushes. My new bunches pull at my scalp, and her scent makes my eyes water. Zulima walks on the other side of Nanny Souad, her nose to the sky, as we pass out of the blue tin gates and on to the road. The nannies say that all the girls at the Institute for the Protected are my sisters; all the boys are my brothers. Then they say Zulima is my real sister. I don't know what they mean. Amal is my sister. Amal is buried in my life like the stone in a mango.

A yellow taxi slows down as it passes. Souad shakes her head and it drives off empty. She lets go of my arm and goes into a kiosk to buy paper tissues. She comes out looking cross and says the shopkeeper only gave her aspirin for change and when she complained he took back the aspirin and gave her chewing gum. She chucks the gum at Zulima and says that

---

some people have no respect; her gold earrings fly about her face, glinting in the sun.

When I remember again where we are going, I feel my feet lifting from the ground. I could jump up to the balconies over the tops of the shops, or on to their flat roofs where the sheets hang out to dry like pieces of paper. Souad clicks her tongue. I am not allowed to skip; the dust will dirty my socks. But I feel like skipping. I say the word again to myself and look around, expecting someone to be able to hear. Mother – it's a word like God. You can't know what it means and it's dangerous to say it out loud. Mother.

She will wear a bright-coloured *tobe*, like Lublubah's mother does. She will have a handbag that shuts with a click, and she will smell of perfume. She will call me 'daughter' and lift me into the air and kiss me. I don't know what will happen after that. I asked Nanny Souad what mothers did and she said they were like nannies except they didn't get paid for bringing up brats. But Nanny Samia said that mothers were nothing like nannies and not to listen to Souad. She said I would understand when I grew up, what a mother was.

A group of men pass us. As we go by, they all turn their heads to stare at Zulima. Their prayer beads hang from their fingers and the hems of their *jellabiyas* are brown at the back where they trail on the ground. A man drives by in a car with a sheep on the back seat making a terrible screaming noise. Even the sheep turns its head to look at Zulima, its nose poking out of the top of the back window. Zulima is meant to look at the ground when she walks along but I can feel her eyes roaming over everything. Zulima is a bad girl. All the nannies say so.

Zulima has spots around her nose and on her chin. At night she holds her face up close against the mirror and squeezes them between her nails. She wears a bra, a red one, not a baggy old white one like Souad's. She dries it under her pillow so no one can see it and in the mornings the padding is all flattened.

Zulima is the oldest girl in the Institute. She's fifteen. The oldest boy is called Rashid. He's sixteen. Zulima and Rashid are enemies. They stand around in the dark under the trees talking in loud voices and pushing each other on the shoulder while the nannies are inside having their supper. Sometimes Rashid grabs hold of her wrists and swings her around and she makes a funny noise that isn't laughing and isn't crying either. Then she slaps him and goes off with the other girls, and he goes off with the boys.

I stop walking and clamp my legs together. Nanny Souad holds her *tobe* out in front of me while I squat down. A dark stain spreads between my feet. I can feel the sun on my back, and hear Souad puffing. She blots her face with tissue. 'I haven't got all day,' she says. 'What's the matter with you, girl?' I scowl at her. I haven't decided yet if I want to be a girl.

We get off the bus outside an enormous building behind high railings. I'm surprised that my mother lives here. Two men with guns propped between their knees sit by the door, one on each side. Nanny Souad has to talk to them before we're allowed to go inside. In the hallway, the air is still and hot; it feels thicker than outside. It's dark. Nanny Souad begins to climb the steps one at a time, holding the banister with both hands. I hurry to catch up with her.

I don't want to live in this place. There are no children here. I don't think there have ever been any children here. It smells like the toilets at the Institute. On the landing, through a half-open door, I see a woman sitting in a kitchen by a silver kettle. She has jars with dried leaves and roots in them around her, and one big one full of yellow sugar. I wonder whether she is my mother. Zulima brushes past and pinches my arm, a small tight pinch between her nails. She has shiny stuff on her lips as if she had just licked them.

'What are you staring at?' she asks.

'Will you tell her about me? Will you remind her? In case she's forgotten.'

Zulima pauses for a second and shoves me so hard I almost fall over. 'Get lost, idiot,' she says. 'What's the matter with you?'

At the top of the stairs we go down a long corridor and the three of us wait in an office. There are two telephones on one of the desks and sunflower-seed husks scattered on the floor underneath. I sneak a look at Nanny Souad to see if she has noticed but her eyes are still; her hands lie in her lap holding a square of paper tissue. Zulima leans against the wall and chews gum. I stand near the door. I'm wondering, what is the matter with me?

I hear a howling noise from along the corridor that reminds me of the sheep. I put my head round the door and see a woman with long white hair creeping along the corridor with two other women in green overalls holding on to her elbows. 'Oh, Prophet,' the old woman cries. 'Prophet, forgive me.' It's the same as what Nanny Sara kept shouting, the night she got a migraine and rolled around on her bed under the moon while the holy man put his hands on her head and all the other nannies burned incense around her and slapped her and poured water on her. There is a bird flying up and down the corridor over their heads; none of them notices.

The woman lifts her head and sees me. The air fills with the noise of her slippers shuffling along the tiles. I jump back into the room to hide under a desk but it's too late; she clamps her arms around me so my face is squashed into her stomach. Nanny Souad and the other women begin to cry. I feel the hot flood between my legs but no one sees because the woman pulls me on to her lap and starts to rock back and forth, wailing like the nannies do when someone goes to Paradise.

I can feel her bones under my bottom, her breath warm on my face. After a bit, she calms down. She licks her fingers and starts dabbing at my eyes and cheeks. Then she pulls the new bunches out of my hair, brings a bottle of oil from inside her clothes, and starts doing them again. The feeling – of her hands plucking at my hair, sorting the strands, but gently and slowly, not like the nannies – reminds me of something. The oil is bitter. I breathe in the smell of it again and again. I remember that I don't like bunches because they mark me out as a girl. I jerk my head away from her hands and open my eyes. Zulima is sitting on the edge of one of the desks. Nanny Souad leans back with a glass of tea in her hand.

No one is talking, so they all hear when my stomach rumbles.

One of the women in overalls asks if I haven't had my breakfast yet, and Souad says that of course I have, all the orphans at the Institute for the Protected get two meals a day plus supper, and don't they have eyes in their heads to see Zulima?

'Do you think a girl grows a shape like that on fresh air, by God?' she says. The women start squabbling about whether the woman in overalls meant we weren't looked after properly.

Zulima uncovers her face and moves a bit nearer although she still doesn't look at the old woman; she's only interested in her nails today and her gum is lasting forever. The old woman gets hold of Zulima's hand and kisses the back of it again and again. She holds it against her forehead and starts on some more about being forgiven. Zulima pulls her hand away.

'Where is my father?' she asks. 'I've got a right to know.' She whispers it, as if she doesn't want Nanny Souad to hear.

'Where can I find him?' she hisses.

The woman moans and holds on to me more tightly. No one has ever held me like this. I think she's going to squeeze me right into her bones. All the time I'm wondering what happened to our mother. We were meant to see her today.

Nanny Souad drains her tea and belches. She stands up and pulls her *tobe* over her round stomach, knotting it at the sides. I slide my feet down to the floor. I don't want to get left behind. My dress is warm and damp against my legs. One of the telephones rings but no one answers it. The old woman feels in the bottom of a faded plastic bag that she has by her feet and brings out two oranges. She hands one to Zulima and holds the other out to me.

'Child, take it. I saved it for you.' Her voice sounds strange;

the words come out separate from each other. I open my mouth but I can't speak. Nanny Souad shoves me forwards with her knee. The orange is shrivelled up, light and hard in my hand. I'm trying to stuff it into my pocket when the old woman grabs me again in her strong, skinny arms and starts to howl just as she did at the beginning.

'Come on, Queen,' says one of the women in overalls. 'Back to the ward. By God's grace, your daughters are alive.'

'Queen?' Nanny Souad laughs. 'Is that what you call her?'

'Just wait till you see the rest of them,' the woman says.

'Mother?' Zulima says. 'Please . . .' But they've pulled her away again, down the long corridor in front of us. Her white hair hangs right down her back.

As we walk out through the gates, Zulima hurls her orange into the drain by the side of the road. It floats, beside a cigarette packet and a dead branch. Sweat trickles from my hair into my eyes. It's the time of day when your shadow disappears underneath you. A woman sits on the ground holding out arms that end in two shiny stumps. She has an open umbrella propped up behind her and an empty bowl in front of her.

'God will provide,' Nanny Souad says as we pass. When we have gone a few steps further, something in my head makes me run back and put my orange in the bowl.

'God bless you, my daughter,' she says.

'You're not my mother,' I hear myself say. 'My mother's in there.'

'God bless you,' she says again.

*

18

I wake up the next morning with an ache in my chest. I'm pressing my fingers against my ribs to make it go away when the bell rings. Amal gets out of bed with her eyes still closed and pushes her feet into her flip-flops. I try to fold my sheet, but I keep getting the corners mixed up. The others have gone. Their beds are empty, the sheets folded neatly at the end of the striped mattresses. I pile mine on the end of my bed in a heap and run to the dining room but Nanny Skinny stops me at the door and snatches my hands up to her nose. 'With soap, girl,' she shouts in her high-pitched voice, pushing me back towards the bathroom. 'Wash with soap.'

By the time I get to the table there is only one chair left, at the far end. Nanny Souad and Nanny Samia sit at the top of the table, mixing milk powder and sugar in the bottom of the tea glasses. Nanny Souad lifts the thermos and pours a thin black trickle of tea, which Nanny Samia stirs with a spoon until it dances round and round. I am the last to get some. I bring my mouth down to the edge of the glass, pressing it against my lip so that it burns. It smells warm and spicy; some of the milk still spins around in lumps.

Rahel, one of the big girls, is sitting next to me. Rahel has far-apart eyes and a face like a grown-up's. She has finished her tea and is staring at mine. I hold the cloudy glass tight between my two hands. The bell goes and everyone begins to scramble out of the room in a rush of chair-scraping and quarrelling. I dip down on to the floor and hide under the table. When I see Nanny Samia's heels walking out of the door, I crawl up to the far end as fast as I can, jump out and fill the pocket of my skirt with milk powder from the big blue tin. I walk out of the room as slowly as I dare, my hands hanging by my sides, my eyes vacant.

Amal is waiting for me by the water pitchers, resting her elbow on one of their wooden lids. I put a little heap of powder in the palm of her hand and she licks it all up in one go, stretching her tongue out of her mouth so I can see the roots straining underneath.

'More.' She holds her arm out like the beggar woman.

'God will provide.'

'Give me,' she whines. 'Or I'm telling.'

'Get lost.' I knock her hand out of the way. 'Go and get your own.'

'Where did you go yesterday?' she asks.

'Mind your own business. I didn't go anywhere.'

I kneel down and hold out my hand and, after a minute, the white cat comes out from behind the wall of the storeroom. Its tongue is rough against my fingers; its belly looks as if it has swallowed a grapefruit. Two of the boys run by and it disappears up over the wall. I wipe my hands on my dress and get up again. Amal's gone. She says cats are bad luck. She's frightened of everything – cats, dogs, the rats that squeeze under the kitchen door at night after it's locked. She's even scared of ants.

The garden is already too hot as I walk across the grass to the lime trees at the far end. The ground is warm and soggy under the soles of my feet. There are patches of sticky mud where the grass has worn away. I sit down in the shade of the trees next to a pile of leaves with curled-up edges. The roots of the trees look like fingers, grabbing the ground. I can hear the clatter of glasses from outside the kitchen and the vegetables man in the distance shouting out that he has potatoes, tomatoes, greens and onions on his cart. He shouts the same thing every morning. A breeze comes through the branches and a few more leaves drift down through the air.

The milk, its weight light against the top of my leg, is my secret. It makes me feel as if I've got something of my own. It doesn't work today. There is a space where I had the happy thoughts of meeting my mother. I don't know what to think about my mother now. I search around in my mind for other happy thoughts. I eat the powder as slowly as I can, pinching it up from my pocket a few grains at a time, but by the middle of the morning there is nothing left. I'm spitting out bits of grit and cotton.

In the evening, we have yoghurt with sugar and bits of torn-up bread left over from lunch. I like yoghurt because we eat it with spoons. The nannies say you will always be hungry unless you eat with your fingers, but I like the curve of the spoon against my tongue, smooth and reliable. When we've finished, the long table is scattered with spoons with bent handles and the two big china bowls are licked clean. The chairs around the table make me think of Musa's teeth, all higgledy-piggledy. There are twenty-four of them, one for each kid and two for the nannies.

After supper, I stand and look at myself in the bit of broken mirror on the back of the cupboard door in the girls' dormitory. It's dark but a little light from the hall comes into the room and after a while my eyes get used to it. I stick my tongue out. I roll my eyes from side to side and draw a finger across my throat like a knife, like the big girls do if we go into their room. My hair is enough for three girls, Nanny Souad says. It's in six thick bunches, three on each side of my head. It looks horrible. I wish I didn't have hair.

I bring my face close to the glass and stare into my eyes until I start to feel dizzy. I wish I hadn't given the orange to the beggar woman. I want to feel its lightness in my hand again. I want to hear the old woman's rusty voice saying that she saved it for me. 'Oh, Prophet,' I whisper to myself. 'Forgive me.' Something catches my eye and in the mirror I see Nanny Souad standing in the doorway with her arms folded over her chest. I want to ask her if it's true that that was my mother. But I keep quiet. I feel the ache again, deep in my chest.

'Malish,' she says in a soft voice. 'Never mind.'

*

Amal, two others – Affaf and Hiba, the younger girls in our dormitory – and I stand in a line in front of the Director's wooden desk, looking at the top of her head. In the middle is the skin of her head, brown and shiny along the wide parting. The hair grows white for a short way, then black. Her pen scratches its way across the lined paper in front of her. High up on the wall behind her there is a picture of the President of Sudan. We have learned his name at Kindergarten – it is Jaafar Mohamed Numeiri and he is the *patron* of the Institute. I don't know what a patron is.

The picture has slipped inside its wooden frame, so the President is falling over backwards. There are curtains over the windows, long red and yellow silky striped ones, and behind them the wooden shutters are open. The light coming through is bright and soft. She has lifted her head up and she is looking at us. My heart always starts punching my chest from the inside if I enter the Director's office, even though she never hits us. Just being in the room makes me feel I must have done something wrong. I don't dare to salute her in here.

'It's time you started school,' she says, finally. She carries on talking, in her quiet, serious voice, but I don't hear much after that. The word 'school' is racing round inside my head, making me want to jump in the air. She clears her throat and tells us to listen carefully. 'Education will be your father and mother. I'm relying on you not to let down the Institute for the Protected – or its patron.' She turns her head and smiles at the picture as if it can hear her.

'There is no reason why you should feel ashamed of your-selves, girls. And remember –' her voice gets more certain '– God sees everything.' We stand in silence until she waves her hand for us to leave the room.

I have an uncomfortable feeling in the top of my head for the rest of the day, as if I'm being spied on. I look up but the sky over the Institute is as blank as ever, with no clouds, no birds – not even a disappearing puff of the smoke that aero-planes leave behind.

*

I can't wait to start school. It's a new happy thought. I skip when I'm going down the long, dark corridor in the middle of the Institute and Nanny Souad says that if she has to listen to my singing any more she will go crazy. Sometimes, I hide in Musa's hut, just so I can think about school with no one bothering me. The walls are made of mud and there are little tree trunks holding them up. The roof is made of thick yellow straw that smells musty. It's dark inside and his spare *jellabiya* hangs on a string that goes from one side of the hut to the other. A chicken sits under the bed.

When Musa went to school he had to make his own ink, out of black stuff from the fire and something his mother made in the kitchen. He had to find a strong bit of straw and make it sharp to write with. He breaks a bit off from the roof of the hut and shows me how he held it in his hand. Only boys went. They wrote bits from the Holy Book on a special wooden board. Musa knows everything. I think about asking him what mothers do but I decide he must have forgotten by now.

The Director makes our school clothes herself on a sewing machine that she brings to her office. She draws the dresses in white chalk on the cloth and cuts them out with a pair of giant scissors. Mine is green, with a square bib at the front and back and a wide skirt that does up with a button on each side. It's stitched with white cotton and the lines go along the bottom of the skirt in little steps. It's the first dress I've ever had that was made specially for me. When I try it on, with its white short-sleeved shirt underneath, I feel that my whole life has already altered, and that the girl looking back at me from the mirror is someone new – someone better than me, more important. The dress is loose and hangs down below my knees. I run to the Director's office, to show her.

I stand in front of her desk and salute her as hard as I know how. She laughs and comes round to the front of her desk. She hugs me and says it's good to see a smile on my face at last.

Amal's dress is identical to mine, but looks shorter because she is taller. We always end up wearing the same clothes. She keeps asking me if I know what school is. I'm not sure what it is, except that it's something to do with Kindergarten and all the older kids go there every day on a bus. When they come back there is something different about them. They talk more loudly and sometimes they have writing on their hands.

'It's like a mosque,' I tell her. 'But for kids. They go there and eat holy words.'

'Liar,' she says. 'It's a place for books. Rahel told me about it. I'm going to be a teacher when I grow up.'

*

It's Ramadan and the nannies are extra bad-tempered. Samia says it's from fasting. Some of the kids are fasting too – Rashid is, and Ekhlas. Ekhlas says she won't even swallow her spit.

There are more boys than girls in the Institute. Three girls live in the big girls' room: my sister Zulima, the girl with the far-apart eyes, called Rahel, and another called Ekhlas. Ekhlas is quiet and wears a headscarf when she goes out. Rahel picks fights with everyone. Zulima likes dancing and laughing. She doesn't like peeling potatoes or washing sheets in a tin bowl with Omo. Zulima always gets into trouble with the nannies.

Nanny Samia says she was shaped in Paradise, and that's why the other nannies don't like her.

Five girls live in our dormitory now: me, Amal, the two younger girls, Hiba and Affaf, and the baby of the Institute, whose name is Quarratulain and who has one hand. Her bed has bars round it but she has learned to climb out, gripping on to the top bar with her hand and her chin. She's not scared, even of the boys, and if she doesn't get what she wants, she whacks us with her hand, or pulls at our mouths when we're talking to her.

A van arrives one morning and two men carry a carton into the storeroom. There are red letters on the side of the box and Amal says they spell 'Bata'. She pretends she can read. Later, when the nannies have chosen what they want, we are allowed to go in there. There is a mountain of shoes mixed up on the floor and all of us rush at them, screaming. Rashid elbows me in the face as he reaches for a huge white shoe that looks like a boat. I have already decided that I want boys' shoes too. I grab the first ones I see, clamp them against my chest and run outside.

The light is blinding and I feel dizzy. My nose is bleeding. It drips down the top of my lip and splashes inside one of the shoes. I force the shoe on to my foot but it takes me a long time to get the buckles done up. When I succeed I stand up, carefully, so my nose doesn't start off again. The shoes are heavy on my feet and one is too big.

'All right, kid?' asks Rashid. It's the first time he has ever spoken to me on my own. He's wearing two of the big white shoes, with the laces in long, silky bows. He looks at my face then kneels down in front of me. I'm so surprised I can't speak. He undoes the buckles in no time with his long, thin fingers and does them up again, pushing the silver fork through holes further along the strap. The shoes feel better. He nods and walks off, whistling.

That evening, the younger boys play with the box. They push it up and down the path with one walking inside it with his head sticking out of the top, making *rat-a-tat-tat* noises and the rest slashing at the bushes with sticks. They say the box is a tank, and they all laugh when they jump up and down and say they killed a rebel. I think it's stupid. I'm trying to whistle but all I can hear is the rushing of air through my lips.

Nanny Samia says the war is over now and the country is at peace with itself. Nanny Zeinab says the country will never be at peace, with infidels occupying half of it. Nanny Zeinab's youngest son was killed in the war; he is a martyr and has gone to Paradise. Musa has a picture of Paradise on the wall inside his hut. It's a green place with a river running through the middle of it and flowers growing on its banks. There are five chicks now in his hut, as well as the chicken. He calls her the mother hen.

On the last day of Ramadan, Musa comes through the gate pulling a sheep with its front feet tied together. He puts down water for it in a bowl but it doesn't drink any. It's still standing there beside his hut when we go inside to sleep. In the morning it's gone. The ground beside the storeroom is dark and sticky. We have a special lunch for Eid and Rashid gives me a big bit of meat from the tray that was meant for the older boys. Rashid says to Zulima that she ought to look out for me more. He says it is her *duty*, and as he looks at her the round thing that looks like a pebble in the front of his throat moves up and down.

*

At first, I think the bus has stopped outside a place for animals. There are lions and crocodiles and giraffes painted all along the white wall. When we get off the bus, I hear a wave of girls' voices and for a minute I think I'm going to have to go to the toilet immediately. I press my legs together under the scratchy green skirt and the urge passes. Amal and I walk through the tin gates into a crowd of tall girls. They're all wearing dresses the same colour as mine, with white shirts underneath. They laugh and walk along the path in big groups, so we have to jump out of the way. For a while we just stand there, holding hands. A woman says we're late and pulls us into a room.

There is a blackboard stuck to the wall and torn netting over the windows. The desks are in pairs, with seats fixed to them. The woman pushes us into one of them and goes away. The teacher asks us our names but when I open my mouth to tell her I am Leila Aziz, nothing comes out. I look at Amal to see if she will say my name for me but the seat next to me is empty. She's under the desk. I feel the punching in my chest. The teacher will think I am deaf and dumb, like Nanny Souad's niece.

Her name is Mrs Khadija. She has black-framed glasses and on her feet she wears flat brown leather sandals. The light from the open door makes a shadow of her over the blackboard as she stands there with a pointer in her hand. She starts to write, making one downward line then curved ones with dots under or over them. They look like birds, flying across the bumpy surface of the board. As she writes, she makes sounds. 'Alif. Ba. Ta.' The squeak of the chalk makes me shiver, even though it's stuffy in the classroom. I get a feeling in my head that the other girls are staring at me. When I look round, they look away. I kick Amal under the desk, to make her get up on her seat, but she just stays there, whimpering, with her head between her knees.

At the end of the day, Mrs Khadija says she hopes everyone will welcome the new girls and make them feel at home. When I realize she is talking about me and Amal I feel proud. We are new girls, just as I thought when I first saw myself in the green dress. Our life is beginning.

On the bus on the way home, Amal starts showing off.

'Why is she teaching us the alphabet?' she asks. 'When we learned it at Kindergarten?'

'How do you know what she was teaching us?' I reply. 'When you spent all day on the floor?'

'I've got ears, haven't I? It was just kids' stuff that I know already. Rahel said there would be books to read.'

Her face is sulky and her dress is brown with dust. After school we play henna, pasting our feet with mud flowers like the nannies do on Fridays, pretending we are grown-up women. I only play it because Amal wants to. I don't ever want to be a grown-up woman. Where will I live? The Institute is only for kids.

*

Zulima tried to refuse to come but Nanny Souad said she had to. Zulima talks to herself under her breath all the way to the bus stop, and kicks little stones so they skip away down the road in front of us. I wonder if the old woman will give me another orange. The light is ugly today, flat and dull. I don't feel like skipping, or even walking. The hot air on my skin makes me tired and the smell of the rubbish smouldering on the corner of the main road sticks in my throat.

A man winds down his car window and asks Zulima if she's feeling hot today. Zulima says she can't move without people bothering her and Nanny Souad says: what does she expect, walking along with her hands turned outwards like that? Zulima mutters something I don't understand and Nanny Souad swings her fat arm at her but Zulima jumps out of the way. A passing woman clicks her tongue and says: what shameful behaviour is this between mother and daughter, families ought to sort out their problems in their own homes, not on the street. When she has gone, Nanny Souad says Zulima will be thrown out of the Institute if she carries on like this and that her blood pressure is getting the better of her, and if she drops dead Zulima will know whose fault it is. Zulima says it will be Nanny Souad's fault because she didn't want to come anyway and Nanny Souad says Zulima always has to have the last word, doesn't she, and Zulima says no, Souad always has to. After that, no one says anything until we get off the bus outside the same big building.

The guards still have their guns between their legs, as if they have not moved. But this time we don't go upstairs to the office. We go to the *ward*, around the back. There is a gate with bars on it and the old woman stands on the other side of it in a room full of people. The others look different from her. They have silver stubble on their heads. They wear torn shifts and their skin hangs from their arms in little folds. When they smile, they look like Quarratulain did, before she grew teeth. 'Goodbye, Queen,' the nurse says when she's got the gate unlocked. 'Have a good time with your daughters.'

We sit on a concrete bench in the big, dry garden. There's a tree behind the bench and the shadows of the leaves move over my feet. She wears pale powder on her face and a yellow dress with right angles of stitches over it. Her white hair is in one long plait down her back. I can smell her sour smell again, with a trace of the oil mixed in underneath. Before long, Nanny Souad says she is going to drink tea with the nurses. When she has gone, we sit in silence for a while. I begin to tell her about school. I describe Mrs Khadija's sandals and how she tells us stories about a man called Jabber, who always makes mistakes. I tell her that I write with my right hand and Amal writes with her left hand and the water at school tastes salty and some of the girls don't want to sit near us because they say their mothers won't let them.

I tell her how Affaf falls asleep on the seat of the bus every day after school with her thumb in her mouth, and Zulima has to carry her down the steps of the bus when we get back to the Institute. And that Nanny Souad says I shouldn't think that just because I go to school now I can get *above myself*, and we have to take our uniforms off as soon as we get back to the Institute because we will *ruin* them otherwise.

She doesn't say anything. After a while, I stop talking. I can hear the people in the hospital in the distance. They sound like the birds, making high, short noises that float on the air. A man comes around with a box of cold lemonade and Pepsi on the back of a bicycle, clicking his bottle tops between his fingers. I feel thirsty. He slows right down when he gets to us and clicks extra loud but our mother doesn't seem to notice him. Zulima sits on the far end of the bench, looking in the other direction.

The Queen has her carrier bag with her again. When the man has passed by, she digs about inside it with her skinny fingers and brings out a teaspoon. I don't say anything because if Zulima thinks I want it, she won't let me keep it. I keep my face stiff and look at the dead grass on the ground, the way it has gone white like our mother's hair. When she holds it out towards me, I take the spoon and put it in my pocket without saying a word.

'You don't like it,' she says, in her rusty voice. They are the first words she has spoken. I was beginning to think she couldn't talk at all any more. She gets another teaspoon out of the bag and holds it out to Zulima. Zulima picks it out of her hand and chucks it towards the bushes with the white flowers.

She grabs our mother's shoulders and begins to shake her.

'Where is my father?' she asks. 'Tell me, for God's sake.'

I get the pain in my chest. It isn't right for Zulima to shake her.

'Where's *her* father?' Zulima asks, rolling her eyes at me.

When the old woman still keeps silent, Zulima sits down on the bench again.

'I might as well be dead,' she says, and she puts her face in her hands. There are dark patches under her arms, on the cotton of her shirt.

I'm sick on the bus on the way back to the Institute. I know it's my job to take care of this woman called my mother. That is how I think of her now. She is the woman called my mother. She needs me to look after her. I don't know what Zulima means, about my father and her father. Nanny Souad says I've made the whole bus stink. Zulima goes to sit at the front and she leans her head against the window and stares out of it as if she has nothing to do with me. I wipe my mouth on the hem of my dress and sit up very straight, like we have to at school. The teaspoon makes my palm sweat.

*

Two new children come to the Institute. They are brothers. They look the same and they're both as tall as each other. Samia says they're *twins* and that the other nannies think they'll bring bad luck, and that's why they don't like them. Amal and I are given the job of looking after them. One is called Mohamed and the other one is Mahmoud, but some of the nannies can't tell which one is which. They tie a string around the arm of one of them and they still can't remember, so they start to call them 'with string' and 'without string'.

'With string' is Mohamed and without is Mahmoud. One day, the string breaks and I find I know which one Mohamed is. They look the same but they are nothing like each other. Mahmoud is bossy and not frightened of anything. Mohamed follows him like a shadow, running where he runs, sitting where he sits, watching everything he does. The nannies call both of them 'boy' after that.

Musa sings in the early morning when he goes around the garden with his hosepipe, trickling water over the leaves of the bushes along the edge of the path and around the roots of the lime trees. However often he waters them, the bushes are brown with dust by the end of the day and the grass behind the Institute is scratchy and dry underfoot. As he walks around, he sings songs about his beloved and how her face is like a lamp in the dark night. It makes me and Amal laugh so hard our stomachs begin to hurt. Musa only uses his hosepipe to water things, never to hit people.

If no water comes out of the tap when he turns it on, he sits on his three-legged chair outside his hut and carves birds out of cow horns. They stink. He tells us about the time when he was a boy in his village, and he says that that was *long ago* and *far away*. I like hearing about Musa's village, with its mosque in the middle painted green and white and the shopkeeper lying on his back next to the bean pot and the men going off to the fields in the mornings on their donkeys with their slippers nearly touching the ground. Sometimes, when Amal isn't around, I try singing. It's strange to hear my voice vibrating through my chest. I think I must have another girl inside me, and she is the one that sings.

I am always hungry. There is a new cook in the kitchen and she makes a stew I love, with greens and tomatoes and little scraps of meat in it. We have our lunch in two big groups. I'm in the younger kids' group. Nanny Samia sometimes sits down with us and teaches us how to eat. She says you should-n't reach right across the tray, you should eat from the food nearest to where you're sitting. Eat with your right hand, except for Quarratulain whose right hand got cut off in the hospital after it got *infected*. Don't lick your fingers. She says that eating is not a race and that we will make ourselves sick if we don't chew. But it is a race, whatever she says, because if you don't eat as fast as everyone else you don't get enough and the plate is empty and wiped clean with the remains of the bread before you've even started to fill your belly.

I can eat faster than anyone except when it's dried fish. Those days, I eat only bread. I hate dried fish, especially the one that they say if you eat it dogs will follow your hand. The smell comes up off the tray as if it were still a fish, swimming through the air. It makes me want to be sick. I eat my bread with my right hand and hold my nose with the other, but later, when they've taken the tray away, I can still smell it in my hair when I chew the ends of my bunches, and on Amal's breath when she whispers in my face.

Nanny Zeinab catches me one morning with my hand in the milk-powder tin. She drags me to Nanny Souad, who is sitting in the kitchen, and makes me open up my pocket. She says that Souad must have brought me up like a heathen, because I am a thief. Nanny Souad starts shouting that Zeinab is a fine one to talk and she wants to know how her son can afford to live in a house with two storeys when he is meant to be occupied as a clerk at the health ministry. Nanny Zeinab says that Souad is jealous because no man in her family ever had a responsible government job and all they were ever fit for was mending the shoes of their betters. Nanny Souad gets so angry she faints. Nanny Skinny has to go to the shop for vitamin pills to revive her.

While they're all still shouting and quarrelling, I hide under Musa's bed. Later he comes in and sits on the bed and sings a song about a girl who ate honey every day in her mind, and how it made her sweet. His heels are cracked like the mud under the lime trees and his toenails look like the hooves of goats. When Nanny Souad comes looking for me, he says he hasn't seen me, and hasn't she got anything better to do than try to cure hunger with slaps? It's dark by the time I come out and I think she might have forgotten, but she grabs me as soon as she spots me and whips me with the short bit of hosepipe that she keeps in the kitchen. It hurts so much everything goes dark behind my eyes. I curl up in a ball on the floor of the dormitory but I can't get away from her until Nanny Samia makes her stop.

At school the next day, I can't lean back on my chair. Mrs Khadija asks if I've hurt myself. Did I fall over? She makes me stay behind in the classroom at break time so she can look at my back. When I lift up my shirt, she makes a noise like sneezing and says, 'Oh my God.'

That night, I still can't get comfortable. As I lie on my stomach in the dark, listening to Nanny Souad snore, I pray to God to make her have an accident. I imagine the Director calling us all into her office and saying in a sad voice that Nanny Souad fell into a drain in the dark and broke her leg. She can't run after children any more. Or her hair caught fire when she was frying doughnuts. She doesn't want to show her scarred face in public. Or – I only think this quickly because I know it's wrong – Nanny Souad got malaria in her head. She died *tawaaaaali kida*. That's what the nannies say when they mean 'straight away', 'immediately', with no time to alter anything.

*

Girls at school are different from us. They have shiny skin and plump arms. They smell of Lux perfumed soap. They have *shoe bags* and fathers who drop them off at school in the mornings from white cars with blue windows. They don't fight but they cry at the slightest thing and they laugh all the time. I don't know why they laugh so much. I feel as if I'll never know what they are laughing about. 'Why don't you ever laugh?' I say to Amal one night after school. I practise laughing, throwing my head back and showing all my teeth.

'What's the matter with you? Did you turn into a hyena?' she says, and puts her head back into her book.

For homework, we have to copy out words in our exercise books. I don't like homework, so I don't do it. Amal loves homework. She writes *sentences*. She is always begging the nannies to buy her a Bic pen or give her some paper to write on. She takes the Director's old newspapers from the kitchen and lies on her bed in the dormitory, moving her finger along the lines and making sounds. After a while, she stops making the sounds and just looks at the words without saying anything. She's given up trying to read. The nannies say she's lazy.

Soon, I know everything about school. I know which class-room is ours and how to get from the gate to the water pitchers. I know where the toilets are but I never use them, because the other girls whisper if I go in there. I know how to push and shove in the line for a breakfast sandwich, and the names of everyone in our class. I know what school uniform is. Some of the girls have dresses with pleats all around them. Some of them have green ribbons in their hair and socks with lace around the tops. I go hot when I first notice the lace. I thought my dress was the best in the world, but now I can see that it isn't.

My favourite lesson is general knowledge. Mrs Khadija tells us funny things, like how to tell a real pearl by biting it between your front teeth to see if it feels gritty, and that pink flamingos go round in groups of seven. She says that in some countries women can be President, and that a man once left his footsteps on the moon. At the end, before the bell, she asks, 'Does anyone have anything to tell the class?' Wifaq always has something to tell the class.

One morning in general knowledge, she asks us what *facts* we know. While she is turned away to the board I imitate Wifaq, jiggling on my bottom and thrusting my hand towards the ceiling fan. Everyone laughs. 'Yes, Leila?' Mrs Khadija says, without turning round. All the girls twist on their seats to look at me. My heart starts its punching routine. I put my face close to the desk and pretend to be working in my book. I hear Wifaq's voice.

'Sudan is the biggest country in Africa, miss. A hundred piasters make a guinea.'

'Thank you,' says Mrs Khadija. 'Now, who else has some general knowledge? Amal?' Amal doesn't answer, as usual. Mrs Khadija is kind to everyone. But I'm sure she doesn't like Wifaq.

The other girls don't know we're from the Institute. Our teacher doesn't know either, because she smiles at me if she walks past me and always says hello in the mornings and asks me how I am, as if she were talking to a grown-up, or someone important. She says hello to Amal too and tells her she is *top of the class* in reading and writing. After half-term, the whole school is going to the zoo. Everyone has to bring a pound, she says. 'Tell your parents to give you the money in the morning.' She looks over at us. 'Except the Institute girls, of course. You don't need to bring anything.' She smiles and brushes the chalk dust off her fingers, then glances up at me. Her face changes. She turns round to clean the blackboard and says we can go to breakfast early.

I can't eat my sandwich. The bread is sponge, and the sludge of cold beans in my mouth makes me sick. I spit out the first mouthful and throw the sandwich, still in its newspaper wrapping, over the wall. I squat down and hold my knees tight against my chest. The dress doesn't cover them any more. The other girls are playing hopscotch on the far side of the compound; the wall throws a strip of dark shadow over their feet. In the distance the teachers laugh inside their staff room. Mrs Khadija comes out. She walks back to our classroom with one arm full of books and the tea glass on a saucer in the other hand. Usually I like carrying it for her, in both hands, making sure none spills. But today I ignore her.

Amal stands next to me, one foot bent against the wall. I can hear her breathing through her mouth, like she does when she's concentrating. She has bits of splintered wood and lead on her bottom lip, where she has been chewing her pencil. Two buttons hang from my white shirt like teeth waiting to fall out. My bunches have lumpy brown rubber bands wound round them. I do not know how fast light travels or whether the flowers of the jasmine plant are poisonous. The other kids are right – there is something wrong with us.

I lift my head from my knees and shade my eyes with the palm of my hand. Wifaq stands on one foot with her hands on her hips. Her hair is in thin, oiled ropes with coloured beads on the ends that click when she shakes her head. I imagine banging her head against the white wall, her face turning ugly as she starts to cry. She looks over at me from the other side of the yard. Our eyes meet and I stare at her until my eyes begin to burn and I have to look away. She laughs, jumps into the last square with both feet and throws her hands in the air. That is when I decide to fight Wifaq.

Chapter 3

SCENTED SMOKE

It's May and very hot. In the afternoons, the rain hurls itself at the Institute as if it wants to dissolve it. There are pictures of floods in the evening, on the Sudan Television news. There's a shot of a boy swimming in a river that has telegraph poles and tree tops sticking up out of it. It's Sennar, on the Blue Nile, the man says, and lots of people and animals have *drowned*.

It's the school holidays and there's nothing to do except sing. There's a pile of jigsaw puzzles in the Director's office but we are not allowed to play with them because we will lose the pieces. Amal likes the rain; she stays on the veranda all day long, telling stories to Hiba and Affaf and Quarratulain and getting them to write their names in the sticky dust with their fingers. Amal always wants to play soppy games, like making henna patterns, or mixing up incense from stones and leaves. She doesn't like marbles, she doesn't like playing catch. She hates football. I love football. Rashid is the captain of the team. Sometimes he says I'm just a girl so I can't play. Sometimes he says they need me in goal, and that I'm as good as any boy. He sounds like a man when he speaks; his voice is deep. I ask him why he and Zulima aren't friends and he rubs the top of my head and says I ask a lot of questions, by God.

I'm sitting on the floor outside the dormitory one morning, picking at a scab on my knee, when Zulima comes out of the Director's office. She walks along the corridor as if she hasn't seen me and goes into the big girls' room. I hear her crying – muffled, as if she has her face in the pillow. It goes on and on. I've never heard Zulima cry like that before except on the first day we went to see our mother. When we came back to the Institute afterwards, she went into her room until it got dark and missed supper. Nanny Skinny took a cup of tea and some biscuits on a tray into the big girls' room. A bead of blood appears on my knee. I put my mouth to it, feeling the strange, metallic taste. I'm rolling my tongue, trying to make the sides curl up towards each other, when the Director darts out of her office.

She is wearing a black skirt down to her ankles and she walks along the hall in quick little steps, shouting for Nanny Souad. Souad hurries out of the kitchen, trying to swallow a big mouthful of something, and they both go back into the office. I slide over, nearer to the door. A man has been to the Institute, to ask to marry Zulima. He has seen her walking by on her way to school. He works as a guard at one of the big houses nearby. He wants a good Muslim girl, serious about her faith. When the Director says that, Nanny Souad gives a laugh like a dog bark.

'He brings a dowry of three hundred pounds,' the Director says. 'I wonder if he's too old. Mind you, he can't be forty yet.'

Nanny Souad snorts. 'We'll talk to her, madam, don't you worry. She won't get a better offer. I happen to know his sister-in-law. I saw her at a wedding last week.'

'I see,' says the Director, and her voice is cooler than before. 'I thought he seemed to know rather more about our young ladies than I would have expected. In fact, I tried to persuade him that Ekhlas was the most devout. What exactly did you . . .'

Their voices go quiet and I can't make out what they're saying after that.

The floor is hard and dusty underneath me. Some of the tiles are cracked from one side to the other; some have missing corners. I'm waiting for the kitchen to be empty. Sometimes after lunch they leave food out on the table – an open tin of tomato purée or a bowl of peanut butter or some bread – and they don't lock the door. I can eat anything, as long as it's not dog-will-follow-your-hand fish. But Nanny Skinny is in there, talking to Musa. She talks and he doesn't. Just occasionally, I hear his voice saying, 'True. True. Isn't that true?' He sounds as if he is half asleep.

I press my back against the wall and try to think about Zulima. She has sharp nails and small feet. After school, she watches Egyptian soap operas on the new black-and-white television the nannies have on the veranda. She sits on a chair with her elbows on her knees and her face on her hands and stares at the screen so hard it's as if she isn't in the Institute for the Protected any more – she's living with the people on the television instead. She puts cream on her face, out of a sachet, and when it's empty she squeezes it between two fingers from the bottom to the top to get a bit more out. She dances with her friends. They laugh too loudly and they won't get out of bed in the mornings until the nannies start pulling at their ears.

Before school, it's her job to sweep the ground outside the Institute. She does it with one hand behind her back, bending down from her waist, holding the grass brush in the other hand, singing to herself. Swish, swish, swish. When she bends over like that you can see her narrow waist from the back, and her wide hips. From the front you can see her breasts inside the neck of her *jellabiya*, spilling out of the red bra. Even when she puts on her school uniform with the white shirt, she does-n't look like a student.

I dig my fingers down as far as they will go between the tiles, feeling the gritty cement under my nails. I lick my knee and think about what it means to get *married* and why Zulima won't get a *better offer*. The remains of the scab have gone soft. I rip it off and see the raw shine of new skin that has been growing in secret underneath. It hurts.

*

The nannies splash tea on the table and give everyone extra sugar and a whole packet of biscuits. Nanny Zeinab lifts both hands up over her head and starts clapping and moving her scrawny hips round in circles, her white hair waving up and down on her head like the drawing in our science textbook of someone who has had an electric shock. She walks over to where Zulima is sitting.

'Good morning to the bride,' she says with her mouth by Zulima's ear, but so everyone hears.

Zulima stands up so fast her chair falls over backwards behind her. She rushes out of the room, leaving it lying there. I get off my chair and pick it up for her. Without thinking, I follow her to the big girls' room.

She's just standing in the middle of the room, doing nothing. But instead of shoving me back into the corridor she points for me to sit on her bed. She opens the cupboard and gets a carton of chocolate milk out from underneath her clothes. I think for a moment she's going to give it to me. But she looks at me as if she has forgotten I'm there and drinks it until she's sucking up air. Her eyes are red where they should be white. As the sides of the carton squash inwards, I wonder if our mother has died. I hold my breath. Sometimes I think that if I hold my breath I can stop things happening. I close my eyes as well. I don't want her to say that the Queen has gone to Paradise. I haven't looked after her yet. It works. She doesn't say anything at all. I sit there for a long time, until I hear the chairs scraping the floor in the dining room. I open my eyes.

As I do, I realize that my sister is looking at me. Right at me. She has never looked at me like this before. Her face is smeared with snot and tears and she has chocolate milk in a line over her top lip. Her eyes look as if they are melted. They are the shape of almonds. I get a little shock as I look into them, like when Amal and I touched tongues. I've never looked at her before, either.

'I'm getting married,' she says. 'They've settled it all between them.'

I pull my eyes away from hers. My feet dangle off the side of the bed. I can see my big toenails through the holes in my plimsolls, one on each foot. I still don't know what *married* is.

'I don't know what to do,' she says.

I try to think about what she should do. I can't think of anything, except asking Mrs Khadija to help her. Mrs Khadija says there is *no hurry* for girls to get married. I open my mouth to say that but something else comes out.

'Why don't you ask our mother what to do?'

She starts to laugh. I notice again how small her hands are, nearly the same size as mine even though she is years older than me.

'She can't do anything in this world,' she says. 'I need my father. Otherwise, my life is finished.'

I don't know what she means.

'Wifaq called us bastards,' I say. 'She says she's not allowed to talk to us.'

It's not true but it works. Zulima springs round, dropping the carton on the floor. 'Little bitch,' she says. 'You have to fight her. You beat her up properly. If you don't, I'll kill you.' She draws her fingers across her throat and stares at me with her puffy eyes open extra wide. I feel relieved. She has gone back to being Zulima.

In the morning, Rashid doesn't come for his tea. He's not on the bus to school, or at the big kids' tray at suppertime when they gobble down the leftover rice. When it's been dark for a long time, I ask Nanny Samia where he is and she says she doesn't know. The Institute isn't the same without him and in the days that follow I am always listening for his deep voice in the air, or the sound of his whistle. I don't say anything to Zulima. You'd think she would be pleased that Rashid was gone but she goes round all the time with a face like thunder and even the nannies are careful about what they say to her, as if she were a snake that might bite.

*

On Friday mornings, the nannies lie head to toe on the beds in the *rakuba* after breakfast, blackening their coffee beans in a skillet on the charcoal stove and telling each others' fortunes. Sometimes one of them is predicted to get a refrigerator, or a television. Or one of them says to another that soon her husband will buy a car. Or that the junior wife will be infertile, or that her hair will all fall out. One day, Nanny Zeinab asks if she will see her son again. Nanny Samia throws the cowrie shells and they all go quiet; the seven shells lie on the ground for a long time, scattered and in no particular pattern. In the end, Nanny Samia says without even looking at the shells that Nanny Zeinab will be re-united with her son in Paradise, if God wills it.

If there is no wind, one of them drags a big electric fan out from the kitchen. It turns its head from side to side and sends the cool breeze from one corner of the room to the other. If the electricity stops, the nannies get us to make fans out of folded newspaper and swish the air over their faces. The *rakuba* has wooden posts driven into the ground in each corner and a roof of papyrus reeds, long and straight and yellow, tied to round poles. The sides are open, shaded with sheets of pink cotton that move with the breeze. The floor is made of hard, smooth mud. It is a private place, out of sight of everybody, and the boys aren't allowed to come in.

One day Musa is in there, digging. He makes a round, deep hole in the ground in one corner and after he has finished, he goes out of the Institute gates with an empty bucket in his hand and an old scarf wrapped around his head. He comes back as it's getting dark, with mud he says he has brought from the sea. That's what he calls the Nile, even though Mrs Khadija says it's a *river* not a *sea*. In the morning he lines the hole with mud, and by lunchtime, when it has dried out, he covers it in another layer, slapping it on with his hands and smoothing it all out, wiping the sweat out of his eyes on the shoulder of his *jellabiya*.

While he's doing it, he tells us a story about a man in his village who stabbed his daughter in the stomach. He buried her body underneath a tree and told all the neighbours she had run away to Khartoum. After that, the trunk of the tree began to swell up in the shape of a woman's belly. Nine months later, the tree split open and gave birth to a girl. When I ask him why the man killed his daughter, Nanny Samia calls out that we are stopping Musa from doing his work and we should get out of his way.

'He killed her because she was *pregnant*,' Amal says later.

'Oh,' I say. 'Of course.'

Afterwards, I see Musa going back to his hut by the gates. His hands look as if they are made of mud, grey right up to his elbows. When he sees me looking at him, he waves them at me and I run away.

The next evening, the nannies drop coals into the bottom of the pit, all glowing red with a coating of silver ash starting round the edges. They heap on wood and bits of leaves and roots and grasses till a thick smoke pours off it. They are talking and laughing more than usual, as if it were a holiday. Nanny Souad and Nanny Zeinab are friends again and Nanny Souad has a new ring on her hand made of a big round gold coin.

Zulima sits on the edge of one of the beds, biting her nails and swinging her legs backwards and forwards. She has to take off her *jellabiya*, right there in the *rakuba*. She is wearing faded old pants that are much too small for her. When she takes off her bra, I have to look away. Nanny Samia wraps a blanket around her shoulders and she crouches over the smoke on a straw mat with a hole in the middle of it.

Nanny Zeinab turns the bucket upside down and starts drumming on it with her hands very flat, singing a song about a girl who is the same to men as a lamp is to moths. The nannies all join in, their voices high and loud. The smoke creeps out from the bottom of the blanket into the *rakuba*. It makes my throat hurt. Zulima calls out that she is on fire. Nanny Zeinab stops drumming. 'You be patient,' she says. 'By the time of your wedding, you will be light as the moon.'

Zulima has darker skin than mine but it's not as dark as Amal's. Everyone knows men prefer to marry women with pale-coloured skin; I don't know why. Nanny Zeinab starts drumming louder, and faster. She is sitting on a low stool with her knees open, with the bucket on the ground between them. Her bangles fly up and down her wrinkly arms.

Zulima is moaning and coughing. Her eyes stream with tears. Nanny Zeinab shouts over the drumming that girls of today are feeble. She used to do *dukhan* for three hours at a time and on the day of her wedding she had only just begun to see the blood of women.

'Things have moved on since then, Zeinab,' Nanny Samia says, getting up and giving Zulima a drink of water. She has to hold the plastic mug against her lips because Zulima's hands are under the blanket, along with the rest of her.

Nanny Zeinab shouts that young women have no respect. She says girls should listen to their elders, like they used to. Zulima starts to scream, saying that she'll die if she has to stay there. Nanny Samia tells Zulima to stand up and takes off the blanket. Zulima's body is wet all over. They rub her down with a flannel and she puts her nightdress back on and lies on a bed while Nanny Skinny fetches her a special thick drink from the kitchen. Nanny Zeinab says she doesn't need it, because she has spent so little time in there. Nanny Samia whispers to Zulima to take no notice, it will get easier every day. But Zulima starts crying all over again. She asks: what is the point of cooking her like a piece of meat?

'Don't you want to get married?' Nanny Samia asks.

Nanny Skinny starts talking about how God has favoured Zulima, because she will be the first wife. She was wife number three, she says, and the senior wives made her life bitter as salt water until her husband married again. Then they all turned on number four, and he used to swear every day that he would divorce them all. I saw Nanny Skinny's husband once, when he came to collect her from the Institute. He looked older than Musa; his hair was white like cotton wool.

No one takes any notice of me. A strange thought pops into my mind.

'Why doesn't she marry Rashid instead?' I say to no one in particular.

'What nonsense are you talking now?' Nanny Samia looks over to the corner where I'm sitting, squashed up against the wall of the house. 'What are you doing here anyway? Clear off.'

*

I'm hiding from Amal, sitting in the front garden of the Institute, in the middle of the bushes that have pink flowers on them – the ones that hurt your skin when you crawl underneath them. Their leaves are dusty and they have pointed tips and sharp edges. They look like closed eyes, long and oval with a line down the middle. My arms are wrapped around my knees, to make myself as small as possible, and I'm not moving. Amal always sees me if I move. The sour, sharp smell of the bushes stings the inside of my nose.

I hear the sound of voices and close my eyes tightly. It isn't Amal. It's a girl, but I can't tell whose voice it is. It must be a visitor. Then I recognize it, with a little shock in my chest. It's

Zulima. I've never heard her talk like that before. So soft. As if she were frightened. She sounds like someone else. I hear a man's voice. Deep. He doesn't say much. He sounds as if he has a sore throat. My foot is going numb and my back is beginning to hurt. I open my eyes, just enough to be able to see.

Zulima is standing at the far corner of the front part of the garden, leaning against the high wall, with a piece of grass in her hands that she's twisting round one of her fingers. Rashid is standing near her. They're not fighting. They are completely still, except for Zulima's hands. They are looking at each other.

I hit my foot with my fist to get rid of the prickly feeling in my toes and I hear Zulima's voice again, soft as water. Rashid stretches his hands out in front of him, to show they're empty; he rubs his face with his hands. Zulima is sniffing. After a long time, I hear his voice again. It sounds as if he has scraped it, like two stones rubbing together.

I hear her laugh a little. And his voice again, more normal now so that I can even hear what he says. He will wait for her till the end of this life and into the next one. He will kill any man who hurts her. Silence again, and for a moment I can't see them. Then I hear feet. I hold my breath, waiting to be discovered, but Zulima walks straight past me, back towards the front entrance to the Institute. Her sandals slap up at her heels with each step and she leaves a scent in the air behind her, a deep, woody, musky smell. After a few minutes more, Rashid coughs quietly. He walks along by the side of the wall towards the gates, so quick and quiet I wonder if I'm seeing a spirit. He is wearing a red shirt and blue trousers, and has a small round cap on his head. His big white shoes are brown now, and cracked. They make no sound at all as he walks by me.

*

It's the start of the new term. Before I even reach my desk, Wifaq starts to laugh. Soon the whole class is laughing, except Amal. She sits down in our usual place and puts her face straight into her book. Mrs Khadija calls me to stand next to her. As I walk up to the front of the class, the room goes quiet. She puts her arm around my shoulder. I can feel her skin on the back of my neck, where my hair used to be.

'If I hear anyone laugh again, that girl will have to find another class to join,' she says.

She tells the others to get on with their sums and pulls her chair out for me to sit on. She gets her brush out of her handbag and stands behind me. I keep very still as she brushes my hair straight back from my forehead in light, gentle strokes. I wish this moment – of feeling the light touch of her palm as she runs it over my hair in the path of the brush, her fingertips on my forehead as she smooths the stray strands back towards my ears, hearing nothing but the sound of pencils scratching on paper and the seedpods of the Pasha tree rattling in the breeze outside – I wish this moment would last for ever. No one ever touched me this softly before.

'Who did this?' she whispers.

'Me, miss.'

'Why?'

I can't think clearly now about what the reason was. It was just that I needed to get rid of my hair.

'I found Nanny Souad's razor blade. In the cupboard.'

'Is everything all right, Leila?' she asks. 'At home?'

I think for a moment of telling her. About the Institute. My mother. Zulima. I don't know where to start. The words won't come out of my mouth. I scowl and shrug.

'Why shouldn't it be?'

Mrs Khadija doesn't say anything. She carries on brushing and I hold my breath, to make sure she doesn't stop.

'Would you like to come home for lunch one day, with me? You and Amal?'

I'm glad she can't see my face because I feel it go hot with pleasure. I think she can feel the heat through my head. Then she says, 'You can meet my daughters. They're nearly your age.'

It had never entered my mind that Mrs Khadija had daughters. She doesn't look married. She has no gold on her arms or her hands. No henna patterns climbing up her ankles or along her wrists. She doesn't cover her hair. She looks free. I have never thought that she had a life away from school at all. I hate the idea of her daughters. Spoiled, stupid girls. Bitches.

'They'd like you,' she says.

I click my tongue and shake my head in one sharp, dismissive gesture, like Nanny Souad does when a man tries to sell her perfume on the street.

'No thanks,' I say. 'We get enough food at home.'

Back at my desk I put my hand up to my scalp, feeling again the way the hair ends more quickly than my fingers expect. I never want bunches again. I feel strong. Like a boy. I have thrown all of them over the wall at the Institute so no one can stick them back on me. Wifaq smirks at me over her shoulder and Amal puts up her hand to go to the toilet. As she squeezes between the other girls, she knocks into Wifaq's desk. Wifaq screams and jumps off her chair; a puddle of blue ink pours from her lap, splashing over her white socks with frills, her patent leather shoes. Mrs Khadija glances at Amal's narrow back, disappearing over the yard.

'Accidents happen, Wifaq,' she says. 'Stop making a fuss.'

*

Everything is different at the Institute over the next few weeks. For a start, the Director calls all the children together just like I hoped she would and stands in front of us looking serious, cleaning her big glasses on her sleeve. But instead of saying Nanny Souad fell in a drain, or her hair caught fire, she says she was getting potatoes off the gas cooker and she dropped the pot. All the water came out on the ground and some of it scalded her foot. There was no doctor there so her neighbour put honey all over it. It got worse, and she had to go into hospital and stay there for two nights.

I don't feel happy like I thought I would.

'It wasn't me,' my mouth calls out, when she stops talking. The Director looks surprised.

'Of course it wasn't you, Leila,' she says.

I thought it would be better at the Institute without Nanny Souad, but I feel as if she is there anyway, watching me. I still hear her voice sometimes, or smell her sharp stinking perfume that makes my eyes water. When I look around, I can't see her. But I know she's there. Nanny Samia says that's impossible: she has gone to her village by train, to get better, and she is at least a hundred miles away.

All the other nannies are excited about Zulima's wedding. Zulima has to have six of everything to get married. Six *tobes*, six pairs of sandals to match the *tobes*, and handbags to match the sandals. Six kinds of perfume. Nightdresses for a bride. Knickers. More bras. One night, they take me with them to the souk. Zulima, Nanny Samia, Nanny Zeinab and I set off straight after evening prayers.

I hold my breath all the way to the bus stop, so they don't change their minds and tell me to run along back to the Institute. But none of them says anything. I think they have forgotten I'm there, trailing a little way behind them. They're talking about whether the money is safe inside Nanny Zeinab's bra or whether it would be better for Nanny Samia to fold it up and put it in her shoe. The air is still pink as we climb up the silver steps of the bus and squash on to the seats. We drive fast along the empty road. There is a sticker on the front window of the bus that says 'God the Merciful', backwards. I'm wondering why when I realize it's for the other drivers to see, not the passengers. And then I realize – I can read. Amal's not the only one.

Zulima is sitting next to me, chewing gum with her mouth open. Her back teeth have little pits of brown in them and her nails are bitten harder than ever, almost down to the half moon at the base. She still has the spots around her nose.

'What are you staring at?' she says, without turning her head. I look away from her. The boy holds on to a pole with one hand and hangs his body out of the open door of the bus.

'*Souk a' Shaabi*,' he shouts out when he sees people by the side of the road. People's Market. When he ducks in through the door again and clinks the coins between his fingers, the man sitting on the other side of Zulima pays her fare. I don't know why he doesn't pay for me too. I stare at him but he doesn't notice me at all, he's too busy brushing his moustache with his fingers. I want to ask Zulima about Rashid, but I don't dare.

When we get there, I understand why it's called the People's Market. The narrow paths between the stalls are full of people. There are people everywhere – boys darting about with matches to sell, or gold watches dangling in pairs off their wrists. Women walk along in twos and threes, wrapped in orange or gold or turquoise *tobes*, their feet stained black with henna. Some of them rush along as if they're in a hurry but most of them stop and look at everything, pulling things this way and that in their hands, as if they've already bought them and they don't like them any more.

Old *habobas*, grannies, sit on the sides on sacks on the ground with heaps of peanuts in front of them, or sesame cakes or salted pumpkin seeds; tailors feed cloth arms and legs into their sewing machines and barbers cut the hair of men sitting on chairs by the side of the path. As I'm staring at everything, Nanny Zeinab calls over her shoulder to hurry up, or I'll get lost. The ground is covered in flattened-out cardboard and dusty plastic bags and mango stones and goat droppings. The air smells of dung and frying and incense.

Zulima walks past coffee pots and trays and stacks of tin buckets painted with flowers, as though she doesn't even see them. We move on to a narrow alley lined with stalls selling sandals; they are heaped high on top of each other, hanging from boards by the sides of the stalls. Zulima shoves her foot into scores of different shoes, in gold and brown and red leather, with beads or sequins, low heels, high heels, cork soles, wooden ones. Seeing so many empty sandals jumbled up together gives me a funny feeling in my stomach. They look like spirits' shoes and I think again about Nanny Souad and whether she is walking along with us in the People's Market, with her gold earrings pulling the tips of her ears down so the hole in them turns into a line. I hold my breath to stop her appearing in the cramped inside of the shoe stall, twisting my ear and asking what I'm doing.

'Too bad Souad can't be with us,' Nanny Zeinab says, cracking a sunflower seed between her teeth and spitting the husk into the dust. 'God willing, she will be better soon.'

As well as all the shouting and hammering and barking, there is music coming from some of the stalls. A woman moans that she wishes her heart were made of iron; next door, a man sings about beautiful eyes. I wonder if they're singing about each other. We pass another old granny, sitting on a crate with little pyramids of sweets spread out in front of her on a white cloth. The sweets look delicious, pink and round and asking to be picked up and put into a mouth. The woman glares at me and calls out to Nanny Zeinab that I'm eating her goods with my eyes.

'That girl eats the world with her eyes,' Nanny Zeinab shouts back.

All the nice feelings I have inside, about being in the Market of the People, like a normal girl, disappear. Ever since the milk-powder day, Nanny Zeinab has been calling me greedy. And ever since, the nannies take the milk and sugar away with them to the kitchen when they get up from the table. Nanny Samia used to like milk powder as well, when she was a little girl. She was always hungry too and her mother used to say she had a worm living inside her. When she told me that, I felt happy. I said, 'You were exactly like me.' But she looked a bit sad and said no, she wasn't exactly like me. We were *similar*.

I think about this, as we carry on down the street of night-dresses, in pink and orange and yellow and red and blue and mauve and green. Zulima fingers them all – I'm hoping she won't choose the green because that's my least favourite colour – but she doesn't choose anything and we move on, empty-handed. It is the same in the perfume section, and in the handbags. After the bras street, Nanny Zeinab folds her arms and stands in the middle of the path, blocking the way.

'Does nothing please you, you spoiled girls of today?' she says in a loud voice, as if she wants the whole souk to hear.

'Hush, Zeinab,' Nanny Samia says, trying to move her out of the way. 'Be patient. She never had the opportunity to choose anything for herself until now.'

'I still haven't,' Zulima says, and she starts to cry again, making blubbing noises. Everyone is looking at us now and two boys are laughing.

'What's the matter with your sister?' Nanny Zeinab hisses at me through her two sticking-out front teeth. 'She's getting married. Isn't that what any normal girl would want?'

'Shut up, Rabbit,' I say, inside my head. 'She is a normal girl.'

'You're just as bad,' says Nanny Zeinab. 'Gawping at me like a fool.'

When Zulima's dabbed her eyes on a tissue that Nanny Samia produces, we go back to the shoe section. She picks out some pink slippers with sequins on the front, and the man hooks them down on a long pole from the top of his display. In the little shop, she sits on a box with a sack on top of it and holds out both her feet. The slippers have gold stitching around the outside and gold soles inside. Her narrow ankles gleam gold as well in the light from the kerosene lamp and she puts her head on one side as she looks at them. She says she'll have them. When the man says they are five pounds, Nanny Zeinab gets off the chair and pulls her *tobe* around her head, as if we are going. The man says that four pounds will be all right and Nanny Zeinab says any fool knows slippers like that are not worth more than a pound. Zulima says she wants them, and in the end Nanny Zeinab reaches under her *tobe* and into the neck of her dress. She digs around so long I think she really has lost the money but finally she brings out two pound notes, both of them worn out and torn almost in half.

The man kneels down on the ground and takes the slippers off Zulima's feet. It takes him quite a long time. When he stands up, he says he has been robbed but, for a girl like this one, he'd give them away for free. As he's putting them into a plastic bag, he says that salt from her mouth would taste like sugar, and that any time she needs shoes she should come to him. He is more like a boy than a man, about the same age as Rashid. Nanny Zeinab still doesn't look pleased when we leave but Zulima smiles a bit and says goodbye in her quietest voice. Nanny Samia gives her a look I don't understand.

At the next stall, she buys a Miss Rose make-up kit, two tubes of Signal toothpaste and a bottle of Dark and Lovely hair dye that Nanny Samia says will make her hair blacker. Then she buys some Nuits de Paris perfume, in a big bottle, Head and Shoulders shampoo, Crème 21 lightening treatment and two short red nightdresses that you can see right through. She buys an orange bra that looks like two little hills on straps. She buys a pair of yellow knickers and some pink ones and three bars of Lux soap. Then she says she's tired, and she hates shopping.

When we get back to the Institute, the nannies are excited. Her husband-to-be has delivered a present and they think it is the wedding gold. It's in a white plastic carrier bag, with writing all over it that says – I know without even thinking about it – 'House of Books'. I can read. I hug the thought to myself. Nanny Souad can't read, and nor can Nanny Skinny. Only Nanny Samia can. And the Director. And Amal, of course.

Zulima reaches into the bag and brings out a gold box. Inside it is a Koran. She puts it away in the cupboard and hides the pink slippers in the suitcase under her bed. I wonder what a *husband-to-be* is. There are so many things I need to know. I go to sleep wondering whether I could bring them up in general knowledge. I dream that I'm teaching Mrs Khadija something, but not out of a book, and all the other girls in the class are tiny. Only Mrs Khadija and I are the same size and I am even older than she is.

Chapter 4

NAMES OF THE ANCESTORS

The fan is at a standstill; the light coming through the gap over the shutters throws a gold strip across the opposite wall. Amal mutters something in her sleep and turns over. I run my fingers over the material of my dress, feeling my hip-bones through the silky fabric, my stomach curling downwards between them like an empty bowl. When I remember what happened the night before, I jump out from under my sheet. I want to see Zulima in the short red nightdress. I want to find out what it's like to be *married*.

The big girls' room is dark and quiet; the bell hasn't gone. Ekhlas and Rahel are still asleep, their sheets pulled over their heads. I stand in the doorway, breathing in their grown-up smell of sweat and breath and blood. Zulima's bed is empty. The suitcase that has been under the bed ever since she got engaged has gone, as has her hairbrush and her pillow. All

---

that's left are her old flip-flops, with the imprints of her toes on the rubber soles.

Nanny Souad limps down the hall from the bathroom, rubbing her eyes.

'Where's my sister?' I demand.

She puts both her hands up to her head and smooths down her hair.

'Where d'you think she is?' she yawns.

Nanny Skinny appears from the kitchen.

'She's gone to her husband. What are you doing still in that dress?'

I scowl at her and walk towards the door. The air feels cool and dry in my mouth as I step out of the back of the Institute and jump down the two stone steps to the sandy ground. The garden – so beautiful the night before, with the coloured lights strung from the trees and the sounds of the musicians' instruments in the air – is destroyed. The white plastic chairs are scattered about on their sides, covered in brown dust. The stage is gone, along with the red and gold awning that covered the heads of the guests. There are bits of torn orange peel in the flowerbeds and ants carrying half-eaten dates over the ground. There is no sign of Zulima.

I walk over the flattened grass to the back of the garden and sit down underneath the lime trees. I lean on the solid trunk of the tree and pull up my knees. I feel the dampness from the ground seeping up into my dress; Musa has been out already with his hosepipe. Musa had to dress in a green *jellabiya* and a red felt hat for the wedding, and carry round trays with glasses of lemonade and paper plates full of meat and chips. He didn't sing at all.

I didn't know any of the guests. The relatives of the nannies came, and the patrons of the Institute, and people from the Ministry of Social Welfare. They were all happy that an abandoned girl could be wanted in marriage by a normal man. They said so in their speeches. Rashid turned up, later than everyone else. He was wearing a white shirt and cream-coloured trousers with creases down the front of them and new shoes on his feet, cut out of old car tyres. When he bent down to shake my hand, his breath smelled like Musa's does on a Friday, when he has been to visit his friends. Rashid said to me that we had to stick together. 'The laughter of Fate echoes everywhere, Little Sister,' he said. 'Can you hear it?' While I was listening as hard as I could, he started to laugh. The stone in his neck stuck out and he had a beard, short and soft, on his top lip and his chin. I was proud that he called me his sister. I like thinking about Rashid.

Rashid called Zulima a bad word before the wedding. *Sharmuta.* It means something like meat, but worse. He said she didn't have to marry that old guy, by God, whatever they said. And she said something back but I didn't hear it properly because she was crying. They were over here again, by the trees. They didn't see me. Later I saw Zulima talking to Nanny Samia, crying again. Nanny Samia was walking up and down the *rakuba* floor, waving her hands around. Crying is something girls do when they're about to get married. Zulima has anyway; ever since the first day she heard about it, she hasn't stopped crying. Rashid doesn't live at the Institute any more, although sometimes he comes to see the boys. He lives with a carpenter that he met at the mosque.

He is learning a *trade* and his long fingers have blisters on them.

The skirt of my dress has ripped at the side; a long snake of curly white nylon hangs from the seam. I have a feeling in my stomach that is different from being hungry. I feel empty. I feel as if the air could blow right through me with nothing to stop it. All through the party, I was expecting to see a tall man walk down the path from the gate, his white turban wrapped seven times around his head. When he saw the bride, he would look at her with bright eyes and say, 'Thank God. I have found her.' Then he would say she could not marry the security guard, she must marry Rashid. Then Rashid would be my *real brother*.

I don't understand why Zulima's father did not come. I thought that if I prayed to God every day for a week, he must come. Even God doesn't like me. He answered my prayer about Nanny Souad and He didn't listen to a much more important one. Zulima was looking for him right up till they brought the paper from the mosque to say that she was married. I could see her, with her head turned towards the gate all the time. When they brought the paper, she gave a howl that reminded me of the cats, the way they scream in the night. She only made the sound once; all the nannies crowded around her and I didn't hear her after that, just the noise of women ululating, and the band playing. She looked so beautiful up on the stage, I wasn't sure if it was really her. She had gold all over her arms and fingers and a red *tobe* and gold sandals. Her hair was piled up on top of her head so that she was taller than her husband.

Someone out of sight is sweeping. Nanny Souad puts her

head round the kitchen door and waves at me to come in. I rest my chin between my knees and pretend I haven't seen her. The nannies don't like coming over here, far from the house. They say bad spirits gather in corners like this. I love to feel the ground underneath me, here by the trees. I dig my fingers into one of the cracks around the roots of the trees, chip off a couple of lumps of mud and put one in my mouth. I roll it on my tongue, against the roof of my mouth and it dissolves and runs down my throat, smooth and clean, taking away the emptiness. Sometimes, I think the earth is alive.

A bird in the branches over my head takes off in a hurry. I look up and see Nanny Souad coming towards me, struggling over the grass, holding her *jellabiya* up in front of her. She is wearing a high-heeled sandal on one foot. The bandage on her other foot is dirty and her toes are grey, poking out of the end of it.

'What did you think marriage is?' she calls out as she gets near. 'Just the party?'

She starts to laugh.

As I scramble to my feet, she reaches forwards to grab me, misses my shoulder and topples over. There is a moment's silence and she starts screaming for Nanny Skinny, saying I pushed her. I run across the grass, around the side of the Institute, past the *rakuba* and down the path, between the long rows of sharp-leaved bushes. I mean to hide in Musa's hut but the gates are open. Musa is quarrelling with the milkman in the kitchen, saying: does he think he's selling milk or water?

I slip sideways through the gap between the gates and I'm on the other side; the milkman's donkey stands there with its eyes closed, one churn on each side of its belly. I start to walk along under the high wall of the Institute, in the direction of the bus for the market. I expect all the time to hear Nanny Souad behind me, shouting for me to come back, or for one of the boys to run up and grab me by the hair, saying the Director wants to see me. Nothing happens. I am alone outside the Institute for the first time in my life.

I don't run, in case I look like a thief and people start chasing me. I walk quite slowly, sticking close to the high walls in front of the houses, jumping over the puddles of stagnant water with soap scum floating on them, dodging around the rusted car on the corner, keeping my distance from the dogs dozing and twitching in the shade. I feel as if I'm getting smaller with every step I take.

I don't recognize anything. There are men buying grapefruits and bananas, and putting them in striped plastic bags. One woman walks along with a bag of potatoes on her head, a baby tied to her back and two more bags in her hands. I walk behind a mountain of watermelons, taller than me, all piled on top of each other. The watermelon man has a huge knife in his hand and one of the melons is lying on its side, sliced in half, with its red insides exposed. There is a shop with animals' bodies hanging from a rail. They have had their skins taken off; they are red and white and their legs look stiff and useless. Underneath, there is a bucket full of yellow chickens' feet all jumbled up, with a couple of cats crouching nearby.

I smell food and drift towards a café, where men crowd around the cashier, all with empty tin bowls in their hands. None of them takes any notice of me. Outside, the ground is covered with red and blue and silver bottle tops. I stoop to pick one up, but it's stuck to the ground. I get down on my hands and knees and dig at them, loosening them one by one with my nails, cleaning them with spit and putting them in the pocket of my dress. The smell of frying makes my mouth water. Sitting back on my heels, looking at my collection, I feel someone's eyes on me. He is sitting at a round table in front of me, on his own. He is a fat man, leaning back, with the tube of a hubbly-bubbly pipe between his knees. He breathes out and the smell of the tobacco arrives in my nose, all mixed up with the meat.

'Dropped your money?' he asks.

He is speaking to me. I feel excitement run right through me. It must be Zulima's father. He has been looking for us, just like I knew he would. I pretend to be searching for more bottle tops.

'Here,' he says. 'I've got something for you.'

I wipe my hands on the front of my dress and stand in front of him.

'What happened to your shoes? Where is your mother?'

It is him! Why else would he ask about the Queen? He taps the bowl of the pipe on the tray where the coals are, and they gleam red as their coat of ash falls off.

'I am Leila,' I whisper, still looking at the ground. 'Zulima's sister.' I look up at him, waiting for him to let out a great shout of joy and call to everyone in the café to witness the day he found his family. He grunts. He hasn't understood.

'I am Leila,' I say again, speaking as clearly as I can and more loudly and at the same time smiling a bit, because I can't keep the happy feelings off my face.

He nods. 'You said so.'

He feels in the pocket of his *jellabiya*. He brings his hand out of his pocket and holds it out. I think for a minute that there will be a pink sweet in it. But when he turns it over and opens his fist, it is empty. His palm is covered in deep, dark lines. I can feel my smile collapsing, falling down. He laughs and slaps his knees.

'Here, Leila,' he says. 'Put your hand in my pocket.'

I get a strange feeling. It seems that me being here – this sensation of the slippery, torn, orange dress around my legs, the air warm in my nose, the stickiness of my fingers from the bottle tops – it seems as if this moment has always been waiting for me to come and live it. As if I have been here before, in this exact place, with the same man, feeling the same feelings. The ground is warm and gritty under my feet. I grip my toes against it, feel the sandy surface giving way. This is not Zulima's father, I know, as I step forwards and put my hand into his pocket.

'Keep going,' he says.

I push further into the pocket. His breath comes through the air towards my face, as if he has been running. At the very bottom, there are two coins. I get hold of them and pull my hand out as quickly as I can. They are big and light.

He picks up his pipe again, leans back on the chair.

'Now clear off home, before I call a policeman.'

*

Visitors appear on the steps of the Institute. There are two men and a woman, smiling down at us while the kids crowd around them, calling out *khawaja*, foreigner. I have never seen white people before, except on television. The men have pale eyes and pink ears. One of them squats down on his knees to hold Quarratulain's hand. The woman's hair is yellow. It is straight and thick, and when she turns her head it swings around her face. My fingers itch to touch it.

The Director comes out to greet them, smiling at us kids as if she'd never seen us before either. She makes a speech, saying how all nations must work together for the sake of unfortunate orphans, and that at the Institute we are all one big family. I don't know what she means, because the nannies say we are here because we haven't got a family. The visitors don't speak Arabic. The Director has to tell us what they want to say. She says that the foreigners will take some of us to go and live in a new place, called a children's village. The man says that at the village we will grow up to be as good as normal children; maybe – the Director laughs when she tells us this bit – we will be even better. Only lucky children, with no one at all who might ever want to come and get them, can go to the children's village. The nannies talk among themselves.

The foreigners have brought cakes. Nanny Skinny lays them out on long, silver-coloured platters on the table in the dining room, and gives us a small plateful each. There are round ones with almonds on their tops, dripping with syrup, another type that looks like a bird's nest, and my favourite – parcels of pastry like little pillows, sandwiched with chopped-up nuts, and so sweet they give me a sudden sharp ache in my back teeth. Amal won't eat them; she says they are poisoned. I scoff hers as well, before she changes her mind.

When the visitors have gone, the nannies say under their breath that people with blue eyes can't be trusted and that it's a strange day when children of the natural religion are handed over to *kufar*, unbelievers. What do they want us for, they ask, and what makes them think they know how to raise children like these? Nanny Souad sweeps the cakes off the big table and takes them into the kitchen, banging the door behind her. I hear raised voices coming from inside and soon Nanny Samia bursts out of the kitchen and disappears into the Director's office.

Amal stands next to me, later, while I'm sick on the front steps. She doesn't want to go with the foreigners, she says. Their village might be far away from our school and Mrs Khadija won't be able to bring books for her to borrow. She says they are sure to make us eat pigs, because they are *khawajas*, and that if they take us to their country that is in *Europe* we will freeze to death. Then she says, very quietly, that if anyone ever wants to come and look for us they won't know where to find us, if we have gone from the Institute. 'Who's going to come and look for you?' I ask, lifting my head. She walks off without answering.

I can't wait to live in a village with only children. It's a new happy thought and I pray to God to make the *khawajas* choose me and to say that Amal has got to come too. At school, when we're doing grammar or geography, I don't think about what's on the blackboard. I go inside my head and imagine me and Amal living in a place like the one where Musa grew up. Mud houses with pink flowers tumbling over the high outside walls. A shopkeeper resting on a straw mat by the bean pot. A green-painted mosque in the middle. The air will smell of wood smoke and on the edge of the village there will be the tomb of a saint. All the women who thirst for babies will come on Saturdays, dressed in their best clothes and weeping and fainting in the early morning light like they used to at Musa's place, shrieking out to God that they can't live in this world without a child to call their own, before going away with a handful of sand.

*

The guards recognize us now. The tall one winks at me and jerks his head to say we can go in. Walking towards the ward, I hear the women shriek and call from inside. My mother sits upright on the bench. I can see the bones of her spine through the back of her yellow dress. She has given me a page torn from a magazine, with a picture of a boy on it eating an ice cream. I am trying to read what it says underneath but the paper is limp in my hands; the ink comes off on my fingers. I can read almost anything now. Mrs Khadija says I make her *proud*. I think of telling my mother that and I open my mouth. I change my mind and close it again. Sometimes, I think her silence is catching, like a disease. Sometimes, I think we talk without words. We sit next to each other and we know what the other is feeling. I think of what she might say to me, if she spoke. 'Once I was a Queen, with hair I could sit on, which was blacker than the hair of the woman on the Dark and Lovely bottle. What am I now?' A prisoner, I tell her, silently. A woman of no words. And no colour in your hair. But one day, I will rescue you. One day, I will look after you.

Two fat aunties stop as they walk by us. The air fills with the smell of their bodies, of their smoke baths. 'Ah, Queen,' shouts one. 'How is your colour today? And you girls, God willing you are well?' I scowl at them. One of them has a daughter who lives here in the hospital. She talks to herself, walking along washing her hands in the air. I wipe my forehead on my shoulder. A dog sprawls on its side on a heap of earth, showing a set of long pink teats. She whines in her sleep. I wonder where her puppies are.

Zulima is going on about her wedding. About the six new dresses she got from her husband, the six pairs of matching shoes and handbags. She's sorry our mother wasn't well enough to come to the wedding, she says. She wanted her to be there. She kept hoping she might come.

These days, when the bus stops in the morning to collect Zulima for school, she sits on her own and won't talk to anyone. Sometimes Rashid is there, waiting near the school when we get off the bus, with his leather sling with a hammer in it. She walks past him without saying hello, and goes straight into school instead of hanging around outside with the other girls like she used to.

'See,' I say to Amal. 'I told you they hate each other.'

'No they don't,' she says. 'They love each other.'

Amal is such an idiot.

Zulima looks silly in her old green pinafore and white shirt, with her hands still decorated like a bride's. She looks strange out of her school uniform too, in her embroidered *tobe* and with sharp gold rings on all her fingers. Whatever she wears, she looks as if she's dressed up in someone else's clothes. She holds her hands out in front of her to show the black flowery patterns to our mother. Her nails are bitten deeper than ever; the tips of her fingers bulge out over the top of them. Our mother doesn't say anything. Zulima unwraps a piece of gum out of her bag, and starts chewing it on one side of her mouth. She doesn't offer me a bit.

Our mother sits as still as ever. There is a line around her chin where the pale powder ends and the skin begins. As I look at it, I notice that her face is bruised under the powder. I sit on my hands and stare at the ground. The concrete under my thighs is rough and warm. The grass is worn away in front of the bench, the ground hollowed out by feet.

'You are now a married woman. You must know who your people are.' My mother struggles to push the words into the right shape in her mouth. But I can understand her perfectly. 'Your father was my first husband. He is known as Abu Ali,' she says. 'But he was born Hassan. His brothers are Ahmed, Munir and Mohamed. There was another, Abbas, who died as a boy. Abu Ali's father was Fadl Omar and his uncles were Taha Omar, Abdullah Omar, Suleiman Omar. Fadl Omar's father was Omar Mohamed. And his father was Mohamed Moneim . . .'

The names are disappearing into the air. When she is finished, she goes quiet again. She hasn't said my father's name. Aziz Mohamed Mahmoud.

'Thank you, mother,' says Zulima, in the end. 'We have waited a long time to know about these men. But where are they? Where can I find my father? Or Leila's father? We need their protection.'

Our mother spits on the ground beside her feet, very deliberately, and for a long time it seems as though she isn't going to speak again. Then she lifts up her head and speaks more clearly and loudly than before.

'You call these men?' she says. 'Who never once came to look for me, in all the long years? I have forgotten every single one of them.'

When I ask her to repeat the names, she grows angry. She says there are no men in our family. Only cowards. It is the most talking she has ever done. She closes her mouth into a thin line like a stick. Zulima starts to howl again, saying her life is over and she might as well throw herself into the sea. 'It's not a sea,' I say. 'It's a river.' She ignores me. I carry on swinging the soles of my sandals over the ground in front of the bench, making little soft drifting noises and raising fine, dry dust the colour of cinnamon powder. Sometimes, I think that the only sound I really like is when no one is saying anything.

One morning, soon after this visit, the bus does not stop outside Zulima's new house. I think the driver has forgotten and I scramble up to the front to remind him. We are already quite a way past Zulima's place but he tells me to sit down. After that, Zulima doesn't come to school any more.

Chapter 5

_____

YOU ARE MY LIFE

The bus stands outside the front entrance, with the door open and the engine running. When the Director hugs me and wishes me a good life, I realize for the first time that going to the village means leaving the Institute. Amal and I climb on board and sit together, without speaking. Wagir sits in front of us, on his own. The twins, Mahmoud and Mohamed, are on the bus as well, along with Quarratulain, who snivels, clutching her bag in her one hand. Zulima's friend Ekhlas sits on her own at the front, scowling. Ekhlas has been in a bad temper ever since Zulima got married; her scarf is pinned on more tightly than ever and pulled right down over her eyebrows. I count us up in my head: ten kids altogether. It's hot on the bus and the driver's seat is empty; he's saying his prayers with Musa.

All the nannies stand outside the Institute, waving as the

_____

bus finally pulls off down the drive. Nanny Zeinab bares her rabbit teeth and Nanny Skinny blinks her milky eyes. Only Nanny Souad has her arms folded. It crosses my mind that she is jealous of us, because we are leaving while she is staying. I push away the thought; she could leave any time she wanted. All she has to do is walk out of the gates and go to her house in Omdurman. The Director is standing in the middle of all of them, nodding her head, asking God to protect us. Nanny Samia is waving hardest, fluttering her hand to and fro above her head and wiping her eyes on her arm, smiling and crying at the same time.

As the bus passes through the wide, open gates, Musa salutes me. He keeps his hand up by his forehead and looks straight ahead; the bus rolls away down the tarmac and soon I can't see him any more.

*

We are matched to our new mothers by the colour of our skin. Amal goes to the smiling woman with black skin and a red dress. I go to the tall one. The first thing I notice is her voice. She has a voice like a rustling paper bag, and when she speaks to me I don't understand what she means. We're still gathered in a big group of kids on a bare piece of ground, with empty sachets of the orange drinks they gave us littered around. She leans forwards and takes my hand, then pulls me behind her into a house with a green door. I follow her into a small, hot room. I can make out two beds in the gloom, both with green sheets, and a green chair in between.

She pulls open the shutters; light floods across the tiles.

'So, you are Leila,' she whispers, turning round to me again. 'And quite a big girl already.'

With the window behind her, I can see the straight, narrow outline of her body, her two feet planted flat on the ground. She's wearing a plain housedress and her hair is in braids on each side of her head, hanging down like pods. I give her a wide, stiff smile, the kind we do for visitors, and she smiles back.

She rests her hands on my shoulders.

'I don't suppose you know how old you are?' she says.

I do know. I am nearly ten. I know the date I was born on, because it's in my records. 1 June 1969. Nanny Samia told me. All the other kids have their birthday on the first of January. No one wrote down anything about the day they were born, or if they did it got lost or they threw it into the river, because they didn't want a birthday. That's what they say, anyway. I open my mouth to tell her but she is already talking again, saying that I will learn to be a good girl here and – God willing – a good woman. I will help her with my little brothers. We will be just like a real mother and daughter. Most women only care about sons but not her, she says. Flashes of gold glint from inside her mouth as she speaks.

When she's finished talking, she looks me up and down. I'm wearing the orange dress I had for Zulima's wedding. Nanny Souad said it was the only thing I was fit to be seen in and she wasn't going to send me out in school uniform, looking like a prisoner. She went through the bag I had packed and pulled out nearly all the clothes, saying they were good only for rags and why hadn't I reminded her I needed new ones? She found the teaspoon in the bottom and said she was putting the spoon back in the kitchen where it belonged and I grabbed her hand between both of mine and bit it. She dropped the spoon on the floor and went down the corridor, shouting that I had made problems for her up till the end, just like my sister before me. Afterwards, Nanny Samia came in and said she would miss me almost as if I were her own daughter. Amal was hiding in the bathroom, saying she refused to go. And suddenly the bus was waiting for us. I didn't have time to say a proper goodbye to Musa, or the white cat, or the lime trees.

The bodice of the dress cuts into my armpits; I yank it down towards my knees and realize that my new mother is speaking to me.

'Red, of all colours,' she says, shaking her head. 'Tomorrow you can choose something more suitable.'

'It's not red, Miss. It's orange.'

'Call me Mama,' she whispers. 'I am your Mama Luban. God willing, you'll be happy here. God wants all the children to be happy.'

One of the boys begins to scream from somewhere further inside the house and she leaves, half closing the door behind her. 'This is your room,' she says. 'All for you.'

There is a doll on one of the beds, tipped against the pillow. She has round gold earrings sewn on to each side of her head, a white scarf around her face and a brown felt mouth in a smile. She is wearing a green dress. I don't dare touch her. I step over to the cupboard and look at myself in the mirror. My hair is lumpy, as if someone had been taking bites out of it. My face is empty. It looks like the lid on a pot.

A roar comes from overhead; it sounds as if an aeroplane is about to crash into the roof. I grab the doll and dive under the bed. The noise passes; nothing happens. I stay hunched up under the bed, smelling the smell of the doll's head, feeling her soft body in my hands. When the woman comes back, I am still there. She lifts the green sheet and peers at me with her face upside down.

'I see you found your dolly,' she says. 'I made her for you.'

I come out, and stand in front of her.

'Miss, where is Amal going to stay?'

She doesn't say where Amal is. She says again that she is my new mother.

'I've got a mother. She's a Queen. She lives in a great big house, like a palace.'

She takes the doll from my hands and straightens her scarf around her face.

'It's a sin to tell lies, Leila,' she says. 'If you had a mother you wouldn't be here.'

She hands the doll back to me and hugs me.

'This is the start of your new life. It's your chance to lead a good life.'

*

Later, she calls all the kids together and says she's going to show us everything about the Green house. It has two bedrooms for boys on one side, and two for girls on the other –

mine, that is, and hers. There is a big room in the middle with a wall that only comes up halfway, so the air blows through the mosquito netting above it. We will eat our meals there, around a table. There is one bathroom for the girls and another for the boys, and you have to sit on the lavatory as if it were a chair and wash your hands afterwards with pink soap. There is a kitchen just for the Green house, with a refrigerator in it that we are not allowed to go into. Mama Luban reaches into the neck of her housedress and holds up a piece of string with several keys on it.

In front of the Green house, there is a yard where we will plant onions and greens, she says. Around the back of the house are two taps and a plastic barrel for when there is no water in the taps. There are two wide, shallow silver bowls for washing clothes propped against the wall, and a smaller one for washing dishes. We have to use the powdery blue stuff in the cardboard box for our clothes, Mama Luban says, and the hard blocks of white soap for the dishes. We can use the low stool to sit on while we do it. When we've finished doing the washing, we have to chuck the water far away from the house, otherwise we will get malaria.

There will be nine of us living in the Green house. Mama Luban, one girl – that's me – and seven boys. The twins, Mohamed and Mahmoud, were already brothers but the other kids are new brothers and sisters, she says. We are a family now, and we have to help each other and take care of each other. One of the kids, a boy called Faisal, cries all the time for his mother. The twins are calling him 'Lamb', because he bleats. Another one has drips coming out from both sides of his nose.

I make sure I'm not sitting next to him when we sit around the tray on the table to eat lunch. We have lentils and crisp-edged pieces of fried liver and my favourite kind of bread – long, soft white sticks with brown tops, the sort that comes from a shop.

'I see you were hungry,' the woman says when I look up from the tray. She pours out eight glasses of pink grapefruit juice and lumps of ice bang against the side of the glass jug; one of them slips into my glass and I take it into my mouth and feel its hard coldness burning my tongue.

After I've washed my hands with the pink soap, I go out-side and find Amal. She's wearing a new dress like I am, and some flip-flops that are too big for her. She has tracks down her face, under her eyes. We find a big heap of rocky earth near the gates to hide behind. I dig out a lump of mud, with my nails, from under the dry surface. The earth tastes differ-ent here, grittier, and all wrong. Amal watches as I spit it out. When she starts to cry again, I cry too. I haven't cried for a long time. As I wipe my eyes, I tell myself that I'm not crying at this village, whatever happens. I'm not crying any more.

That night, lying under the green sheet, I can't sleep. The mattress has no hollow in the middle to roll into; it is hard and uncomfortable. The door to the room stands open a little way; a dim light comes in from the hallway. After a long time, the voices of the boys go quiet and there is silence all around me. I thought it was going to be the best thing that had ever hap-pened to me, to move to the children's village. Now I'm not so sure. The cupboard looks bigger in the darkness. I fix my eyes on the door, to see if it moves. I think once that I hear Amal calling me, but although I strain my ears, I don't hear the sound again. I hold the doll more tightly. Her head is smooth and soft, under my nose. I'll call her *Waheda*, I decide. One.

*

The first day becomes the second, and then the third. Soon, I lose count of how many days I have been at the village. Amal lives in the Blue house. Her new mother sings to herself when she's in the kitchen making meals for the Blue house kids, when she's braiding Amal's hair or embroidering flowers on the edges of pillowcases. Quarratulain is in the Yellow house; her mother, Mama Hajji, is a grandmother with milky-looking eyes that don't see well. She has to ask Quarratulain to cut her nails for her and sometimes she puts her shoes on the wrong feet. Ekhlas is in the Red house, with Mama Miriam. Mama Miriam is always cleaning and sweeping and washing; Ekhlas has to help her and she complains that she barely has time to say her prayers.

It doesn't look like I expected a village to look. There are piles of sand, scattered heaps of broken bricks. No trees. The houses are all the same, but their windows and doors are painted different colours. There is no shop, and no mosque. There are a lot of grown-ups, who work in the office, and two of the *khawajas* are still here. The land is big and empty and when the wind blows the dust lifts and blasts into my eyes and nose. Over everything there is a hot, sour smell I can't get used to. Planes swoop in over the village one after the other early in the morning, and again in the evenings, so close I can see the heads of the passengers through the windows. They look as if they are in another world, flying through this one.

A man comes and plants pink and orange flowers all the way along the path from the gates to the office. He marks out a pitch in the middle of the empty ground and the boys play football all day. After school and on Fridays, from our place behind the forgotten hill, Amal and I hear them shouting, and the traffic from the main road, and the aeroplanes, and the mothers calling their children, all mixed up together. Mama Luban can't shout; she has to bang on a saucepan with a stone when she wants us.

The food at the village tastes better than at the Institute and there is always bread left over when everyone has finished. One morning, as I'm putting on my school clothes, Mama Luban comes in and asks me what I want for lunch. I am so surprised, I can't think what to say. I stare at her, and she says I am a funny child. Next time she asks, I'm ready. I tell her I want lamb stew, fried fish, meatballs, and the pudding called *Umm Ali* that has milk and raisins and sugar in it. She clicks her tongue and says that no good comes to greedy girls. But when we come running back for lunch at the sound of her saucepan, the smell of *Umm Ali* fills the Green house.

I soon get used to my brothers. Everyone wants me in goal; I'm the only one who's not afraid of the ball. All the boys apart from Faisal like football. Faisal's father died and later he lost his mother in the market. She sent him into the baker's shop to queue up for bread; when he came back outside, holding three loaves in his arms, she wasn't there. 'The bread was still warm,' he says, in a voice like a baby's. Mahmoud says that his mother lost him on purpose, and all the kids laugh. Faisal cries harder than ever.

On Fridays, after we have washed our clothes in the morning and the boys have been to the mosque, we are allowed to play. Amal lines the little ones up and makes them do writing with sticks on the ground. Faisal sits down, with his legs crossed, and writes his name and his mother's name. No one else likes playing schools. Quarratulain pretends to have to run to the toilet, and goes to play jacks with the other kids from the Red house. Even the twins, Mohamed and Mahmoud, refuse to play now we are at the village; Mahmoud says they are not about to be bossed around by a girl.

One day, we play thieves. Amal and I look in Mama Hajji's handbag and take her chewing gum while she is praying. When she accuses us, we deny it. Amal opens her mouth to show her it's empty. Mama Hajji sniffs her breath and doesn't say anything. Afterwards, Mahmoud says we will die, because that's what happens if you swallow gum. Mohamed stands beside him, nodding his head.

I wear the same thing every day – a green towelling shorts suit with a zip up the front that is the best thing I have ever had in my life. The zip has English letters on it that Amal says are YKK; it makes a nice sound when I pull it up to my neck. Mama Luban says shorts are for boys. Mama Luban prefers boys. I know she does, from the way she talks to them. She doesn't want me to be like one, though. She wants me to be more like a girl. She keeps on saying that soon she'll be able to plait my hair again.

When the barber comes, I line up with my new brothers. He cuts my hair with his long scissors that make sharp sounds around my ears; he goes up the back of my neck with his silver razor, pressing it hard against my skin.

'Good lad,' he says when he's finished, flicking the hair off my shoulders with a cloth. As I get out of the chair, he winks at me. He doesn't know I'm a girl.

Sometimes Mama Luban lets me play in her room. It has two beds in it and a chair where her prayer mat sits rolled up tight when she's not using it. In her cupboard, she keeps her prayer beads on top of a thin pile of folded white *tobes*, with a tin of sweets hidden underneath. On the bottom shelf, there is a plastic tub of Vaseline with no lid, a tin of coconut oil with a picture on the side of a group of palm trees, a plastic comb, a mirror with a red frame and a stick with a ragged end for cleaning her teeth. She has a verse from the Koran in a frame on the wall, saying that you get the reward for the life you live on earth when you reach Paradise. I don't dare play thieves in the Green house.

In the day, I forget that everything has changed. But at night, on my own in the bedroom, I remember. Sometimes I feel as if I'm living the wrong life, as if it doesn't belong to me. I strain my ears for something that isn't the crickets, or the dogs that yelp in the distance, or the passing cars. I don't know what it is that I want to hear. I listen for it anyway. I have ripped Waheda's smile off her face. I like her better without her mouth, with just her round black eyes, for looking, and her ears that must be hidden underneath her white head-scarf, even though you can't see them. The feel of her in my hands, the musty, familiar smell of her head under my nose, makes me feel better.

*

Soon after we move to the village, Zulima appears at the door. She pushes past me and sits down in the big dining room in the middle of the house, sticking her legs straight out in front of her. Her ankles are not as narrow as they used to be and the pink sandals have lost most of their sequins.

'Did they cut out your tongue?' she asks. 'I thought you'd be pleased to see me.'

She gets a red apple out of her bag and thrusts it at me.

'What happened to your hair?' she asks, through a mouthful of fingers. 'Where's Amal? This place is miles from anywhere, by God.'

Mama Luban comes out of the kitchen.

'This is my sister,' I say. 'Zulima. And this is my new mother. Mama Luban.'

'I can see the resemblance,' Mama Luban says, as they shake hands. 'Same mother, same father. Anyone would know.'

Her eyes are very bright as she looks at Zulima. She sends me to get the tin of sweets from her cupboard. Zulima takes a peppermint, drops the wrapper on the floor and sucks it noisily.

'You're well, God willing?' she asks in a flat voice, after a long time.

Mama Luban thanks God for her health and asks Zulima how she is, and how is her husband. I had forgotten about him. Zulima looks around the room, and says that she's *nus nus* – so so. Mama Luban's mouth goes into two straight lines.

'May God bless you,' she says, glancing again at my sister's body, wrapped in its pink *tobe* with swirly patterns on it like puffs of smoke.

I want to ask Zulima if she's seen Nanny Samia, or even Nanny Souad. But I keep quiet. At the village, we don't talk about our old life. When Zulima gets up to leave, I go with her. Mama Luban seems as if she's coming too but Zulima stops in the doorway and turns and says goodbye to her.

Mama Luban goes back towards the kitchen, calling out to me not to go outside the gates.

'Nosy old woman,' Zulima says, before we're even out of the Green house garden. 'Don't tell her anything. And don't call her mother or I'll slap you one.' She rolls her eyes at me murderously.

We call in to the Blue house so she can greet Amal, and the Yellow house, where Quarratulain is. I want to visit Ekhlas in the Red house too but Zulima says that all these houses are getting on her nerves. When we're nearly at the gates, she stops and turns to me. She pulls her *tobe* forwards just enough to make it stay up on her head but so you can still see her gleaming hair parted in the middle; she is wearing tiny gold earrings with red dangling stones that jump about as she moves.

'Has Rashid been along to find out how you are?' she asks. I shake my head.

'Not yet. But he will,' I say. 'He is my big brother, no matter where Fate scatters us. He said so.'

She hardly says goodbye. It's lunchtime and the traffic is building up on the tarmac road outside the gates. She pulls her *tobe* tight over her behind and steps out on to the road to get to the other side. A blue-painted truck comes screeching to a halt, and the metal drums on the back of it all bang into each other. Zulima doesn't seem to notice. I don't want her to go. I didn't realize how much I had missed her.

'When are we going to see mother?' I call after her, over the noise of the car horns and the men's voices and the music coming from the cab of the lorry.

'Soon,' she shouts back. 'I'll come for you.' She's already feeling in her bag for a coin for her bus fare. She's getting fat, I notice as she stands there. She looks as if she's carrying a sack of potatoes under her pink *tobe*.

I've still got the apple in my hands. I've never had one before. I eat it, walking back to the Green house. I eat it bite by bite, thinking about my sister but not thinking particular thoughts, just letting Zulima fill up the whole of the inside of my head. I hardly notice the apple.

*

Amal's new mother is called Mama Amaani. She has a tape recorder and she has *cassettes* of an Egyptian singer called Umm Kalthoum. She pounds peanuts and aubergines for salads and slices tomatoes in the round palm of her hand and all the time she sings songs, about sweet hearts who are parted and people who have lost each other. Umm Kalthoum has passed away, she says, but she lives on through her music. Her favourite song is one called *Inta Umri*, which means 'You Are My Life'. She closes her eyes when she sings and sometimes she moves her body, sticking her shoulders back and shaking her hips in a way that makes me want to watch her. I ask her one day who is her life and she laughs and taps me on the head with her red-painted nails and says her husband is, of course.

Mama Luban bangs on her saucepan for me to come back to the Green house when she hears Umm Kalthoum on the cassette player coming from the Blue house. I pretend I can't hear. I love to listen to the instruments, the shivery sounds like wailing cats, and the drumming that gets faster and faster and the clapping from the people when Umm Kalthoum's voice goes up high and trembling in the air. After a while, when Mama Amaani sings *Inta Umri* at the same time as Umm Kalthoum, I start to join in as well. Listening to the music, how right it is, how it goes along just the way it's meant to, as if it couldn't be any other way, I forget that I don't know who I'm singing it for.

Next to football, I like singing more than anything now. When I sing, I forget if I'm hungry or thirsty, I forget if I'm cross with Amal, or in trouble with Mama Luban. I even forget – or at least I don't remember it in the same way as usual – that I'm not like other girls and that my mother lives in a *hospital*. I only remember the sound of my voice in my own ears, in my own chest. I can hear myself with my whole body.

Mama Amaani always asks after the health of my mother – she means Mama Luban – and how are all my brothers today, are they strong? Mama Luban doesn't ever ask about Mama Amaani. She pulls her *tobe* tight around her head when she sees her. She pretends to be weeding the onions when Mama Amaani walks past the Green house on the path, or looking in the hair of one of the boys. After Mama Amaani's gone, Mama Luban talks under her breath, asking how she's meant to bring up a respectable girl, when adult women behave like . . . She says a word I don't know.

In the mornings, a white car with black windows stops outside the village. The watchman jumps off his stool to open the gates when he hears the horn and the car drives fast up the path to the office. Before it has even stopped, a man jumps out of the passenger seat and holds open the back door. A woman with gold bracelets all the way up her arms climbs out of the car and goes into the office. Two men go behind her, one of them carrying her shiny white handbag with the gold chain on it. It looks funny in his big hands. For a long time after they have gone inside the dust drifts down, on to the orange and pink flowers that grow by the path, and the skin of our faces and arms.

Mama Luban never had children of her own and that is why it was the will of God for her to work at the village, she says. The President of Sudan has no children either and that is why he cares for the orphans as well. President Numeiri doesn't have time to come to the village, Mama Luban says, but the woman in the white car is his relative. She is married to his brother and that means she is Second Lady. Second Lady doesn't have any children either. 'Does she go to tombs, to pray to the saints?' I ask Mama Luban. But she says that a woman like that doesn't pray for anything you can find in this world.

President Jaafar Numeiri is the patron of the village as well as of the Institute, and he is going to *inaugurate* the village. We have to get ready. In the evenings, in the week before he comes, every kid in the village – there are forty-two of us – gathers on the football pitch to practise singing songs about how the President is the father of the nation. A man comes to tell us what songs to sing and how to sing them. He listens to everyone singing, and he asks me to sing a special song for the President, alone. I'm going to wear a dress made of red and green and black material, like the Sudanese flag. I have to wear a headscarf too, because of my hair.

I practise all the time. Mama Luban doesn't like me singing but she can't say anything about it, because the manager of the village and the foreigners are organizing the show. Amal's got to wear a yellow T-shirt with the village symbol on it, like the boys, and a brown skirt. She says I'm a show-off. Mahmoud pretends to sing like me, putting his hands on his chest, closing his eyes, opening his mouth as wide as it can go and screeching. Mohamed copies him. One morning when Mohamed does it in front of everyone, I pick up a stone and chuck it at him as hard as I can; the blood runs down from above his eye and he starts to scream. Faisal laughs.

Mama Luban comes out from the Green house, wiping her hands on her housedress. She slaps Mohamed, and says she wants to see me inside. I run off to the hill for a while and hide behind it, eating a few lumps of mud. I've got used to the taste of the earth here. It's not as bad as I thought it was when we first came.

I hear the stone banging on the saucepan, fast and cross-sounding, and my feet drag as I go back towards the Green house. Mama Luban sits at the big table in the middle of the house, passing her prayer beads through her fingers.

She goes on about how families have to stick together because there are enough people in the world to quarrel with without falling out with your relatives. I open my mouth to say she should tell Mohamed, not me, but she grabs my arm and holds on to it tightly.

'Please understand that I am trying to help you, Leila,' she says. 'You will always have to behave better than other girls. Wherever you go in this life, people will judge you.' She pauses, and wipes her eyes. 'Is that mud on your face?'

*

The President is not a giant, like he seems in all the pictures by the side of the road that we see from the school bus. He wears a green safari suit and brown leather sandals. He looks like the uncle of the President in the pictures, with white stubble on his chin and small eyes.

All the grown-ups are at the far end of the football pitch, on a stage under a red shade held up on wooden poles. The President is in the middle, in the front row, with his wife, First Lady, sitting next to him. Second Lady sits behind him. The manager is there, in a long white *jellabiya* and a big turban, and the foreigners. Mama Amaani is wearing a bright red *tobe* with gold-coloured embroidery on it; her glittery bangles sparkle in the sun. She's wearing red high-heeled sandals and red polish on her toenails. Mama Luban is wearing a yellow *tobe* instead of her usual white one, and her hair has been newly braided into tight, straight lines over her head.

We do the songs we have practised, and the dances, while the big people chat to each other and sip at their lemonade through striped straws. When it's my turn to step in front of all the others and sing to the President, I think I'm going to fall down. The microphone is slippery in my hands and my heart is beating fast. My mind empties. I can't remember a single one of the words to the song. I can't even remember the tune. All the people on the platform are looking at me. An aeroplane goes over the top of us and one of the women on the stage laughs.

Mama Amaani climbs down the steps from the stage, holding her red *tobe* in one hand. She stands in front of me and smiles at me, and as she opens her mouth I breathe in and begin to sing. I close my eyes. I don't see the big people any more. I sing as if I'm standing in Mama Amaani's yard while she chops up tomatoes. I don't sing the song I am meant to sing, about how the President is the first among the sons of the country. I sing *Inta Umri*. 'You Are My Life'. And as I hear it running through my body, I know who I am singing it for. It is for my country. Sudan.

When I finish, there is silence. One person begins to clap. It is the President. Everyone else starts clapping too. He wipes his face on a big white handkerchief, and beckons to me. He stands up as I approach him, shakes my hand and gives me a red velvet-covered box from the table in front of him. When he speaks to me, I can't answer.

We have practised walking backwards down the steps off the stage, because it's rude to turn your back on the big people. I walk carefully, one step at a time, until I feel my foot back on the hot, soft ground. I go back to my place, with the others. All the kids turn their heads and stare at me. Only Amal doesn't look at me, as I sit down beside her. I try to hide the box up my sleeve. It is so light. It feels empty. Everybody sings the last song, about the end of the war between the two halves of our country. Even the people on the stage stand up and join in. 'There is no north without the south,' the words say. 'There is no south without the north.'

When it is all over, I run back to the Green house and into my room. The box has a rounded lid with a hinge at one end and a thin gilt clasp at the other. I undo it and lift up the lid. Inside is a fine gold chain. I pull it carefully off its white satin pillow; it trickles between my fingers, so thin and glinting it seems to be made of liquid. I will wear it, I decide. I will never take it off, because it was given to me by the President. I'm trying out the little catch that fastens it, when Mama Luban appears beside me.

I look up at her and smile. I'm certain, for once, that I have been the kind of girl she wants me to be.

'The President says I have the voice of a woman, Mama. In the body of a girl.'

The smile disappears from her face. She looks at me for a moment, then snatches the necklace out of my hand.

'Singing will bring you nothing but trouble, Leila,' she says. 'From today, you must forget it.'

Chapter 6

CRUSHED FLOWERS

The big stones that edge the flowerbeds by the side of the drive were whitewashed for the President's visit; since then the paint has flaked off, leaving awkward brown shapes that look like the *continents* on the globe at school. Some of the stones are easy to balance on, some want to tip you off the moment you give them your weight. My legs are not long enough to reach from one to the next in one stride; I have to make a bit of a jump. I'm wearing Mohamed's brown canvas shorts; my green ones are drying behind the house. I think about the Queen, how she says you can trust nobody in this world, and at the same time I jump from one stone to the next, holding my arms out to each side. A strong, warm smell rises from the flowers where I have landed on them.

The first thing I see is a pair of black and yellow leopardskin shoes, the sort that Zulima says only country bumpkins

---

would be seen in. His feet are planted far apart from each other on the path, pointing in different directions, and out of them come legs in the bottom part of a faded grey safari suit.

'*Walad*,' he says. 'Son. Is there anybody here at all apart from that fool of a watchman?'

He asks if he is in the Orphans' Town; if he is he can't see many young 'uns running about, and where are they all? He says: what do I think of this set-up and is it a decent place for a young lady to grow up? Or a lad, he adds, looking at me in a distracted way as if he is thinking of something else. He breathes in quickly at the end of his words with a little sighing noise. I jump off my stone, land neatly with both feet together and point at the office, which wobbles in the distance behind a shimmering heat haze.

'The big people are in there,' I say.

'What big people?'

I shrug. 'The Manager. The *khawajas*. Maybe the President,' I add, for good measure.

I can hear his feet as they flop away along the path. It's quiet: the boys are on an outing with the Rotary Club and Mama Luban is inside. I'm thirsty but I want to get to stone number ten before I go and get water. I lick my tongue over my top lip, tasting its salty flavour. Feel the sharpness of the stones against the soles of my bare feet. Time seems as if it has got stuck on this moment, as though this feeling will last for ever and ever. I'm thinking this, at the same time as concentrating on balancing, when I hear an urgent banging coming from the direction of the Green house. Mama Luban hurries towards me, waving her arms in the air. I jump off stone number nine – it is annoying to be interrupted again – and skip along to meet her.

'What have you done?' she rasps, grabbing my arm.

I shake off her fingers. 'Nothing.'

'They want you in the office.'

I know I must have done something wrong. But I can't think what it is.

'Look at you! Where are your shoes? Run!' She pulls me along, twisting her *tobe* around her head and smoothing down her braids as we go.

'God forbid that any of my children have committed a wrongdoing,' she mutters.

On the path, I remember the chewing gum. By the time we get there, I am too frightened to knock on the office door. The Director of the village is there, as is the President's relative. The man in leopardskin slippers jumps up from his chair. 'You?' he says.

'Come here, Leila Aziz,' says Second Lady, reaching through the door and pulling me inside the room. Two men stand behind her with their arms crossed. She's wearing a gold chain around her neck with the arms of her spectacles attached to it. She sits down, still holding on to my arm. Her nails dig into the insides of my wrists and I can feel her breath on my face.

'On a day like this,' she says, 'the stars hold still in the firmament.'

I look at her, blankly.

'The angels bow their heads.'

Leopardskin Slippers steps forwards and stands in front of me, wiping the palms of his hands on his trousers.

'*Binti*,' he says. 'Daughter. You have lived all your life among strangers. But it is not my fault. After your mother and I divorced, I . . .'

I hear his sighing in-breath but I don't hear the words he says after that. The shiny tiles are flat and cool under my feet. I sneeze, from the cold air. I hear grown-ups' voices around me but I don't listen to the words they are saying.

The man digs in his pocket and brings out a creased piece of paper, which he holds out in front of me. There is a picture at the top, a drawing of a pair of scales. He points to my name on it, Leila Aziz. He points to another name, which he says is his. The tip of his finger is missing, I notice, as his hand disappears back into his pocket.

'Daughter,' he says. 'We want you to come . . .'.

Second Lady interrupts, asking why he waited till now to come looking for me.

'She'll be married within the year if she goes with you. She will never see the inside of a classroom again. And I will have to answer to my God,' she says, clutching both hands towards her throat.

The man shuffles his slippers, mops at his face with a dirty-looking towel.

'She's our girl,' he says. 'She belongs with us.'

Mama Luban pokes a shoulder through the door and Second Lady tells me to go back to the house with her. We walk along the path in silence; shortly afterwards the man arrives at the Green house. Mama Luban invites him inside and he lights a cigarette and puts his hands on his knees. I go out of the back of the house to the clay water pitcher and lift its wooden lid. I reach my arm down to where the tin mug floats cold and white on the dark surface, and dip it full of water. I go back indoors, putting one foot deliberately in front of the other, concentrating on not spilling any. I'm trying to feel the happiness that I knew this moment would bring me, but I don't feel anything at all.

I can't look at him, as I offer him the water. The hand with the missing fingertip closes around the mug. He is talking about the bus that he took to the village, how it broke down near the People's Market and the boy kept hold of the money honest citizens like him had paid. There are thieves from the top of the society to the bottom these days, Mama Luban agrees.

He grinds his cigarette out on the leg of the table and stands up. He says he is planning to work in Saudi Arabia. That once he gets his papers – and by God the people of offices don't know what labour is – he will set sail for the Gulf. He will make a lot of money there, where they know how to reward a skilled person like one who cooks for others. He will be able to send me fine presents, things that young ladies like. I stare at him and his eyes slide away from mine.

'I'll write to you,' he says, his voice rough and broken again. 'I'll write to you, *binti*. I waited a long time for this day.'

I watch from the garden as he plods along the path towards the gate, in between the stones and the crushed flowers. He will turn back. He will realize that he has forgotten to explain everything to me. And he will come back into the Green house and talk about the things I need to hear about. When he turns around, I will run to him. I will greet him as a father. And he will greet me as his daughter. Everything will be as it should be.

His shoulders stay set in front of him. He reaches the gate, walks through it, and disappears.

*

Abir is the cleverest girl in the class, next to Amal. She even wears glasses, round ones that make her eyes look huge. Abir is not one of the popular girls. But I like her more than any of the others.

For her breakfast, in her sandwich, Abir has yellow squares of processed cheese, or white circles of something she says is chicken, which comes out of a tin. She has biscuits with pink icing on them and cartons of mango or guava syrup to drink through a blue and white straw. It all fits into a plastic box with a red lid that she snaps off with her fingers. Before she starts to eat, she always offers to share her breakfast with me. I always refuse. I say it looks funny and it smells funny and she raises her thick eyebrows and wishes me a good appetite. My sandwiches are wrapped in torn pieces of newspaper. They have beans in them, sometimes lentils. I never offer them to her.

One day, as we sit eating on a bench in the shade of the classroom wall, she invites me to go home with her.

'You can meet my brother, Hassan,' she says. 'We can have anything you like for lunch.'

I feel twice as tall, immediately. Leila! Chosen by Abir, to be her friend!

'My mum will take you back to your place afterwards.'

All the nice feelings disappear. Abir must know I'm from the village. All the girls at school know it, although since the time of the zoo trip Mrs Khadija has never said anything about it. If her mother finds out I'm abandoned, she won't want me to go to their house again. She will tell Abir she's not allowed to talk to me.

That night in bed I think about Abir going to eat her sandwiches with Wifaq instead of me, looking over at me from the other side of the yard, laughing with the other girls. I wipe my eyes on Waheda's head. Mama Luban is right; I have to be stronger than other girls.

The next day, I tell Abir that I will go home from her house on a bus.

'Mummy has a car. What are you worrying about?' she says through a mouthful of crisps.

How can Abir be so clever and so stupid at the same time? If I go, it will be the end of my friendship. If I don't, it still might mean we are no longer friends. At break times, I start to avoid Abir, so that she doesn't have a chance to ask me again. By the end of term, she is eating her breakfast alone.

*

It's the beginning of the summer holidays and Mama Luban is in a good mood. She hurries around between her room and the kitchen and the yard, sweeping and sorting and washing. Several times, she twists her white *tobe* around her narrow body and hurries off down the path to the big gates, catching a bus into town. She comes back late with plastic bags full of tins of jam and fish, measures of herbs and spices tied up in newspaper cones, and flat paper parcels that look like new clothes. She locks the things in her cupboard, and starts to pour sesame oil and crumble white cheese on to the dish of beans for supper, still busy in her own mind. She lets the milk boil over in the mornings and burns the potatoes at lunchtime. When the twins pester her for sweets, she hands them her special tin as if they were visitors and tells them not to bother her. I wonder if she is going to have a *child of her own*, like she says she always wanted.

I am ten but my feet still haven't grown long. My front teeth remain too big for my face; the gap between them is wide enough to get my thumbnail into. And something strange is happening on my chest. I've got swellings, on both sides. Sometimes, in bed at night, I think they're going away. Other times, it feels as if they're getting worse. I can hardly do up the zip on the green shorts suit. Amal says I've got a disease. Her chest looks like two mosquito bites, as it always did.

One week after the holidays begin, I am in my room when I hear whistling outside the window. I fly outside, shouting his name. Rashid is standing next to the chilli plants that are growing in front of the house. He is taller than before, and his hair is cut short and neat so it's the same length as his beard. He's wearing a blue shirt with the sleeves rolled back over his wrists. When I see him, I can't speak. He laughs and rubs my head and says he wouldn't have known his Little Sister at all, if it weren't for the gap between her teeth.

All the boys come crowding around him, pulling at his

hands and asking his name and wanting to look at his watch. He plays a game of football with us for a while, showing my little brothers *ball skills*. But when Mama Luban invites him to stay and have lunch with us, he says he has to be going. He is meeting his friends at the cinema. He picks up the big bag he has with him and brings out a small wooden stool. When he says he made it for me, I am so happy I forget that I feel shy. I grab his hand and kiss it. I knew he hadn't forgotten me, and I told Zulima that he never would, I shout out. As he goes, he says I must be sure to let her know that he always remembers us. Both of us.

The stool is just the right size for me. It has three carved legs with patterns of leaves on them and the top is made of fine strips of white leather, woven together. I put it by my bed. I'll show it to Zulima next time she comes, to prove that he came. I told her my father had been and she didn't believe me. She said I must have misunderstood, and that he couldn't come and just disappear again. She said it was *mish mumkin*. Not possible.

I like having my own room in the Green house now. When I come back from school and shut the door behind me, I feel the inside of my head getting clear and empty. Sometimes, I just stand and look out of the window, at the leaves of the lime trees that Amal and I planted moving in the breeze, or the planes disappearing into the blueness over my head. I imagine all the people up there looking down on the village and seeing the flat roof of the Green house, and all the other houses, and the sheets hanging on the lines and the brown dust of the football pitch and the pink and orange flowers along the side of the path. When I turn back to the room, it looks small, and private. Even the people on the plane can't see in here. No one can.

Waheda has lost one of her eyes as well as her mouth; her arms and legs, which used to be stiff, are floppy now; when I sit her on my pillow she falls over. I take hold of her and put her head under my nose. It is seventy-two days since my father visited. I have decided that when he comes back, I will go away with him. I will tell Second Lady that I don't care if I never *see the inside* of a classroom again. I practise in my mind what I will say to her to make her see why I have to go with him, even if he is a poor man who can't give me as good a life as they can at the village, like she said. He might have lost the address of the village. It might have fallen out of the pocket of his green safari suit.

'Daydreaming again?'

Mama Luban stands in the doorway, wiping her knobbly hands on a cloth.

'Are you well?' she asks. 'Strong?'

I nod, half-heartedly. She must want me to do the washing for the boys. Or carry a bag of rice for her, from the store.

'Good,' she says. 'Because this is a special time for you.'

She keeps on rubbing her hands, even though they must be dry by now.

'You want to be clean, don't you?' she says. 'Pure?'

I nod again and she opens her mouth as if she's going to say something else. She turns round and goes back into the kitchen. I can hear her busy with pans and bowls but not banging them around, as she does when she's cross. For a moment, I even think I hear her humming.

Crushed Flowers

The girls at school talk about *purification* sometimes, when the teachers are nowhere near. They say a girl who hasn't been purified will never get married, because no one will want her. She will gape open like a heathen, they shudder, screwing up their faces. I agree, and screw up my own face as hard as I can. I hate the feeling that there are things that everyone but me knows. In the mornings, I rub my skin hard with the loofah in the bathroom, and use the sour-smelling pink soap all over. The idea that there is more to purification than washing keeps nagging at me.

I can't ask Mama Luban, in case it is the wrong question. There are a lot of things she thinks girls shouldn't talk about. Amal probably knows, but I don't want her calling me an idiot. Zulima is always thinking about her own things. I could ask Mrs Khadija, but I never get a chance to talk to her on my own. There are always other girls around, and if they heard me they would think I was stupid. They would say that it was because I'm not like them that I don't know what purification is. The thought makes me angry. I chuck Waheda back on the bed and run outside to play with the boys.

*

Mama Luban calls me and Amal into the Green house yard. She is sitting on the low stool in her old housedress, mixing henna powder with water. She scrapes the mixture off the sides of the bowl with a spoon and gathers the last of the dry powder into the thick, greenish paste; the smell makes me want to sneeze. She has a small bottle of oil on a tray, squares of newspaper and a box of matches.

'Tomorrow is your special day,' she says.

She tells us to sit on the bed, and she brings all her things over and sits in front of us on the stool. Amal claps her hands in excitement. Mama Luban rolls a piece of newspaper into a cone, and spoons the mixture into it. She pulls Amal's foot into her lap, rubs strong-smelling oil all over it. She holds the cone like a pen, squeezing a thin, wobbly line all the way around Amal's foot. When she's finished, she begins to cover the sole with the henna paste, spreading the mixture around with a matchstick. She finishes one foot and moves on to the other. She is humming again. I didn't imagine it. The question I haven't dared to ask bursts out of my mouth.

'Mama Luban? Are you going to have a child of your own?'

Her expression changes, but she keeps her eyes on Amal's foot.

'What kind of empty talk is this?' she asks.

Amal begins to laugh silently; I can feel her next to me. Mama Luban must be able to feel it too. She slaps her leg and tells her to hold still.

She makes a circle of henna on each of Amal's palms, and covers the ends of each of her fingers with a cap of the paste, pressing it round to make it stick. It's my turn. I stick out my feet and she draws a wobbly line around them. All the time she's doing it, she talks in her croaky voice about how we are going to become women, even though it's late, how fortunate we are, how we will make her proud if we act as women should. I don't know how women should act, except that they shouldn't speak loudly or eat greedily, especially in company.

When I feel the cold henna paste on the palms of my hands,

I feel excited. I feel as if I am going to be someone different. Stretching my hands out and keeping them still in front of me makes my shoulders ache. Mama Luban shakes her head at me.

'From now on, you have to be strong,' she says. 'You must be proud. Keep your suffering to yourself.'

She drops the empty henna cone back into the bowl and says she's finished. Amal and I sit side by side with our legs stuck out in front of us, until the shadow of the kitchen wall has moved off us and we are in the sun. The boys are shouting to each other in the distance; birds gather in the trees beyond the back walls of the village. The noise they make reminds me of visiting the Queen, the sound of the other women in the ward, the way it grows louder when visitors come to the gate. As the visitors walk away, calling over their shoulders that they'll be back soon, the sound of the patients dies away.

Zulima hasn't taken me to see our mother lately, because she's had a baby. A girl, called Jamila. I've only seen it twice and I was disappointed that she didn't name it after me. When we went to visit, the Queen gave me a small, empty bottle with the words 'Girl of Sudan' on the front. She didn't look at the baby much and we didn't stay long because Zulima said she was *exhausted*.

Amal sits very still. She won't talk to me in case it stops the henna working. It's boring, doing nothing. I move around a bit, and some of my henna falls off. I pick a bit more off with my fingers, just to see how it's developing underneath, and that breaks off big lumps of the stuff from my fingertips. I get an itch on the sole of my foot and have to rub it against the leg of the bed. By the time Mama Luban says it's time to get ready for bed, most of my henna has already come off.

We wash off the remains together, scraping it under the out-side tap with a scrap of loofah and no soap, like Mama Luban tells us. Afterwards, she rubs more oil into our skin and says the colour will get darker in the night. She disappears into her room and comes out with new dresses for each of us, red ones, and two small gold rings, and special bracelets of silk thread with beads and charms to ward off the evil eye. We put on the bracelets, and the rings, and she says we can wear the dresses in the morning, because that's when we are going to become women. I'm relieved; I hate wearing dresses. Amal is disap-pointed; she wants to sleep in hers.

Amal comes to stay the night with me in the Green house and we talk in the darkness for a long time. I can't sleep. It's part of the strangeness of the day, the way everything is changing minute by minute from my old life to a new one that I don't know yet. Amal says she can't wait to be a woman so she can be a teacher like Mrs Khadija. I say that I can't wait either, that I'm in even more of a hurry than she is.

I wake up when it's still dark. I hold on tightly to Waheda. What will happen to me when I can't go to school and live at the village? I ask her silently. Who will give me food? Where will I sleep? I pray to God not to make me grow up.

*

The omelette is just how I like it, salty and soft with bits of onion in it and tomato. We have my favourite drink too – *tebaldi*, the one made from the seeds of the tree of life, that is sweet and sour at the same time. Mama Luban pours me and

Amal a big glass each then goes to the door and looks out down the path towards the gates. She pops back into her room, muttering to herself. She has made us have a bath and put on the new dresses; now we have to stay around the house. We are washing the dishes at the back of the house when we hear a lot of voices, all shouting and calling at the same time. Amal drops her scourer and begins to cry.

They crowd around us, smiling and joking as if they are at a party. All the mothers are there from all the houses, along with two other women that I've never seen before. One of them, the fat one, is carrying a black bag in one hand. Mama Amaani has a clay drum and a big smile on her face. Something about the way they are so excited makes me feel afraid.

Mama Luban tells Amal to come with her, and all the grown-ups go inside, leaving me in the yard. I can't concentrate on the dishes, there's so much noise coming from inside the house. There is drumming and all the women make loud noises in their throats, as if they were at a wedding. Mama Luban comes rushing out and fills a jug with water from the zir, then disappears inside again. After what seems like a long time, she comes to the back door and nods her head for me to follow her.

All the women are crowded into my bedroom. The shutter is closed and the electric light is on, as is the ceiling fan. Amal is lying on the other bed, facing the wall. She is all covered up with a new shawl; the colours – purple and orange and gold – look rich and exciting in the dim light. Mama Amaani is sitting by her, with her hand on her shoulder. The air is thick with smoke from a big incense burner by my bed but I can see a tin basin on the floor with blood in it and lumps of something else that I don't recognize. All the mothers are there, and the two women I've never seen before. The fat one – she has big hands – tells me to hurry up and take my knickers off and lie on my back on the bed. She says she's wasted enough time with the other one fighting like a cat and that if I've got any sense I'll keep still and everything will be finished before I know it.

Mama Luban sits by my head, half on top of me; she covers my eyes with her fingers and two of the other mothers yank my knees apart and hold them so tight I can't move. I start to shout for help – it's all happening so quickly, I'm not ready. I feel a slap on my leg and hear Mama Hajji, the old one, say there is no need to cry, no one has touched me yet. After that, I don't know exactly what happens but I feel a horrible sharp pain between my legs and Mama Luban says it's an *injection*. Straight away after that, I feel a different kind of pain, a sharp agony that drives the breath out of my body. I try to kick the women off me but two of them have got my legs trapped between their arms so I can't move. The room is full of noise: drumming, women's voices shouting out to me to be strong, and all of them making the wedding cries from deep in their throats.

I think they might be killing me. I scream at them to stop, as loud as I can. Mama Luban splays her fingers to clamp them over my mouth as well as my eyes and I glimpse the woman, standing at the bottom of the bed with a big curved needle held in fingers covered in blood. She pulls the needle away from me, with a length of bloody thread behind it. The hand comes back over my eyes.

Mama Luban gets off my arm and stands up; the breath is coming into my body in great gasps. The fat woman drops the needle into a bowl and wipes her hands. She kisses her fingertips with a smacking sound.

'Just like a watermelon,' she says. 'No way in at all.'

I feel someone pulling my dress down over my knees, the silky lightness of a shawl being thrown over me. The women crowd out of the room, and soon afterwards everything goes quiet.

There is a burning pain between my legs. My body feels as if it doesn't belong to me. My throat is raw. I see Waheda on the floor, by the cupboard, but as I think of getting off the bed to go and get her, I realize my legs are tied together. Amal is whimpering on the other bed. I call her, but she doesn't answer. The shawl is slippery between my fingers. Waheda's face has no expression at all.

The next day it's still agony, although I can get off the bed and move around the room and eat the special lunch Mama Luban makes. Amal develops a fever. She can't pee. At night, she doesn't make sense when she talks. She has to be taken away in the Director's car. She doesn't come back to the village for a week and when she does, she can't stand up. Mama Amaani makes her wear a *hejab* pouch around her neck that has a prayer in it to make her better, and she spends most of the rest of the school holidays lying on a bed in the shade of the *rakuba* at the back of the Blue house.

Mama Amaani says that Mama Luban chose the wrong

woman to do the purification, and that if she had taken her advice and brought someone younger there wouldn't have been any problems. Mama Luban says that the woman who came is famous for her clean scars and that Amal will be perfectly all right as time goes by, God willing. Mama Amaani says Mama Luban shouldn't have employed an old woman who can't see the moon in the sky, let alone the bud in a rose. I'm sitting by Amal's bed under the palm-leaf shade of the *rakuba*; they are in the kitchen. After Mama Luban has gone, Mama Amaani sniffs and talks to herself. Soon, she puts on one of her cassettes and I can't hear her any more.

I still don't know what purification is, except that I can't go after the ball in goal properly any more. I can't jump from one stone to another either, coming along the drive. Peeing takes me a long time. It comes in drops, where it used to come as if from a tap. Mama Luban says I shouldn't be playing football any more, anyway.

Chapter 7

GREEN COFFEE BEANS

The year is 1979 and the month is June. It is written on the blackboard, next to the Arabic date. Mrs Khadija stands in front of us and fans her face with an atlas that has lost its spine.

'You've changed, girls,' she says, looking at me and Amal.

I go hot under the short plaits that Mama Luban has insisted on twisting my hair into for the new term. The henna patterns have worn off my hands but the ends of my nails are still stained orange. I'm afraid she is going to ask us about our purification in front of the whole class. I stare at the desk and Mrs Khadija tells Amal to get out the exercise books. She starts to talk about her holiday in Egypt and how her daughters went inside the Great Pyramid.

I was dreading going back to school, because I didn't want to see Wifaq again. She looks at me as if I'm not really there.

She uses a sugary voice to say hello to the other girls and ignores me and Amal. But as the day goes on, I decide that I am glad to be back. In general knowledge, Mrs Khadija says that you should write the good things that happen to you on a piece of stone and the bad ones in the sand. I like hearing about Big Ben, and how to tell the difference between a sheep and a goat, and all the other funny things she tells us.

At break, I feel happy. When Wifaq comes walking by with her friends, I smile at her and say hello.

'Sorry,' Wifaq says, loud enough for me to hear but no one else. 'My mother won't let me talk to daughters of sin.'

After school, I wait outside the white-painted wall. My right hand is closed over a handful of dust. I am holding it so tight, my fingers hurt. Everybody is looking at me, even the woman who sits behind a box selling tea. She scrubs out a tea glass with a bit of dried grass, watching me all the while. Amal waits on the other side of the road, under the tree. As I look at her, she gives a shout. I turn round and see Wifaq coming through the gate with her shoe bag dangling from one hand.

'Something hot burns like fire,' I yell, and chuck the dust in her face. It is how kids start fights.

Her arms are still by her sides as I launch myself at her. I feel her shirt sleeve against my lips as my teeth close through the white cotton on to her flesh. She smells of milk. She screams and drops her bag. I claw at her back with both hands, feeling her solid body.

She is wiping her eyes on her knuckles and crying for her mother. I shove her and she falls over and curls up on her side in the dust, covering her face with her hands, whimpering that she doesn't want to fight. I don't feel angry any more but I know the others are watching. I kick her in her side, not hard, and she starts to scream again. Her socks are round her ankles. I kneel down and put my mouth close to her ear.

'Next time, I swear to God I'll cut your throat.'

'I'm sorry,' she sobs. 'I don't know what a daughter of sin is.'

Wifaq's parents complain and the head of the whole school calls me in to the office. When she's finished telling me off, she gives me a letter to take back to the village. She says that if my teacher hadn't spoken so highly of me, she might have had to ask me to leave.

When I come out of the office, Wifaq is waiting for me. I push past her and start to walk back towards the classroom but she grabs my arm and says she's sorry for what she said; she didn't know what it meant. The following day, she gives me her pink pencil case and the day after she asks me to play with her and her friends at break. I don't want to but Amal does. So we join in. After that, I'm not quite sure how it happens but Wifaq becomes our friend.

*

Abir has been to London for her holidays. At break, the day she comes back to school, she comes over and sits next to me. She asks me again to go to her house. I can't think of an excuse quickly enough, so I say yes. Her face lights up.

'I was beginning to think you didn't want to meet my family,' she says. 'Which day will you come?'

Abir's mother wears a white skirt that shows her ankles, a dark-purple cotton shirt with white embroidery on it and black sunglasses pushed up on the top of her head. Her hair is as straight and silky as Abir's and her skin is the colour of milky coffee. Around her neck is a string of purple beads that match her blouse and make you notice her shining, smooth skin. I can't stop staring at her.

Their house is painted white on the outside and has two storeys, with curly metal bars over the windows. Inside, the floors are tiled with smooth, creamy-coloured squares like the ones in the office at the village. There are plants in shiny metal pots that look as if they are made of gold.

Abir's father is a newspaper editor, she says, and reads books even when he is not at work. The shelves of books go from the floor to the ceiling. There is a whole row of giant books that all look the same as each other, dark blue with gold letters across their backs. Abir says it is the *Encyclopaedia Britannica*. She says everything you might ever want to know is in there, arranged in alphabetical order.

'Can you find out what's going to happen in the years to come?'

She laughs. 'Of course not. Dad says no one can predict the future.'

Her bedroom is *upstairs*. She has a row of dolls with pink plastic faces and long yellow hair and sharp, solid eyelashes. Her room has windows leading on to a balcony that overlooks a green garden, where machines turn around in circles sending a spray of rain that patters on the wide leaves.

'Are you OK?' she asks. 'You're not usually so quiet.'

I can't think of anything to say. Abir's house is so beautiful; it makes me feel sad to think that I will never see it again. Her mother calls up the stairs, asking if we want our lunch. Abir looks at me. I shrug. The idea that she can eat when she wants to is so unexpected, I feel stupid. I don't know if I'm hungry or not. It's lunchtime. I must be.

We eat our lunch off china plates; Abir picks up a knife and fork and although there is a pair put out for me I use my right hand as usual to eat with. I have never used a knife and fork. Abir's mother pushes hers aside and eats with her hand as well. There are more dishes than I have ever seen, except at a party. Five different bowls full of stews and vegetables, a fried Nile perch fish lying on a pillow of rice, and two sorts of juice in tall flower-patterned jugs with matching glasses.

'So, girls,' she says. 'Did you have a good day at school?'

I have just taken a big mouthful of chicken, so I don't answer. Mama Luban has taught us never to show what is in our mouths as we eat. Mama Luban says it's rude to talk while people are eating.

'Not bad,' says Abir, with her mouth full.

Her mother looks at me and smiles.

'What do you like at school?' she says, in a kind voice.

'Koranic studies,' I say, in the most pious voice I can manage.

'Oh really? That was never my favourite, I must admit. What do you enjoy outside school?'

'Football.'

She laughs. 'Good for you. Why should boys have all the fun?'

After we have finished eating, a woman comes out from the kitchen with a big round tray and takes all the dishes away. She comes back with mango ice cream in glass dishes and fruit salad and small biscuits like the ones Abir has in her plastic box. I eat all mine and, when I've finished, I lick the sides of the bowl. Abir's mother offers me more ice cream. I refuse. Girls should not eat much, especially when they are guests in someone else's house. She spoons more into my dish, saying it's from Egypt and will help me score goals.

'I'm usually the one in goal,' I say. 'I'm bigger than most of my brothers.'

'Do you have enough for a team? Goodness.'

Abir shows me the coloured pencils she got when she went to London with her family. They stayed in an apartment, she says. In London, grown-up women wear trousers. Even the Muslims. There is so much food, they give it to the birds. Cats live inside houses, with the people. At school I make Abir laugh. But I can't think of anything funny, here in her echoing house. After today, we won't be friends any more. So it doesn't matter.

'What did you do in the holidays?' she asks.

'I had my purification. Thanks be to God. I got a ring and a shawl.'

Abir doesn't say anything.

'What did you get?' I ask her. 'When you had yours?'

She looks towards the window, out at her green garden.

'I didn't have it done. My parents say it's barbaric.'

She laughs, apologetically. 'I'm sure it isn't really, though. I mean, I know I'm the only one, at school . . .'

When it gets dark, we climb into the back of the white car, on to the soft, smooth seats. Abir sits next to me. She is quiet too. We pass our school and from there I can't think what to do, except to direct Abir's mother out along the airport road, all the way to the gates of the village. I will never go to the cool, quiet house again. Never sit with Abir at break, or make her laugh when she's meant to be doing algebra. It crosses my mind to explain to her that I'm not the same as the other kids at the village – I have a mother and a father. But I keep quiet. She wouldn't believe me. And anyway, I am like my brothers and sisters. I am exactly like them.

When I see the big gates of the village, with the picture on the wall of a boy and a girl, I call out to stop the car. Abir's mother looks over her shoulder into the back seat.

'Right here?' she asks.

'That's what I said, isn't it?' It sounds rude, although I don't mean it to.

She pulls the car to the side, jerks up the brake and leans round to the back seat again. Her brown eyes are the same shape as Abir's. The beads lie on her neck like boiled sweets. I've never seen a grown-up woman go out without a *tobe* before. She seems like a film star.

'Did you know?' she asks Abir.

'Of course,' says Abir.

'Why didn't you tell me?'

Abir lifts her shoulders. Her mother gets out of the car and opens the door for me. I climb out, lugging my school bag behind me.

'Come again soon,' she says. 'You are welcome at any time.'

She reaches down and kisses me. It makes me dizzy, feeling her soft hair brush my face, breathing in her scent of soap and almonds.

'I mean it,' she says. 'Come soon. Abi likes you so much.'

'You won't say anything, will you?' Abir says, rolling down her window. 'At school?'

When I understand what she's talking about, I shake my head.

As I walk up the path towards the Green house, Faisal and the twins race towards me, along with the new boy from the Red house that they call Paper Bag, because he is light enough to blow about in the wind. I recognize them without seeing their faces. I know them by their shapes, by the way they move. When I look at them, I see myself. I know it's the same for them. We are family. Mahmoud takes my bag and runs ahead to the Green house, shouting to Mama Luban that I'm home.

*

Every morning after that, Abir brings two sandwiches with her to school, in her navy-blue rucksack with the *Union Jack* on it. I love these sandwiches. I love their tastiness, their textures and colours. But more than that I love the thought that Abir's mother remembers me each morning, wraps a second sandwich in thin, clean paper and snaps the lid on another plastic box with her ringed fingers.

I begin to visit Abir's home regularly, and once she has permission from her father she comes home with me to the

village as well sometimes, on the bus with the others. We practise singing in my room, or play with my brothers, or just sit
and talk with Amal. One day, Abir plays football with me and
the boys; afterwards her socks are around her ankles and her
eyes shine behind her glasses.

When they've been to their farm in the countryside, Abir's
parents send boxes of mangos or tomatoes to the village for all
of us. At Abir's house, her mother always tells me to study,
that it will help me in my future. Abir helps me with my
maths, when I let her. At the village, no one knows if you do
your homework or not. If you want to study, you can. If not,
it doesn't matter.

I look up to Abir and try to be like her. But I don't have as
much space in my mind as she does, for geometry and history.
I still wait every day for a letter from my father, or a message
to hurry to the office to find him sitting in the visitor's chair
again. Only Amal shares this secret with me and she waits
with almost the same impatience as I do. Because when Aziz
Mohamed Mahmoud returns, he will be taking both of us into
our futures. We are ready and waiting, even if his letter has got
lost in the post.

*

A new Director has come to the village. He is Sudanese but he
trained in America. His hands are still decorated with henna
from his wedding; he is young. He and his wife come and live
in a house in the village; he is the first Director to live with us
and he calls in to the houses at any time to say hello to us or

have breakfast with us. The mothers don't like it but they have to get used to it. He speaks to us politely, as if he really wants to know about us. He plays games with us and learns all our names. He asks us to call him Father Sayf but after a couple of weeks I have dropped the 'Sayf', and so has every other kid in the village. We just call him Father.

There is a new boy in the Yellow house. He is eight years old but he looks younger. He fights with his brothers, throws mud at the clean washing and pisses in his trousers. Mohamed has nicknamed him *Jabbad*, Glutton, because of the way he begs for food, pulling up his shirt to show his belly.

His mother, Mama Hajji, says she hasn't been able to get anything done since he arrived. One day, soon after the new Director has come, he finds Jabbad with a rope around his waist, tied to a bed in the Yellow house.

That night, when it gets dark, Father Sayf holds a big meeting for all the mothers and all the children. He says that no child will ever be tied up in this village ever again. He says we are human beings, not animals, and all the time he is around we will be treated like human beings. He says that any child in the village can talk to him if they have problems they can't work out alone, or with their mothers. All the time he's talking, he walks up and down on the football pitch, where the goal is. Mama Hajji isn't at the meeting and the next day we see her dragging a big bag out of the gates of the village.

Mama Luban and the other mothers are a bit quiet after the meeting. Mama Luban says to Mama Miriam that a young man like him doesn't know what these kids are like. He thinks they are like any others, agrees Mama Miriam. Mama Amaani interrupts and says we are just like normal children, if anyone gives us a chance.

Mama Luban doesn't hit us much, or tie anyone to the tree. But if my cupboard isn't tidy, she tips everything out on to the floor. It makes me angry. Next time I come home from school to find my clothes on the floor, I complain to Father Sayf and he comes to talk to her about it. When he's gone, Mama Luban pulls the key to my room off the string that she wears around her neck and throws it at me. After that, I keep my room locked when I am outside the house. My room is my own private world where I can sing, or have Amal to stay with me, or just sit on my special stool with Waheda and think about the things that have happened to me so far in this life.

*

The car bumps over the metal railway tracks, down a wide side street and stops outside a tall house with two white-trunked palm trees in the front garden. I follow Father Sayf under the trees and around the side of the house to a mud-plastered room with a narrow veranda in front of it. Some dented saucepans are balanced on a wooden rack outside, next to a heap of charcoal and two empty bottles. There is no shade and the sun is so hot it makes the back of my head prickle.

Inside, my sister Zulima lies on a bed, with her head on the pillow. She's wearing a red housedress, open at the neck; her hair needs combing.

'At last,' she says, raising herself on her elbow.

There is a baby beside her, lying on a cloth, dressed in a yellow vest. Its eyes are shut tight and it has no hair. It looks old. The baby begins to mew and Zulima picks it up and pulls down the neck of her nightdress. Her breast is bigger than its head. She tells me to put my bag under the bed, and fetch some water for her. Father Sayf clears his throat. He gives me two pound notes and says that I must make myself useful and telephone him when I'm ready to come back to the village. He puts down the tin of toffees that Mama Luban has sent for Zulima and ducks back out of the doorway.

I try not to look at the baby in case it brings bad luck, but I want to stare and stare at her. Her skin is pale. She has long feet curling up uselessly at the end of her thin legs and fine, dark fur covering her face. She looks as if she has hatched out from an egg. On her tummy, where the vest ends, there is a withered stump of flesh. It makes me feel sick. I wonder again where she came from.

Zulima sent a message to the village for me to come and help her with the new baby. Her first one, Jamila, is being looked after by her husband's mother until she feels better. I decided when I was packing my bag to come that I was going to ask Zulima a question. I open my mouth to ask it but Zulima is moaning, shifting her body under the sheet. She doesn't look like she normally does. Her face is puffy and she has shadows under her eyes. There is a dried aubergine plant hanging from a nail on the wall behind her.

I go outside to have a look around. No one seems to be at

home in the big house. Zulima's husband Ali is the guard here but in the day he goes to his other job, guarding a bank. There is a latrine with a broken wooden door and on the side of Zulima's house a tiny, dark kitchen just big enough for one person, with a table crowded with plates and jars and papery onion skins.

Zulima calls me back inside. Her neighbour is coming. I have to get the coffee beans. Light a piece of charcoal over the gas ring in the corner of the room and fan it with a mat. Fetch the dried ginger, and bring the six small coffee cups, and some sugar. The round-bottomed clay coffee pot and the beaded ring to balance it on are under her bed.

When the coals begin to glow, I squat next to the stove on the stool and tip the beans into the pan, shaking it over the heat like Mama Luban does, throwing the beans up in the air and catching them again.

'How's everyone?' Zulima asks. 'How's Amal? What's happened to Quarratulain? Have you seen any of the others?' I tell her about all the kids from the Institute, and their mothers and what they have been doing. I enjoy talking about them, giving her all the news, but when I look up from the skillet she's asleep. I haven't even given her Rashid's message yet.

The neighbour arrives with her own baby in her arms, a noisy boy, grabbing at her necklace with fat hands. By the time the beans are black enough to satisfy Zulima, my arm's tired. I tip them into the mortar, take up the pestle and start to pound them. My palms rub and slip against its metal sides.

The neighbour sings a song. 'Don't visit me today,' she sings. 'Not by the window, not by the door. My husband has returned.' Zulima giggles on the bed. She groans again and tells the woman not to make her laugh.

'Did she sew you up nice and tight?' the neighbour asks. 'Good as new?'

Zulima closes her eyes. 'I suppose so,' she says, in a flat voice.

I put the fine coffee grounds into the tin jug of water, add the pounded ginger and set it on the coals. The baby has fallen asleep again; a dribble of yellow comes out of the side of her mouth. By the time the coffee boils in the jug, more women have crowded into the room and are sitting along the edge of the second bed, in a row. They all seem to know Zulima; they're giving her advice about what she mustn't eat and mustn't do. One of them says she knew a midwife that went blind from seeing so much blood. Another one says that child-birth is death. They all agree she might get a son next time, God willing.

Zulima complains that her husband's mother interferes in everything.

'She's buried the afterbirth in the yard,' Zulima says, jigging the baby up and down. 'So she won't go far away. Why? What kind of a life is this for her?'

I shift about on the low stool and wipe sweat off my face. I pick the jug off the coals, pour the coffee in a thin stream into the neck of the coffee pot. Its round bottom is blackened from use but its neck and handle are still red. I stuff the bit of fibre into the neck of the pot and settle it back on to the stove.

The first neighbour takes a coal from the stove and scatters incense over it. She holds the tiny coffee cups over the incense burner. They fill with smoke even though they're upside down. She puts them on the tray, spoons sugar into the bottom of them and pours the coffee so full that a bit spills over the brim of every cup. Mama Luban does the same thing; she says it brings *prosperity*. I pass the tray around.

The smell of the coffee mixed with sweet, woody incense makes my head spin. It makes Zulima's ugly room seem more beautiful. My back is sore and my hands are stinging but I would rather be here than at the village, I decide. The only thing I miss is Amal. The women take cup after cup of coffee; the more they drink, the more loudly they talk and laugh and quarrel. I have to refill the sugar bowl twice and go to the shop for more green coffee beans. It's dark by the time they go and Zulima is in a bad temper.

'Go and wash the cups,' she says. 'I swear they would stay all night if they dared.'

I decide it's not a good time to ask her anything.

Her husband comes home late; he changes into his *jellabiya*, eats his food and goes to sleep on a bed at the front of the big house in case thieves come over the wall. I sleep in the room with Zulima and the baby. Several times, I wake up to the sound of it crying and lie on my bed, waiting for Zulima to wake up. The bed here is soft, with a big round hollow in the middle of the mattress, like the old beds at the Institute. I have got used to the hard beds of the village; I feel suffocated and hot.

Before long, the days all seem the same; I get up early to

make tea for Zulima's husband before he goes to his job. When he has gone, I boil water with a special tree bark, for Zulima to wash herself with. I rinse out the baby's dirty clothes and drape them over the bushes to dry. I hate the stink and my fingers go wrinkly from so much washing. Several times a day, I walk under the tall palm trees of the big house, out of the gate and down to the shop on the corner. Sometimes Zulima doesn't have any money. Those days, I have to say that she sent me and she'll settle the bill later. The boy serves me extra slowly and flings the milk powder or the sugar down on the scarred counter with a disapproving look.

When we've had our tea, Zulima washes the baby, holding her in the crook of her arm and splashing water over her then wiping her dry and rubbing sesame oil into her skin. The stump at her middle gets smaller every day. By the time it falls off, it looks like a bit of string. Sometimes, I put my little finger in her mouth to feel her hard gums, her mouth sucking. I'm getting used to the baby. After she's had her milk, she waves her hands in the air as if she's swimming, and sometimes she sneezes. Zulima wants to call her *Habibi*, which means Darling, but her husband's mother thinks she should be called something else.

The neighbours visit every day. The one with the fat baby shows me how to make a milk pudding with fenugreek seeds, to help Zulima's breasts fill up. I sweep the floor and sprinkle it with water before they come, burn incense to keep bad spirits away from the house, iron shirts for Zulima's husband Ali to wear to work. I run back and forth to and from the shop for packets of tea, or matches, or dates for the guests.

It's hard work but I feel proud, because I'm helping my sister.

One morning, Zulima rolls herself off the bed and hobbles out to the latrine. She still can't walk properly. She is gone a long time and the baby begins to yell. I whisper at her to be quiet but she carries on crying. I stroke her face a bit, and fan her with my hand in case she's hot. She yells louder than ever. I can't stand the sound any longer. I take hold of her two hands and lift her into the air, like the nannies used to pick us up at Mygoma. She is silent for a moment and her face turns dark. She lets out a shriek that goes into my chest like a knife. Zulima rushes in and grabs her, shouting what have I done? and that she told me not to touch her. I try to say that I was only trying to help but Zulima slaps me and tells me to shut up. The baby grizzles all day and doesn't move her arms at all. Zulima won't let me near her; she gives me a pile of sheets to wash in the yard, then I peel potatoes till my hands ache.

That evening, Zulima's husband takes the baby to the clinic. He comes back with her wrapped in a white cotton shawl, and hands her to Zulima. The doctor had to return the baby's wrists to their sockets, he says. They were dislocated, from when I picked her up. It has cost him a week's wages to get it put right. I lie on my bed and curl up towards the wall. I have decided to make Zulima ring Father Sayf tomorrow and tell him to come and get me.

When the baby goes to sleep, Zulima shakes my shoulder.

'Never mind,' she says. 'I know you didn't mean to.'

'I'm going back to the village,' I say.

'You're not,' she says. 'I can't manage without you.'

Later, she sprays some of her scent on my hair. After that, she lets me hold the baby on my lap for a bit. I sit outside on the stool in the cool darkness while she tries to get a picture on the old television set. The baby looks at me with her calm eyes and reaches up to touch my face.

'Sorry, Habibi,' I whisper to her.

Zulima's husband comes out of the room, on his way out again. His stomach is so round under his white *jellabiya*, he looks as if he's going to have a baby. He never says anything to Zulima, apart from: where is his food? or what did she do with the money he gave her? But every time he sees me, he calls me 'Auntie Leila'. And every time, it makes him laugh.

'So, Auntie Leila,' he says. 'You'll be more careful next time, eh?'

*

That night, I see blood in my knickers. The next morning there's more, on the sheet of my bed. I'm scared I'm going to die. It's a punishment for hurting the baby. I tell Zulima about it.

'You became a woman,' she says, 'even if you don't look like one.' She says this will happen to me every month, and I must take care because it can come at any time and it's shameful to be seen with blood on your dress. It's time for me to start fasting properly at Ramadan, she says, not just going hungry till lunchtime.

All the while, I wait for Zulima to answer my question, even though I haven't asked it yet.

'Baby girls,' I say. 'I expect each one is different?'

She shrugs. 'Not really. Why?'

I try again. 'You knew about babies, before you became a mother . . .'

'Are you kidding?' she says, through her chewing gum.

After another week, I can't wait any longer.

'What was I like? When I was born?'

I think at first she's not going to answer. She is sitting on the edge of the bed, looking in the mirror and pulling little hairs out from her eyebrows with a pair of tweezers.

'I used to carry you round all the time,' she says. 'On my hip. I was so happy to have a sister.'

She wipes her eyes on the back of her hand.

Our mother used to go out to work, in the market, she says, selling traditional bread. Zulima used to wake up early and see her sitting by the big stove, scraping the pieces up off the hot metal tray. The room would be warm, thick with the smell of the batter and wood smoke and the deep, woody smell of our mother. When she had finished cooking, she would fold the bread into flat squares, wrap everything in a clean cloth and wash herself. Her hair was long and black and she combed it every morning with scented oil before she went out, wrapped up in her *tobe*, with the bundle of goods tied in the cloth and balanced on her head.

I can hardly breathe, I am listening so hard. The baby snuffles in her sleep and a train whistles in the distance.

'At first, she used to take you with her,' Zulima says. 'Later, I had to look after you. She would leave a bowl of milk, with a plate over it, for you. She used to lock the door behind her.'

'What happened to us after that?'

Zulima shakes her head and flings the mirror across the room.

'I can't remember,' she says. 'Leave me alone, will you, for God's sake.'

Forty days after I arrive, Father Sayf comes to pick me up. I am waiting, my bag packed. Zulima has given me a photograph of me holding the baby, to take back to the village. I look at it in the car as we jolt back over the railway line. My face looks startled in the flashlight; on my lap, Habibi swims through the air.

Chapter 8

SWEET SLEEP

While I was away, Mama Luban has made a new dress and headscarf for Waheda, in green felt. She's sewn on a new mouth and replaced her missing eye. The new eye is bigger and blacker than the other; it makes Waheda look angry. The top of her head feels scratchy under my nose, and she smells of onions. On my first night back at the village, I get out of bed in the dark and hurl her into the back of the cupboard. She isn't Waheda any more.

The following week, Abir and another girl, Nadia, come back to the village with me after school. Our friend Amira wanted to come but her parents wouldn't let her. It's windy in the morning; by the time we get off the bus, the air is thick with red dust that makes our hair stand away from our heads. We walk up the path towards the Green house with our scarves pulled over our mouths, our eyes nearly closed. Mama

Luban promised to make my favourite lunch, the stew of meat and spinach called *mulokhia*. I have told Nadia about her on the way back to the village, saying what a good cook she is. As we get closer, the smell of lamb cooking drifts from the Green house.

The three of us go into my room to change. Under her school uniform, Abir has a petticoat, with lace around the edges. Nadia is wearing a bra on her flat chest. The girls at school call her 'the remains'. My vest and pants are grey from washing, and the same style as when I was a kid. I pull on my shorts as quick as I can, and drag an old T-shirt over my head. Abir is sitting on Rashid's stool, looking at the picture of me at Zulima's. Nadia grabs the photo out of her hand so she can see my new niece.

'Don't tell me you're baby-crazy too,' says Abir. 'When I get married, I'm informing my husband I don't want any.'

Mama Luban is always telling me to be quiet, and I never can be. But I am often quiet with Abir, these days. Abir's future already belongs to her. It is definite and solid; you could reach out and touch it. I am stuck with the *unfuture*.

'How will you keep a husband if you don't have children?' Nadia asks. Her father owns a factory that makes sweets, and he is married to three wives.

'I'll be working as a scientist,' Abir says. 'I'll have time to talk to him, because I won't have kids around the place.'

'Some girls go to university these days but none of them get jobs when they come out,' says Nadia. 'That's what my dad says.'

Abir doesn't bother to answer. She has had her hair cut; her eyes look bigger than ever behind her glasses. She keeps the long tail of hair in a drawer at her house. It is crinkly from her plaits, with one sharp, bristled end where the scissors cut it off.

'You needn't act all superior, Abir.' Nadia's voice is sulky.

Nadia's twin half-sisters are in our school but they don't speak to her. Wifaq says the third wife is only a little bit older than Nadia. She says Nadia's mother looks like 'remains' too.

'Who would want to get married?' I say loudly. 'Not me.'

When the wind has dropped, after lunch, we set off for a tour of the village. Abir points out the lime trees that Amal and I planted. I show Nadia the different-coloured houses, and the gardens where some of the mothers grow chillis and aubergines. Mama Luban got cross when she saw that Mama Amaani had started to grow roses. She said to Mama Miriam that she'd like to know who could feed kids on flowers. We grow onions and greens, like we always have. I show Nadia the office and the store, where all the things donated for orphans are kept.

I'm proud of my home but sometimes when I bring girls back to the village they cry, and say how sorry they are for me. Or their mothers do. A gang of kids trails behind us as we walk around the edge of the football pitch. They are as curious as I used to be about children from normal families. They want to know what makes us different from them. Because when we look at other children, they might have better clothes, or shoes that shine, or teeth that aren't chipped. But apart from that, they look the same as we do. I shoo the kids away and they hang back a bit but they still follow us. I'm about to take them back indoors when Father Sayf comes out of his house. I let go of Nadia's arm and jump up and down, waving at him. I want to introduce her to my handsome father.

I run towards him, calling his name. I am puffing when I reach him.

'Father,' I begin, 'this is Na–'

'What do you think you're wearing?'

I look down at myself.

'What I always wear.'

'Go and get changed.' He sounds angry.

'What do you mean?'

'It's unsuitable, drawing attention to yourself like this. Look at your friends. Put on something decent, Leila.'

He puts his briefcase down on the bonnet and starts wiping the dust off the windscreen of his car.

The three of us walk back to the Green house in silence. I run to my bedroom, lock the door and throw myself on the bed. It's dark when I come out and the others have gone.

'Why did he have to say it in front of my friends?' I ask. 'My real father wouldn't do that.'

Mama Luban sniffs and tuts.

'The time of shorts is over,' she says. 'Put on a dress and come and eat. I made *Umm Ali*.'

*

After that day, Mama Luban is always telling me that now that I'm a young woman I have to behave like one. The first thing is that I can't wear shorts ever again. I have to give her all three pairs out of my cupboard. The second is to keep my voice down, like she's been saying from the first day I came to the Green house. But that's not all. I can't chew gum or look around myself in public. If a man in a car hoots at me and Amal on the way to school, we mustn't speak to him. 'Men want one thing. It is up to you to know that.' She doesn't say what the one thing is.

I don't tell her what happened to me at Zulima's place. The same thing has happened to Amal. I know, because I see blood on her skirt one day. She didn't tell Mama Amaani, either, but she gets bad stomach aches and sometimes she can't walk, so Mama Amaani notices. Mama Amaani buys Amal cream for her face, and hair bands with beads on them. She shows her how to apply black pencil underneath her eyes and how to rub her nails together at night to make them strong. She says that becoming a woman is an adventure, and that Amal has her whole life ahead of her.

Mama Luban just tells me what not to do. She tells Amal as well, because she says Mama Amaani doesn't *set a good example*. We can't wear red. Anything tight is unsuitable. Make-up is for foolish girls. Modern hairstyles make a girl look cheap. The cinema is forbidden. Going out of the village alone is asking for trouble, as is going to weddings or birthday parties without your brothers and sisters. Talking to boys, apart from my brothers, we must always be in groups.

Amal and I are more at risk from men than ordinary girls like Nadia, or Abir, she says. We can't receive letters from them, make jokes with them, meet them by the Nile or hang around under the Beard of the Pasha tree after school, like she's seen other girls doing. We can't even think about boys.

Because they already believe, whispers Mama Luban, that we will be like our mothers. Mama Luban doesn't even like Amal chatting with Faisal. Any boy who grew up in a different house isn't a *milk brother,* she says.

It makes me nervous. I understand from this time on that it is boys, and the men they will become, who can spoil my life. I begin to realize that abandoned children are the result of men and women relating to each other in some secret way. And I decide in my heart that I reject this, and that if I can't look at a boy as my brother I won't look at him at all.

Our little sister, Quarratulain, stops every day after school to talk to the man that works in the photography shop. He sits on the counter in front of a board covered with pictures of different people, swinging his legs. He has a comb stuck in his hair and he wears bright patterned shirts. When he sees Quarratulain coming down the road, he jumps off the counter. Sometimes, Quarratulain says he's bought her a cold Pepsi, and she's going inside the shop to drink it. She asks me and Amal to tell Mama Badriya that she got delayed at school. I tell her it's wrong, but Quarratulain says she doesn't care. Amal says it's in God's hands. I avoid Mama Badriya on these days. I feel relieved when I see Quarratulain hurrying up the path, with her school bag in her hand.

*

Abir's mother is taking us to the souk in Omdurman. She is buying new shoes for Abir and she wants me to choose some too. We drive past the white palace where the President lives, past the big hotel where the foreigners sit out on the veranda and on to the bridge that goes to Omdurman. You can see the funfair underneath on the bank of the river, with its merry-go-rounds and the long silver slide that kids crouch on mats to speed down. In the middle of the calm water there are small islands with patches of vegetables and maize, and on the other bank men repair their boats by the edge of the water. Her mum says you can see where the Blue Nile and the White Nile join. There are two different shades in the great mass of water that flows under the bridge. But they look more like the grey Nile and the green Nile.

We come off the bridge and drive past the line of restaurants facing the river. It is afternoon, and the cafés are crowded with people. The smell of frying fish comes in through the car window and my stomach begins to rumble.

Abir's mother turns in to the road that leads to the souk, while Abir and I joke in the back. We are excited about getting the shoes and about being in Omdurman. Abir's mum has to go slowly; the road is full of boys riding bicycles – one pedalling and the other sitting on the back seat, feet dangling – and women walking in the road, holding their babies. We pass a boy with no legs, rolling himself along on a low wooden trolley, wearing leather pads on his hands. Any time I go out to a new place, despite what Mama Luban says, I look at as many men as I can. I am always searching for the face of Aziz Mohamed Mahmoud.

We walk through the souk, looking for the shoe stalls. We go down the alley of nightdresses and brassieres, just like when I went shopping in the People's Market with Zulima before she got married, and the one for curtains made of beads. In the gold section, the windows are full of matching sets of headdresses, earrings and rings for brides. We pass through the tourist section, where they sell carved white brooches made from camels' bones, and dusters made of ostrich feathers.

Abir's mum walks in front of us, striding along in her loose blue skirt with her hair gleaming. People turn their heads as she passes, women as well as men. I hold Abir's hand tight. Mama Luban says Omdurman souk is full of thieves. One goes in front with a knife to slit your pockets, she says. The other walks behind to pick up the money when it falls to the ground. I don't have any money. I don't even have any pockets. I'm wearing a plain dress with white buttons down the front, and a white scarf over my hair.

Abir and I both choose the same shoes; black patent ones with a silver buckle attached to the side by a bit of elastic. Abir's are size seven; mine are size four. We spend a long time in the souk, and afterwards we stop for ice cream at a place by the river. It's cool by the water; mosquitoes bite my wrists and cheeks. The new shoes rub my heels. I'm glad when we get back to the car. Abir's mum puts on a cassette of music from America and turns it up loud.

She is driving back on to the bridge when a soldier steps out in front of the car. He has a gun across his shoulder, pointing into the air. All the varnish has worn off its wooden handle. His face looks young; he has spots on his cheeks and his beard is as soft as Mahmoud's and Mohamed's. Abir's mum turns off the music and rolls down the glass.

'Can I help you?' she asks.

He asks where we are going, and if we are her daughters.

'Ma'am, where is your headscarf?' he asks.

Abir's mother's neck is long and straight. She doesn't look at the soldier. Her hands grip the steering wheel.

'How dare you?'

He takes a step back. 'Sorry, ma'am.' And he waves his gun to say we can go on the bridge.

The sound of the car wheels on the metal bridge roars in my ears. I look down at the big wheel turning in the air, the children shouting and laughing in the little painted carriages. When we get to the other side of the river, the road past the Palace is closed, and we have to go round the back. Abir's mum doesn't put the music back on.

That night, Abir and I watch the television news with her mother and father, and her brother Hassan. President Numeiri stands by the river outside the grand hotel we passed earlier. He has a bottle of whisky in each hand and he is emptying them into the water. It makes Abir's father angry, even though he doesn't drink Johnnie Walker. He says the President is a stranger to God and he will lead the country backwards, not forwards. He shouts for his driver, and says he's going back to his office at *News of the Day*. Abir's mother asks him not to go, and after he's gone she keeps walking around the house; the phone rings again and again.

I can't sleep, lying on the spare bed in Abir's room. I admire her parents. But President Numeiri spoke to me. He gave me a gold necklace. I feel sorry for him, because he doesn't have any children. We are due to transfer to senior secondary school soon and Abir is going to a school in the area called Garden City, where she can study science better. I pull the sheet over my head and wrap it around me as much as I can; I have never got used to air conditioning. I like thinking about Abir being a famous scientist and inventing a cure for malaria like she says she will.

*

Mrs Khadija tells us to come back often and see her; she says her daughters are still waiting to meet us. She gives Amal a book of Sudanese poetry and me a cassette of Sudanese music from all over the country. She hugs us and tells us that we will *go far*. Mrs Khadija hasn't been my teacher for the last couple of years but she's still my best and favourite teacher ever, and I tell her so.

Our new school is all right but I don't make a friend like Abir. The other girls talk about boys all the time, about their cousins and their brothers' friends, and the weddings they've been to. Some of them buy long tails of Cleopatra hair to put under their headscarves and dab talcum powder on their cheeks to make them white. My teacher doesn't seem to like me and one day, when I get something wrong, she throws a stick of chalk at my head.

Amal misses a few days of school nearly every month, lying in the *rakuba* behind the Blue house, holding on to her stomach and taking aspirin. I don't mind being absent from school, but she hates it. She says she'll never get to be a teacher if she can't study. Sometimes, I stay at home to keep her company.

We play the music Mrs Khadija gave me on Mama Amaani's cassette player, or just lie around waiting for the heat to pass, not talking much. I like being at the village when the kids are out at school. It's quiet and the smell of the mothers' coffee beans hangs on the air. There are odd sandals on the football pitch, and shorts and sheets drying everywhere, and the sound of the village secretary, Alawia, banging on her old typewriter in the office. Sometimes Faisal comes when he gets home from school, and brings Amal chewing gum or a book he's found. He is getting tall; no one dares call him Lamb any more.

I still love singing. I go to youth activities once a week, run by the Ministry of Social Welfare, and learn how to breathe from my stomach. I meet kids from other schools and we put on shows for the President on the anniversary of the May Revolution, or sometimes for visitors from other countries. Mama Luban says songs about the nation are not as bad as love songs, and anyway we wear girl guide uniforms.

In the summers, we go on camp. One summer, Father Sayf sends all of us on camp to Egypt, with abandoned kids from other Arab countries. We begin to understand that there are kids like us all over the world, and some of them have grown up to be important people. Once we get to know their accents, we enjoy being with the others, laughing and chatting together. We do drill and cook our favourite foods. I get to taste the earth of Egypt on this holiday; it is finer and sweeter than the dust of Sudan. On the way back, in Cairo, the Egyptian men stare after me and Amal and call out 'milk chocolate'. We ignore them, just like Mama Luban says, but I still can't help looking for my father's face. He might be working here.

Back in Sudan, Zulima calls for me every few weeks on a Friday, and we go and see the Queen. Zulima has given birth to a boy. She carries him on her hip and feeds him cartons of Chocko Milk. My mother smiles a bit when she sees the children and Habibi crawls around on the scratchy grass near the concrete bench. All the patients stop to talk to her.

My mother is thinner than ever and when she reaches out to touch the children's cheeks, the ends of her fingers are bent. Sometimes I notice her looking at me with an expression that I think must be love. Sometimes she calls out – to Zulima and anyone else who happens to be around – that they mustn't let any man get his hands on me. 'Not even a male fly can land on this girl,' she shouts. She goes quiet again. I always feel empty when we leave her, but I don't cry on the bus on the way back. I'm too old for that. Habibi sits on my lap; she has hair now, soft curls that smell of sour milk.

One day, not long after we come back from camp, the streets are extra crowded when we come out at lunchtime. All that afternoon, after we get back to the village, trucks full of soldiers speed down the road past the gates, with the drivers sounding their horns. We watch from the football pitch; the boys pull sticks down from the trees and pretend they're shooting each other. Father Sayf sits in the office with his radio held against his ear, moving the little dial backwards and forwards; then he comes out and shouts at everyone to be quiet and get into their own houses. The next day, we don't go to school; Father Sayf calls us all together, like he does on special occasions. He isn't dressed in smart clothes this time. He hasn't even shaved. He says President Numeiri has gone away. There is a new government and none of us should talk about it to anybody outside the village.

*

The three years of senior secondary school pass quickly. Sometimes when I wake up in the mornings – to the noise of the aeroplanes approaching overhead, the smell of milk boiling, the feeling of heat building in the small room – I feel afraid. I'm eighteen; my final exams are coming up. It isn't the exams I'm worried about, it's leaving school. The unfuture is getting closer. I have no pictures in my mind of what my life will be when I'm older. Some of the girls at school are getting engaged to their cousins; at the village, we are allowed to marry boys from other houses. Ekhlas, Zulima's friend, married a boy from the Yellow house, and when he joined the army she went away with him. Some of my classmates are going to university. But my school marks are always in the middle and anyway, no kid from the village has ever been to university.

When Father Sayf says he wants me to work in the village, I accept immediately. He gets the guard to carry a small desk into the office outside his. It just fits, in the corner. I have my own chair and Father Sayf buys a new typewriter for Alawia. I get her old one, although I don't know how to use it. There is a telephone on the desk, and on the first day I have to answer it when it rings and take messages. It feels strange at first, being in the office. It's quiet, and they keep the ceiling fan on all the time. Alawia doesn't like me answering the phone; if she's there, she jumps up and picks it up first.

In the second week, visitors come. Father Sayf asks me to show them around and arrange which family they will have a cup of tea with. They leave a donation for taking the children out, and I arrange a trip to the funfair by the river. I understand better than Father Sayf what makes kids happy; he always used to take us to the museum. Father Sayf is pleased; he says I'm making a good start.

But the main part of my job is *sponsorship*. Every time a new kid comes to the village, we have to try and find someone who wants to send money for them. They can come and see the kid if they want to. Most of them don't, Father Sayf says, so we send them letters once a year, telling them how the kid is getting on. Some kids have more than one sponsor; some don't have any. But it doesn't matter because the money goes equally on all the kids.

From the day I begin this job, I jump out of bed the minute I wake up. Father Sayf tries to teach me accounting, and I wish I had paid more attention in maths lessons. He shows me all the letters he writes, asking for sponsorship. Three weeks after I start, a new girl comes to live in the Red house. Alawia is away from work, sick. Father Sayf is going to a meeting. He goes into the filing cabinet next to Alawia's desk and pulls out a brown paper file, which he says belongs to the new girl. He says I should write a story about her, for the letter to sponsors, from the information inside.

After he goes, I open up the brand-new folder and copy out

her name from the top of the piece of paper, and the date she came to the village. The next piece of paper is from Mygoma orphanage. In the section 'police report', it says that the girl was found on a rubbish dump in Omdurman, early in the morning, by a baker on his way home from work. He took her to the police station, and the police took her to Mygoma. They have called her Hannan, and made up names for her father, grandfather and great-grandfather. Hannan Ahmed Mohamed Sid Ahmed.

I forget about writing Hannan's sponsorship letter. I go back to the filing cabinet and read as many children's files as I can find. Some of them just have kids' names in them, and the date they came to the village. One kid was rescued by the police from a latrine, after neighbours heard him crying. Several were found near mosques. They are nearly always found at night. Some of them are abandoned at hospitals. Most are given names by the policemen who bring them to the orphanage, or the workers there. There is no file for me, or Amal, or Faisal or the twins. Only for the younger ones.

When Father Sayf comes back, he sees all the files on the floor. He calls me into his office, and tells me not to speak to any of the kids about what I have read, because it is private. He says in a quiet voice that he should have talked more about these things to me before I started work. 'This is more important than accountancy, Leila,' he says.

Even though I'm eighteen, I have never really thought about how children get to the village. We understand without discussing it that it's better not to know about the past. Occasionally, we read something in a newspaper about a woman going to court for burying her newborn baby alive, or we see on television that a baby has been rescued from dogs after being left by the road. I never realized that these babies are us.

As we grow older, we learn to read the story told in the face. Amal's parents must have come from the African south: she has the dark skin and small, neat head of the Dinka tribe. My face shows my mixed Arab and African roots; my skin is light brown and my nose has an African flatness. The twins, Mohamed and Mahmoud, have the characteristics of the Nubian tribe in the north: sleek hair that grows close to their heads, straight noses and dark skin. All of us can look in the mirror and dream about our stories.

Now I'm working in the office I understand more than I ever understood before. And soon I decide that the unfuture is over. It's my job to work for my brothers and sisters. Not just in the village but all over Sudan. We are abandoned. But we are not guilty.

*

The village pays me a salary of fifty dollars a month. I am proud to be earning money. I still live in my room at the Green house, but now I live there as an employee. Meals, clothes, pocket money, medicine – all these stop. Sometimes, Mama Luban offers me lunch and I eat one of her *mulokhia* stews or *Umm Ali* puddings off the old tray, with my younger brothers. The twins have deep voices now. Mama Luban says they eat enough for a whole tribe. Faisal is taller than anyone; he never talks about the day he lost his mother any more. He has white teeth and an open face and all the kids like him because he makes them laugh.

Sometimes I go hungry, because I'm saving as much as I can. I have something important to do. Some days after work I just eat a piece of bread or some biscuits, or Amal shares her lunch with me. She's still at school; she's missed so much time with her monthly illness that she hasn't been able to take her exams yet. Mama Amaani gives me a matching orange skirt and blouse to wear to the office. I wash them before I go to bed and get up in time to iron them before I go to work again. I light the charcoal on the gas ring in the kitchen and get it glowing red before I drop a couple of lumps into Mama Luban's heavy iron. I iron my clothes on my bed, kneeling on Rashid's stool. I wash and make myself tea before I walk down the path to the office. I buy the cheapest soap, and I don't have lemonade or tea on the street. I save every *piastre* that I can.

Zulima's husband has agreed that if I can pay for it, we will build a room for the Queen at the plot he has bought for himself and Zulima. They have a 200-metre-square piece of land next to where his mother lives with his unmarried brothers and sisters. Father Sayf gives me a three-month advance, and we begin looking for cheap bricks and wooden poles from houses that have been pulled down. One of Zulima's husband's friends is a builder; he agrees to work on the room in his spare time. Once he starts, I go to Zulima's house every week to walk between the foundations on the rough ground. I imagine the walls getting higher, the roof going on, our mother stepping through the doorway.

The weather slows progress. Rain comes down like spears most afternoons, collecting in muddy shallows on the football pitch at the village, and in the yards of the houses. The water evaporates once the rain stops but the mud remains. It squelches over our sandals, spatters our clothes, gets under our nails and into our pores. In the evening, Amal and I watch the news on television in the Blue house with Mama Amaani and the children; parts of Omdurman turn into one great lake; goats are stranded on the roofs of drowned buses and a woman gives birth up a tree.

Finally, the day comes when the men nail on the tin roof. They plaster the inside with smooth mud and get Habibi to make a handprint, for good luck. We paint the walls with a tin left over from the Yellow house. Over the following weeks, I buy two wooden single beds and four chairs, cheap, from the carpenter Rashid works for. I spot a piece of lino in the market, big enough to put down on the floor, and when I cast my eyes down and tell the merchant in a very quiet voice that it is for a sick person, he gives it to me for free and says may God bless him whoever he is. Father Sayf's wife lets me have a cupboard she doesn't need any more, and I put two old-fashioned dresses with deep pockets and hoods at the back, one pair of flat, round-toed shoes, and a bottle of *Bint al Sudan* scent inside. Amal embroiders two yellow pillowcases with the words 'sweet sleep'. Zulima brings some red glittery flowers from her own room, and a small table.

The day before I am going to collect our mother, I stay the night with Zulima. We are up late, talking and laughing and getting everything ready. I go for one last look at the room, standing in the middle of it and breathing in the strong, clean smell of paint, looking at the beds with their matching yellow sheets, the flowers on the low table, the scrubbed lino.

'By God, Leila,' Zulima says to me before we go to sleep. 'You did something good. These children will know their grandmother. She will end her days in peace.'

*

The Queen is waiting by the locked door of the ward, with a few things in a plastic carrier bag. I have brought her one of Zulima's *tobes* to put on for the journey to the house, washed and ironed. The nurses hug her and kiss her and say they are glad to see her leave the place where she has spent her years. They give me a supply of the injections she has to have each month, and I practise squirting water into a grapefruit, as if it were her arm.

While they say goodbye, I climb the stairs to the Director's office. He signs the papers to say that she is discharged from the hospital. He says he has something important to tell me.

'Your mother is not dangerous. She will never do anyone any harm.'

The office door is open. There are people in the corridor, and the tea boy keeps coming in and out. I take the signed papers, and fold them into my handbag.

'Why is she here?'

He says that hers is a strange case. The notes say she was brought to the hospital by the police. She had been in a quarrel and they said she was dangerous. He says she has had a lot of treatment over the years. At first, she had electric shocks to her brain. In recent years, they have given her injections to make her calm. But there has never been a proper diagnosis of what is wrong with her.

My mother sits quietly next to me on the bus, clutching the handles of the plastic bag. Her face is ashen under her powder. I pay the fares to the boy and she stares out of the window as the bus passes along the streets of the city, past the central mosque with its peddlers of religious books and prayer rugs gathered outside, past the big modern block of the Meridian hotel, the railway station, the pharmacies and cafés and furniture shops of Khartoum Two and on to the south of the city, to the narrow mud streets where Zulima lives.

We hear the voices as soon as we get away from the main road. The girls come running along to meet us; they take her hands and pull her towards Zulima's narrow gate. Ali is outside, with the slaughtered sheep, calling welcome. The neighbours crowd around to see as she jumps over the sheep, for a blessing, and steps over the threshold into the yard. Amal is there and Quarratulain and Faisal and the twins, all clapping. I wanted to invite Rashid but Zulima shouted at me that he wouldn't find the girl he used to know anywhere in this house, and why couldn't I leave things alone. Then she burst into tears.

The Queen looks around her, gripping her bag to her chest. She seems smaller than ever, in Zulima's orange *tobe*. One of Zulima's neighbours says she is tired and it is this woman who leads her into her new room for the first time. She comes out later when the food is ready, and sits round a big tray with

Jamila and Habibi, but she doesn't eat anything, just moves a piece of *asida* backwards and forwards in the sauce. When the meal is over, the neighbours drift back to their houses. Amal, Zulima and I scrub all the borrowed cooking pots and trays. By the time we've finished, I have never been so tired in all my life. I look around the door of the new room and see the Queen curled up on one of the beds, with her head on the pillow. On the bus on the way back to the village, I feel content. Our mother looked after us when she still could. Now we can care for her.

Faisal waited till the very end so he could accompany us back to the village. He and Amal sit on the seat in front of me. Faisal even makes Amal laugh.

Chapter 9

SEVEN HILLS

I have been working at the village for just over a year when Father Sayf calls me into his office, in the voice he uses for making announcements. His briefcase is open on the desk, next to a half-drunk glass of tea. He tells me to sit down, and says he is going to come straight to the important matter.

'You work hard,' he says. 'Visitors think highly of you. But your secretarial skills are not good.'

I open my mouth to protest; Father raises his hand for me to be quiet.

'I want to send you for training,' he says. 'In Jordan.'

I can't concentrate for the rest of the day. Jordan is an Arab country but it is far away from Sudan. I imagine myself arriving in a foreign city, at night, alone. Being kidnapped by the taxi driver, and kept prisoner. Murdered, maybe. When I think about leaving Amal, I feel even more frightened. That night, I

---

dig Waheda out of the back of the cupboard and hold on to her as I lie in the darkness, listening to music from a distant wedding party. I can't imagine myself away from my brothers and sisters. My country. Who will I be?

When I report to his office early on Saturday, to tell him I would like to go as soon as possible, Father Sayf is pleased. No one else is. Alawia stops speaking to me. Mama Luban says Father Sayf must have gone mad, when I tell her the news. She winds her white *tobe* around herself and hurries off in the direction of his house, leaving her stew burning on the cooker. Whoever heard of an unmarried girl travelling abroad on her own, she shrieks to Mama Miriam as she disappears down the path.

Amal goes very quiet. I will only be gone for a short time, I say. It is just secretarial training. Not the same as going to university, or becoming a teacher. We are sitting on her bed in the *rakuba* at the back of the Blue house. She is working at the village too now, helping with the new small boys, trying to teach them to read. 'It's all right,' she says. 'I've always known that you were the lucky one. Anyway, I don't want to go away.' She lies down with her back to me. She is so tall these days, inches taller than me. Mama Amaani braids her hair for her in small squares that show off the shape of her head.

Zulima says that she hopes I'll at least send her some money, because everyone knows that Jordan is a rich country. She says that she wouldn't have agreed to have our mother out of hospital if she'd known that I'd be dancing off to have a good life somewhere else. She cries, and says she'll miss me, and that I must look at all the trees and all the people in Jordan with Zulima's eyes as well as Leila's, because there will never be any life for her, not now.

I don't say anything to the Queen. I decide to wait until the day before I leave. She seems content, sitting in her room. She doesn't like being outside any more. Zulima says our mother won't let her comb her hair; she insists on doing it herself and it takes her a long time. The only time she speaks loudly and clearly is when Jamila and Habibi run into the room because Zulima is threatening them with her slipper. She lets the girls hide behind the skirts of her long dress, sits up very straight and says to Zulima, 'Did I ever hit you when you were a child?'

I have tried many times to call my old school friend Abir, but the phone doesn't ring. Shortly before I'm due to leave, I go by bus to her house. I walk down the quiet street, with its big houses with guards at the front gates, and trees waving overhead. When I get to Abir's house, the front gates are padlocked. The leaves of the white-trunked Royal palms in the garden are brown and rotting; the dust is piled in drifts against the front door. The watchman from the house opposite hurries over the road. They have gone away, he whispers. On holiday? I ask. He stares at me. They have *run* away, he hisses.

*

I travel to Jordan via Egypt. When the plane takes off from Khartoum airport, the other passengers start to clap. I stare out of the window as the tops of the trees and the square brown roofs of the houses shrink from view. Soon, there is nothing underneath but the river, fringed with green, winding through the desert. After a few minutes, even that disappears. It's strange to be inside an aeroplane, when I have spent so many years of my life watching them from the ground. My ears hurt and it's cold. I wrap myself in the blanket they give me, close my eyes and pray harder than I have ever prayed before, that one day I will come back to my country.

In Cairo, I wait a week to get the plane ticket for Jordan. While I'm there, I stay at the Egyptian village. On the first morning, the mother at the house where I'm staying says they are going to see the man who used to be President of Sudan, Jaafar Numeiri. He lives *in exile* in Cairo, she says. A group of children goes every month, to have lunch and play in the garden. When I tell her that I have sung for him many times, she agrees that I can go with them. When we get off the bus outside the gates, the guards recognize me immediately as Sudanese, like them. They let in all the Egyptian kids, and the village mothers, but say I will have to wait outside. No Sudanese are allowed in.

I tell them that I want to speak to the President, and they laugh. I repeat that I know him, and that he gave me a present once. Eventually, they pick up the telephone in the guard box. A minute later, the gates are open. Two of the guards escort me up the path to the house, saying I am welcome.

They show me into a sitting room with chairs with carved gold legs and a table with tall stems of furled flowers in a glass vase. There is a huge television in the corner and long curtains. I don't dare sit down. The President comes in and stands in front of me, with the light from the chandelier reflecting off the top of his head. He asks about the village, and I tell him how it has grown, and that I work in the office now and we have new children. He always wanted the best for the orphans, he says. He dabs at one eye with the corner of a white handkerchief and hands me some clean, folded notes out of his pocket. He says that the money is for my studies, and that his people will arrange for the plane ticket to Jordan.

The security officers have told him that he gave me a present, he says. 'What was it?'

I feel the blood rushing to my face. I thought he remembered my singing. Now I realize he doesn't.

'It was a gold necklace, sir,' I say. 'It was beautiful.'

The next day, the people at the village say that the ticket is ready. A Sudanese man comes to collect me in a black car, and drives me to the airport. When we get there, he ushers me through the barriers and past all the officials, right to the steps of the plane. He says it is a pleasure to help a *bint al Sudan*, daughter of Sudan, and that his uncle has told him about my voice.

*

Father Sayf has arranged for me to live at the village in Jordan. I have a room of my own in one of the houses there. I get up at half past five in the morning to be ready to catch the bus that brings the workers to the village. It travels back empty into the city, and it goes past my college. The driver lets me on for free. The first thing I notice about Amman is the hills. The bus goes up and down so much it makes me feel sick. I didn't realize that not all cities are flat.

I arrive at college earlier than all the other students and sit in a corner of the canteen, watching it fill up. Almost all the others are from Jordan. They are Muslims, and speak Arabic, but they seem like foreigners. The girls wear skirts that show their knees, and tight tops with no sleeves. They wear their hair loose over their shoulders, hold cigarettes between their fingers, sit with their legs crossed. Some of them hold hands with boys, walking in the gardens of the college. When classes are over, they climb into their cars and drive off with the windows open and music floating out into the air.

Most of the students ignore me, although there is one who talks to me. She asks me about Sudan, and I tell her about my father, Sayf, and my mother, Luban, and that I have seven brothers in my house, and I live in a village. I don't tell her I'm abandoned. I don't know how to. Her name is Maha; her father has a travel agency and she is going to work for him when she finishes the course.

We study typing, in English. We sit in a large room; everyone has their own typewriter in front of them, and headphones with a voice coming through. Some of the others move on quickly but I have to type out the same thing again and again, until I get used to it. 'The quick brown fox jumps over the lazy dog.' I take my books back to my room at night and stare at the words, waiting for them to make sense. In my mind, the English words are like the people all around me. Strangers. We did English at school, but I never thought it would be useful to me.

Soon after I arrive, Rania, the mother at the house where I'm staying, takes me to buy a coat; I spend eight dollars of the hundred Father Sayf gave me, on the cheapest coat I can find. The President gave me thirty dollars. I keep the money under the mattress on the bed. Everything costs a lot in Jordan, even things like soap and bread. I'm worried that I won't have enough to last. I eat a few biscuits in the morning and I have an omelette or some lentils for lunch when I get back from college. I spend as little as possible. All the mothers at the village take it in turns to invite me to eat with their families. They eat rice at nearly every meal, and sometimes they cook their special dish, lamb with raisins and almonds and yoghurt. I write the recipe down for Mama Luban. On Fridays, they drink coffee together; you have to have at least three cups. They say the first cup is bitter, like life. The second is sweet, like love. And the third is soft, like death. They all taste bitter to me; they make the coffee in a different way here.

When I feel homesick, I get my suitcase down from the top of the cupboard and take out a plastic bag. I sit on my chair, close my eyes and dissolve a chip of Sudanese mud in my mouth, letting the taste and feel of it take me home. One night, as I prepare to go to bed, there is white stuff falling through the air. I sit by my window, watching the flakes drift down. I can't drag my eyes away from their slow fall, the endless supply coming from the sky. The ground gradually turns white. When it's light enough, I put on my new coat and go outside. I hold my hands out to try to catch the flakes. I jump through the snow, looking behind me at the shape of my feet. I pick up handfuls of it and rub it on my face. My teeth begin to chatter. That morning, I miss the bus for college. In the evening, Rania drags me to the shops again. She says sandals won't do in the snow.

Most of the children at the village here are from Palestine. Nearly all the women who work here are from Palestine too. I ask Rania what Jordanian women do with the babies they can't keep. She changes the subject. Then one day she says there are things in this life that every girl must know. In Jordan, she says, there are pills women can take to stop them from ever having babies. She says you can have an operation, too, to get rid of a baby even when it's growing in the stomach. I don't believe her at first but she swears by God that it's true. I feel sad about that. I begin to think that perhaps we are the lucky ones after all.

I am surer than ever that I can't talk to boys or joke with them. If any of the boys at college speak to me, I pretend not to understand. Sometimes, in the canteen, one of them calls me to take away a tea cup, or bring him more bread. They see the colour of my skin and think I work there; they don't believe I could be a student like them. I stop going to the canteen; the smoke irritates my eyes.

*

Evenings pass slowly. I try to imagine what everyone is doing. I think about Amal and the twins and Faisal and Quarratulain. I think about the Queen, in her room, hearing the children playing outside. I still think about my real father. I wonder which direction his feet led him in, when he walked out of the gates of the village, and if he still carries the piece of paper with the picture of the scales on the top of it. Or perhaps he forgot about me, as soon as he left the Green house. Sometimes, I write him a letter in my head. I tell him that it would have been better if he had never come to the village. To know you have a father that doesn't want you is worse than not having one at all.

I watch the news on television with Rania and the children. It rarely mentions Sudan, and when it does it is always about people being killed. There is another new government and the war has got worse between them and the rebels. Rania says: aren't I frightened of going back? I try to explain that the war is in the south, far away from Khartoum. She doesn't listen. Everyone in Jordan is worried about a trouble closer to home: Iraq has invaded Kuwait and Amman is filling up with refugees.

Rania is small and dark-eyed. She cooks for the kids in the house, irons their clothes with an electric iron. She makes yoghurt, and date pastries; she pickles cucumbers and pounds up a spice mix from dried leaves and seeds. In the evenings, her hands fly over her embroidery. She makes cushion covers in gold and silver threads, to sell to a tourist shop. She is surprised that I have never learned to do it. She shows me running stitch and cross-stitch, how to keep the stitches small and even. She talks as she sews. She says the big men make war, and citizens pay in blood. She says we can do nothing in this life but trust in God.

She brings out a big piece of plain cotton and a paper bag full of embroidery silks one evening, and says they're for me. The silks feel soft in my hands: there are pinks, greens, browns, scarlets. What shall I do, I ask her. Amman, she says. Seven hills, and the Citadel and almond trees in blossom. I have to draw it on the material first, with a pen. 'Make something beautiful, in this time of ugliness.'

She is surprised the next morning, when I show her my drawing. It is of a mud house with a flat roof and a small window on either side of the door. In front of it is a lime tree, covered in round fruits, and beside that a water pitcher in a stand, its long body ending in a curved tip. There is a cat crouched on the roof of the house and bougainvillea pouring over the wall. In the distance, on the horizon, a man on a donkey rides towards a round sun, his slippers almost touching the ground. I didn't know what I was going to draw, when I began. But by the time I finished it, I recognized Musa's village. That evening, I begin to stitch it into life.

*

It is a thin, sky-coloured envelope with red stripes along the edges and in the top left corner a stamp with a picture of a black bird with a long, orange beak. I recognize Amal's neat, left-handed writing immediately. In my room, sitting on the edge of the bed, I kiss the letter before I tear it open. She wrote it a month ago. She hopes I am well, by God's will, and that I am strong. Everyone at the village is OK, and Father Sayf and Mama Luban and all my brothers and sisters greet me. Her life is about to change, she says. She has some news that will surprise me.

I put the letter down on the bed beside me when I finish it.

Then I pick it up and read the words over again. She doesn't tell me what the news is. She hopes, God willing, I can be back in Sudan before another year passes. Faisal and the twins have to complete their military service now that they have left school. They are preparing themselves to join the Defence Force. She says that the village is not the same without Leila and that I should finish my studies and hurry back to my home.

That night, as I stitch the cat white, my mind races. Is Amal going to become a teacher? Has one of her relatives come to meet her? Does she have a new job at the village? I change the white thread for pink, giving the cat a round nose between her whiskers. It is time for me to go home.

Over the next months, Maha helps me practise the typing and the book-keeping and the computer skills, to pass the tests I need to get the certificate. We stay on in the big room full of typewriters until the cleaners are emptying the waste-paper baskets around us, dragging their cloths around our feet. I'm getting good at typing and I love working on the computer.

One evening, as she drops me off from her car at the village, I tell Maha about my situation. She switches off the engine and lights a cigarette. Why didn't I tell her before? Didn't I trust her? I can't answer. She flicks the end of the cigarette out of the car window and says she wants to come to the village in Khartoum and meet the whole of my family, now she's heard about them. My heart lifts. She is welcome, I say. My home is her home.

Maha says I have to prepare myself, to show that typing is not the only thing I have learned in Jordan. She sits me in front of the mirror in her bedroom, dabs cream on my face with a sponge and brushes powder over it, then wipes it all off again and says she has to get the right shade for my skin; her stuff makes me look like a spirit. She puts straightening lotion on my disobedient hair, outlines my lips in brown pencil, and makes me practise walking around her room in a pair of her high-heeled mules. She files my nails with an *emery board* and pushes back the skin over the half moon at the base of the nail, with a tiny silver instrument that looks like a shovel. She says it's part of working in an office, to look smart. Anyway, she says, it will help me find a husband. When I tell her I don't want a husband, she doesn't believe me.

Shortly before I'm due to return home, we go to try on skirts and blouses in a big store in the middle of Amman. It disturbs me, to see myself in the mirror in a short skirt that swings as I move, a shirt that clings to my breasts and waist, and shows my naked arms. I tear off the clothes and pull on my old loose long-sleeved top, my skirt with the hem falling down. I feel like crying. These revealing clothes are sure to bring the sort of attention I don't want, have never wanted. But she comes back with another armful of things off the silver rails and eventually I buy a long, ivory-coloured skirt with a narrow belt around the waist and a gold buckle, and a matching blouse patterned with red flowers. The clothes aren't tight and they don't expose my skin, but they make me look more alive. I discover that I love red. It makes me feel happy. I get some red mules like Maha's, but with lower heels, and a set of bracelets that look like gold, which move up and down my arm as I talk.

The first day I wear the new clothes, I feel self-conscious. People at college stare at me in a different way from before. I soon find that I like wearing the pretty clothes. Rania says no one will recognize me. I can see that I look different. My skin has become lighter, away from the Sudanese sun. The make-up shimmers on my cheeks, set off by a tiny pair of gold earrings I got to go with the bracelets. My eyes look different, but not because of the line of black pencil along their lids. Something has changed in my expression.

I still can't imagine getting married. There is no one at the village that I would ever marry. And no one outside the village that would ever marry me.

*

Father Sayf insists that the village can't afford a computer; anyway, he says, with so many power cuts, what use would it be? 'You're not in Jordan now,' he says. My desk seems smaller and more cramped than when I left two years ago. The chair wobbles and the drawer sticks. Alawia tells her friends on the telephone that the office junior is back, thank God, so she has someone to assist her. I try to show her some of the things I have learned at college but she isn't interested. When I explain to her what computers can do, how easy they make our work, she fits a long sheet of blue carbon paper between two thick sheets of foolscap and cranks them noisily into her typewriter. The old ways have always been good enough for her, she says, even if they aren't good enough for me.

I have brought presents back for everyone: T-shirts for the

boys, hair bands for the girls. I got prayer beads for Mama Luban and a cassette for Mama Amaani, tins of pistachio pastries for the other mothers and sunglasses for Father Sayf and Rashid. I brought Amal the best present of all. It is a sealed bottle with an intricate pattern inside made of twenty different-coloured sands – red and yellow and black and white and blue, all from the desert at Petra. It cost more than my winter coat and it's the most beautiful thing I saw in the whole time I was away.

There are two new girls living in my old room at the Green house, so I'm staying in Amal's room with her at the Blue house. After work I fold my new clothes into her cupboard and put on one of my old *jellabiyas* and a pair of flip-flops. It's winter and the nights are cool; we lie on the beds in the *rakuba* under blankets and we talk. Amal breaks her news to me. She has agreed to marry Faisal. He is a good man, serious and loyal. She stares up at the grass roof, stretches her arms. She swings her long legs sideways off the bed and sits looking at me. Her dark eyes shine.

'Why didn't you tell me?' I ask.

'You knew I liked him.'

'Yes, but . . .'

She says she never expected that she could be lucky. She thought I got all the luck for both of us. She didn't dare think he liked her too, enough to propose. No one else knows of their plan; they will announce it to everyone when he has finished his service. She jumps off the bed.

'Let's go for a walk,' she says. 'Let's go and look at our trees.'

She has more energy than me these days; I have never heard her laugh so often.

On the first Friday after I get back, we hold a party at the Blue house. Father Sayf gives us some money to buy food and when we get back from the souk we spend all morning making salads of chopped tomato and onion and peanut butter. We put fish out in the sun, in a coating of cumin and cardamom. We roast chicken legs and stuff long green peppers with meat and garlic and make a cauldron of fluffy white rice spiced with cinnamon sticks and cardamom seeds. Later, we fry the fish and mix up tahini sauce to go with it. We wash oranges and cut them into quarters. We sweep the yard and send one of the boys out for ice and put a cassette on Mama Amaani's player. While Amal is having a shower, I walk to the far edge of the village, where the high grass fence divides our land from the next plot. I dig up a couple of lumps of dry mud with an old knife. I put a lump of earth the size of a marble in my mouth and the other in my pocket and walk slowly back towards the Blue house, with the taste of home running down my throat. I thank God for bringing me safely back.

*

All the kids are excited to be invited to a party, and when I distribute their presents they get even noisier. We prepare special trays for the mothers and find them chairs to sit on, in the shade. We carry round jugs of iced prickly-pear squash, and give everyone a glass. Mama Luban has brought a huge dish of *Umm Ali*, my favourite pudding. When the food is all eaten,

Mama Amaani dances with some of the little girls. Father Sayf calls in with his wife and children. He puts the sunglasses on and says thank you very much, then puts them back in his pocket. He says that I am the spirit of the village, and that I make him proud.

Not everyone is at the party. Faisal and the twins – Mohamed and Mahmoud – are away, in the Defence Force. Zulima couldn't come; she has had another daughter since I left and she said she couldn't bring them all over. The Queen won't come out of her room any more, she says. I didn't invite Rashid. I haven't had time yet to go and find him, and he doesn't have a telephone. I'm sitting there looking at everybody when I realize who else is missing. There is noise all around me, music and voices and laughing.

'Ya, Amal,' I yell, over the heads of some of the kids. 'Where's Quarratulain?' Amal's face darkens; she shakes her head at me. That night, when we lie down to sleep outside on the beds she tells me that Quarratulain's belly began to swell a few months after I left. At first, no one except Amal noticed. She tried to talk to her about it, but Quarratulain told her to mind her own business. She said she was going to be getting married soon. One evening, Mama Luban saw that Quarratulain had swollen ankles. Next, she felt her belly, then immediately fell on the ground in a faint. They got the name of the man out of Quarratulain – it was the one from the photography shop – and Father Sayf went to see him. He said he'd never heard of a girl called Quarratulain; if he wanted a girlfriend, he wouldn't choose one who was deformed.

All the mothers had a meeting, and they took Quarratulain

to the police station. She was flogged eighty times by a policewoman, and afterwards they wouldn't let her come back to the village. They said it set a bad example to the girls coming up.

'Where is she now?'

Amal doesn't answer for a long time. 'Mama Miriam saw her in Souk Libya one night, with some soldiers. Since then, we don't know anything.'

Chapter 10

WATERMELON

The day after the party, Father Sayf gives me the morning off. I catch three buses to the south of the city. Women have to sit separately from men on the buses now. I get off and pick my way along the mud paths to my sister's house, then push open the tin door to the compound. I can hear Zulima's raised voice from inside her bedroom, and children laughing. I slip around the side of the house, into our mother's room. She is sitting on one of the wooden chairs, with her hands on her lap, her long hair combed down her back. She looks at me without surprise. I kneel beside her and kiss her hands, press them against my forehead.

I pull up a chair and sit with her for a while, telling her about the hills in Amman, the dish of lamb with raisins and almonds that the women make there, the snow that falls through the air and covers the ground. I tell her I have learned

---

to use something called a computer. She nods. The pattern of circles on the lino has worn off and the wires for the electric light trail from the ceiling. The yellow walls are covered with children's drawings and the smell of paint is gone, replaced by the smell of dust and lentils.

Zulima screams when I clap my hands and walk into her room.

'By God, what is the matter with you, creeping in like a thief?' she shouts. Jamila and Habibi hang back inside, slim and tall in their blue school shifts. I shake their hands then hug them to me. I give them the sweets I've brought them, and the biros.

When she has dried her eyes, Zulima sends Jamila to the shop for a cold drink. The new baby is asleep on the bed, lying on her back with her arms flung wide apart. She has threads of cotton through her earlobes, and is wearing one of Habibi's old dresses. The boy, Mohamed, is rolling a marble on the floor. While I unpin my scarf, Zulima busies herself lighting a piece of charcoal on the gas ring, straightening the sheets. She apologizes for the pile of washing in the corner, and says: what have I done to my hair?

I give her the dress I brought her from Amman, dark crimson, with a pattern of fine gold threads running through it. Zulima glances into the carrier bag and shouts at her son to go and see grannie. Her husband Ali is out at work, she says, but his mother is present. As always. She throws the bag into the cupboard and starts crying again.

'Do you think you can run away for this long time, and nothing here will change?' she wails. 'Do you think that change is only for Leila?'

She wipes the neck of the Pepsi bottle on the hem of her *jellabiya* and sets it in front of me. She settles herself on the stool, and grows calm. She has important news, she says. She must tell the story from the beginning.

Several months after I left Khartoum, she had a message from the village that someone had been looking for us. She immediately remembered that I had once told her that my father came to find me there one day. She asked God to forgive her, because she had never believed me. Faisal came to this house himself, she says, with a message from Father Sayf. It was a phone number, and a name, on a piece of paper. It wasn't my father, God bless him, who was looking for us. It was her own father. Our mother's first husband.

She put the piece of paper in her cupboard, buried under her clothes. She didn't tell our mother anything about it, or her husband. One day, after this child you see sleeping here was born, she says, she went to the shop to use the telephone. That afternoon, she told her husband to stay at home; they were expecting an important visitor. Her father came after evening prayers, with one of his grown-up sons from his next marriage. She didn't know him; he said he hadn't seen her since she was a small girl. While they were sitting outside the house, drinking lemonade and introducing the man to his grandchildren, the Queen appeared from her room. She said his name – Abu Ali – and the names of his father and brothers, then she returned to her room.

As she speaks, all the hopes I had as a child come to life again inside me, as fierce and bright as ever. With them comes the weight of the years of disappointment. I force myself to smile.

'Thanks be to God, Zulima,' I say. 'You have found your father. This is wonderful news.'

Zulima looks at me with pity in her eyes.

'I'm not finished,' she says.

Zulima tells me that her father knew my father; they were from the same area. Her father saw mine shortly after he came to see me. He was applying for his papers to work abroad. He told everyone that he had found his child, that he would be bringing her home to live with him and his new wife. He was in Khartoum, making his travel arrangements, when he became ill with malaria. He went back to the place where he lived, to get well, but the fever grew worse and he didn't have money for medicine. His wife tried to care for him but he died a few days later.

'He is dead?'

Zulima stands up and begins to wail again, more loudly. 'That's what I said, isn't it?'

I get off the bus outside the village, hurry along the path to the Blue house, and get inside without seeing anyone. Later, Amal comes in, singing. She stops as soon as she sees me. She doesn't ask what's wrong. She sits on the end of the bed until I'm able to speak.

'We will never see Aziz Mohamed Mahmoud again,' I say.

When I tell her what has happened, she weeps.

'In my mind, he was my father as well,' she says.

We stay inside until it gets dark and then we walk out and sit on the ground under the lime trees. I have put on the old skirt and blouse I used to wear when I first arrived in Jordan. The new clothes mock me. I thought I could escape the unfuture.

Have a pretty, bright life, like Maha's. I was wrong. I think of
Quarratulain, wandering the streets somewhere with her baby
with a made-up name. I dig my nails into the dusty ground.
The only thing we the abandoned can be sure of is this earth
that we walk on.

*

It's a cool, early morning and I'm in the office with Alawia.
The only medicine for my sore heart is to throw myself into
my work. There is plenty to do. The list of sponsors' names
has hardly changed since I went away; donations are down,
even though there are new houses at the village and many
more children. Father Sayf is working harder than ever; he
wants me to begin a campaign, to tell people about the work
of the village and recruit new supporters. I have made
appointments to visit businesses in town. Even people who
think it's unlucky to come to the village sometimes give us
clothes or money for the children.

I see the man from where I sit, striding up the path in a
jellabiya, a white scarf flying round his neck, his feet turned
out. I know immediately who it is – and he knows who I am.

'*Ya*, Leila,' he booms, bursting into the office. The draught
scatters my papers on to the floor. I stand up and his fist closes
over my hand.

'Please accept my condolences,' he says, lowering his eyes
for a moment. 'We must know this life is short.'

Abu Ali wears a silver ring set with a rust-coloured stone.
His teeth jostle for space in his mouth and dark hairs creep up

from under the round neck of his *jellabiya*. I feel flustered. I call for tea for him and get back behind my desk. Zulima has told me about him, I say.

'And she has told me about you,' he says, looking at me for longer than is polite. 'I have come to see my new daughter.'

Alawia has stopped typing and is staring at him. I introduce him and ring the bell again for tea. I thought that when I met this man, I would be able to ask him more about my father. Now he's here, I can't ask him anything.

'How is your wife? Your children?' I ask. 'God willing, they are all well.'

'You came from Jordan? You achieved your certificate?'

I nod. I start to tell him about the campaign we are launching for new sponsors, but he interrupts.

'How old are you now?'

'I am twenty-two.'

'Not yet married?'

I shake my head. I have no plans to be married, I say.

He slaps his knees. 'Is it for you, to make such plans?'

He is sitting down, his legs stretched out in front of him. His pockets bulge with rags and keys and coins and packets and scraps of paper, all spilling out.

'We are taking the children away soon,' I begin. 'On summer camp.'

He grunts.

'To Sennar. I have never . . .'

He interrupts again. 'Do you know you have an old uncle there?'

He tells me that my father had a brother, Hassan. He lives in Sennar.

I jump up. 'Is he still alive? Where is his house?'

He shrugs. 'He is a fisherman,' he says.

He refuses the tea when it arrives. He will see me again soon, he says. He intends to introduce me to the rest of the family. He stands up, almost overturning the table, and lurches out of the office, rolling back down the path to the gates. The marigolds and roses tremble as he passes.

Alawia adjusts her *tobe* around her head, wipes up the spilled tea.

'Are these people really your relatives?' she says.

I tell her that this is Zulima's father.

'He seems to think you also belong to him.'

I don't hear her. This man has brought me the first good news I've heard since I came back to Sudan.

*

The boys are dressed in shorts. The girls wear long skirts, their hair hidden under white scarves. Even small girls have to dress like women now. They crowd on to the coach; the driver loads their bags into its belly. They are quiet, for once. Some of the little ones cry as they wave goodbye out of the windows, and Mama Luban and Mama Amaani are wiping their eyes too, and calling out last-minute instructions about saying their prayers and doing what they are told. Once the coach gets on the road, they begin to chatter and quarrel as usual. The soldiers at the checkpoint on the outskirts of the city wave us past and I walk through the coach, drawing the curtains on the left-hand side shut against the hot sun. I sit down behind the driver and watch the landscape speeding by, the scrubby desert ground dotted with *ushr* plants, that no one and nothing can eat, and flat-topped thorn trees. Here and there we pass nomads moving their goats and sheep. They lope along the edge of the tarmac road, their wrists resting on the ends of the sticks they carry slung across their shoulders. The animals' bones poke almost through their skins.

The road follows the river south. We pass small, dry villages baking in the midday sun. Behind them, you can see a fringe of green, where aubergines and tomatoes and cucumbers and sorghum grow, and beyond that the line of shady trees with their roots tapped down into the river that is always out of sight. After a while, I fall asleep.

We spend a week at the camp in Sennar, staying in a boarding school. I'm in charge of the girls and at night I sleep with them in the dormitory – a long, airless room with a cracked concrete floor and rusted metal beds. I tell them stories after supper, the stories that Nanny Samia used to tell me and Amal, about the mother goat going off into the desert to look for food and leaving her kids behind, the blue goat and the red goat and the white goat and the green one, and how the fox tried time after time to trick his way into the house and time after time the kids, with the help of the other animals, survived.

I lie on the uncomfortable bed after the girls have fallen asleep, thinking about my father. I think about him dying, with the memory of me still fresh in his heart. I think about the years I hoped for his return, waited for a letter. I decided when I was a small girl that the time for crying had gone but on these nights I wish I could cry, easily, like Zulima does. My eyes are dry; the pain inside me has no way of escaping.

Days are better. In the morning, all the children do drill, led by a teacher from the school. They throw their arms up in the air, jump forwards, jump back again, all at the shrill of his whistle. It makes me smile, to see how hard they try to follow the instructions, to keep in step, just as we used to. We have breakfast under a grass-roofed shelter in the school grounds, bowls of thin lentil stew with limes to squeeze on top, or pale omelettes dotted with lumps of salt. The children eat hungrily, scooping up the food with rough loaves. I pick the weevils out of my bread with my nails: small, dark bodies that look like cumin seeds. We drink sweet, brackish glasses of black tea afterwards, waving the flies off their rims. The sides of the shelter are open to catch the breeze and the sound of voices floats in the air, and sometimes donkeys braying.

The children try to teach me to whistle and I teach them to sing, how to breathe from their stomachs and throw their voice to a far point in front of them. The girls crowd around me whenever I sit down, feeling my skin, examining my earrings and my nails, trying on my sandals; some of them I know well, like Hannan, but some came to the village while I was away. I tell them about the time I cut my bunches off with a razor blade, the day I fought the girl who called me and Amal a bad name, and how I still have the doll Mama Luban made for me. When I tell the boys I was once a footballer, they don't believe me. I kick my shoes off and have a game with them, holding my long skirt up in one hand as the light fades over the fields and thorn trees around us.

The day before we are due to return, I make a decision. Father Sayf's driver has come with us, in a borrowed car, to collect the food and run errands. When the children are occupied with one of the teachers, I shower and put on a clean blue shirt, long black skirt and blue headscarf. I spray some rose cologne from Jordan on my neck, rub glycerine on my hands and take a long drink of water from the pitcher outside the dormitory. I call for the driver to take me into town.

'Where do you want to go?' he asks, throwing the keys up and down in his hand.

'I don't know. We'll find out when we get there.'

We go first to the souk; the driver stops the car and I tell him to go and ask people if they have ever heard of a man named Hassan Mohamed Mahmoud. A fisherman, I add. He gets out of his seat and disappears into the souk. Fifteen minutes pass; the sound of the muezzin floats through the air. Small boys tap on the window, offering bags of yellow beans, packets of chewing gum, single cigarettes. I'm about to go and look for the driver when he reappears, jumps back in the car and starts the engine. Everybody knows him, he says. We will find him at the river.

He drives to the edge of the town, through residential areas and beyond, the car lurching along an unmade road towards the dam. Where it ends, on a piece of rough ground, he stops beside a couple of dusty white pick-up trucks. We walk towards a line of tall trees and when we get there I stop and stare at the beauty and peace of the scene before me. The Blue

Nile winds like a secret far down below between steep banks, its waters dark and mysterious. Five or six men work on the far side, around upturned wooden boats; further down the river, a group of boys splashes and dives. We cross the foot-bridge next to the long dam, breathing in the smell of mud and stones and leaves.

I shade my eyes and watch as the driver scrambles down the bank to where the fishermen are mending their nets. The men crowd around as he speaks. They call to someone stand-ing in a small wooden dugout a few metres away from the bank. He is lean, his hair white around the edges of his skull-cap. He propels the boat into the bank with a pole and wades ashore, dragging the narrow hull into the mud. He joins them, wiping his hands on his *jellabiya*. They all look up to where I'm standing.

The old man climbs the bank, with the driver following behind him.

'Would you like to be introduced to this young lady?' the driver pants, as they come near. 'She is looking for you, *ya Haj.*'

'You are welcome, miss,' he says. 'I am at your service.'

He is standing in front of me, just a metre away. He is not as old as I first thought. His face is lined but strong; his eyes are bright. He looks nothing like the man who came to the village more than ten years ago.

'Uncle,' I begin. 'You once had a brother . . .'

When Hassan Mohamed Mahmoud understands that he is looking at his brother's daughter, he shouts out thanks to God. He wrings my hand again and again; his smile stretches from one side of his face to the other. He calls to one of the other men, and a watermelon arrives. Hassan draws the knife from his belt, raises it above his head and brings it down on the watermelon; it splits cleanly, showing its pink flesh. He makes huge dripping slices and presents the biggest to me, all the time thanking God for the day that brought me to Sennar, to the river, and to him. He held me in his arms when I was a baby, he says. Do I not remember?

While the driver collects mangos to take back to his children in Khartoum, we sit on the bank and talk. My father was an honest man, liked by all who knew him, Hassan says. He was good with his hands, and he loved food, which was how he got into restaurant work. Hassan only met my mother a couple of times. She was a strong woman; she had been married before and had a daughter already. She sold her goods in the market – bread and spices. She was nicknamed Queen, for her regal ways. Her long hair was always combed and oiled, her back always straight. She came from a powerful family of *sheikhs* in the west. His brother's marriage to her lasted only long enough to produce one child. They called the baby Leila. It means 'of the night'.

After they divorced, my father married again and had a son with his second wife. He lost touch with his former wife but a year later, when he had leave from his job, he went to the city, looking for the child. He went to the district called Bird's Nest, for its straw houses, where the Queen had been living with her daughters. She had gone; nobody knew where. The neighbours told him that they knew her as a quiet woman, going about her business. But one day the landlord came to evict her, to put the family on the street, and they heard her shouting at him, threatening him and his family. The police came and took her away, with the children. No one saw any of them again.

For years, my father kept on travelling to Khartoum when he could, asking people from our tribe if they had any news of the Queen and her daughters. Just before he died, he told everyone that he had found his child. He would be bringing her home, as soon as he made some money. Uncle Hassan pauses, looking out at the river. 'He is buried where he worked, at the sugar plantation. He was proud of the food he made, for hungry people.'

The river glides on below, its surface broken occasionally by a jumping fish. I kiss his hand. I can't speak, except to ask God to bless him. This man has told me more than I have ever known about the people who brought me to this world.

The driver returns; he has unwound his turban and filled it with fruit. Hassan wants to take me to meet the family; the three of us get into the car to drive back into town to his house, near the souk. His oldest son is at his office, he says; he is a university graduate, who works in a Government job. But his wife, his married daughter and some of the younger children are at home. Hassan's wife can't take it in at first; when she does, she becomes dizzy and has to sit down, asking God to forgive her for letting this girl grow up without a mother. I tell her that, thank God, I have my mother at the village as well as the mother who gave me life. The children greet me shyly; one whispers that I'm a 'city girl'. No, says Hassan. This is his brother's daughter. Don't they see the way I cover my mouth with my hand, when I laugh? The set of my shoulders? By God, he would know me anywhere.

By the time we say goodbye, it's dark. I have agreed to come back with Zulima, for *Eid el Adha*, the Feast of Sacrifice. On the way back to the dormitory, I sit in silence in the passenger seat of the car, saturated with the new knowledge I have of my father. And my mother. I feel as if years have passed, not just one long afternoon.

*

Zulima says she will be only too pleased to get away, if her husband will allow it. Father Sayf congratulates me on having found my relatives. He says he hopes they recognize that this girl of theirs is someone special. Mama Luban makes two of her semolina cakes, *bousbousa*, and packs them into plastic bags for the journey. Amal has resumed her humming. She has had a letter from Faisal; he is well, and so are the twins, Mohamed and Mahmoud. They are in the south, in a place called Bahr el Ghazal, which means 'River of the Gazelle'. They hope to be back home soon and they send their greetings to all their brothers and sisters at the village. In the day, Amal keeps the letter in her handbag; at night, she sleeps with it under her pillow.

Six weeks later, I am again on a coach to Sennar, this time with Zulima and the four children. When it pulls into the final stop, Uncle Hassan, his wife and five of the family are lined up in a row, waiting to greet us, the children all dressed in their new Eid clothes. I see them before they have seen me; I sit and look at them through the window. I thank God. He took away my father but led me to my uncle and my cousins. The oldest son is not there, I notice. I pass Mohamed to Zulima and get the sticky parcel down from the luggage rack, and we descend into the warm, dusty air of Sennar.

Zulima's children travel with their new cousins in one taxi, the girls all sitting on top of each other in the back; we go with Uncle Hassan and his wife in another, with the bags in the open boot. It's dark, and the windows are rolled down. The air is balmy and humid; we are 200 miles south of Khartoum. At the house, Aunt Hawa shows us the veranda they have cleared for us, with clean folded sheets on three beds. She has put buckets of water ready in the small bathhouse around the back, and a new bar of pink Lux soap.

I take my bath by candlelight, pouring the soft water over my shoulders, soaping off the dust of the journey. When I have finished I put on a clean *jellabiya*, empty the tin bowl outside and join the others in the yard, where they are gathered around on their wooden beds by the light of a paraffin lamp. Jamila and Habibi have gone with their cousins to explore. Zulima is chatting with Uncle Hassan's wife. Neighbours have arrived to meet us and one of the cakes has been cut up and passed around.

I lie back on the only empty bed, looking up at the stars piercing the blackness overhead, the slice of bright moon. I stretch my arms and sigh; I feel at peace, for the first time since I came back from Jordan. As I think this, I feel a pair of eyes on me. I look up and see a man standing by the open gate to the *hosh*. He is slim, not tall; his hair surrounds his head in a soft cloud and he is wearing the biggest pair of glasses I have ever seen. We look at each other for a moment, then he steps forwards into the lamplight. Hassan Mohamed Mahmoud introduces his son, Muiz.

The next day, we all go for a picnic by the river. Zulima screams when a huge bird swoops down and grabs a piece of meat from her hand; her girls paddle in the water and make pots and cups out of the mud and put them in the sun to dry. The time flies by. We explore the town, we visit Aunt Hawa's relatives, we cook big stews and fry fish caught by Uncle Hassan, we have coffee with neighbours, and at night we lie out in the courtyard, chatting. On the last evening, Muiz invites us to a concert in a park in the town, which he has helped organize. I imagine a park like the one Maha took me to in Amman, a shady garden crossed by luxuriant flowerbeds, with fountains playing in the middle. When we get there, it's a stretch of dry ground with a few trees around the edge and some patches of coarse grass near the entrance. I put my hand over my mouth to keep from laughing. Muiz asks me to hand tickets out to the people as they arrive. As the sun sets, the lines of wooden benches fill with people but more crowd in – young people, old people, children, greeting each other – raising a dust storm around their ankles with their shuffling feet.

The musicians are on the stage, setting up their instruments and chairs. I begin to feel excited; it is the first proper concert I have ever been to. When they begin to play, the crowd falls silent. The sounds of the lute, violins and drums reverberate through the air; I stand to one side, tapping my feet to the insistent rhythms, losing myself in the music. When the singer performs the song called 'Life, the All-time Deceiver', the other musicians stop and listen. He accompanies himself on a clay drum, his voice full of loss, longing and hope. I close my eyes and feel the music running through me as if it were the blood in my veins. Standing in the warm darkness, with the roar of applause around me, I feel at one with the people of my own society; I thank God again for bringing me back to my home.

In the taxi on the way back to the house, my cousin Muiz says the concert was a success because of the pretty girl who gave out the tickets; Zulima says she hasn't enjoyed herself like this since before she got married. Her eyes are shining; she looks like the old Zulima again.

*

Our bus leaves at midday. After breakfast, my uncle calls me from the men's part of the household. When I go in, he stands and greets me, as if he hadn't already seen me earlier. He asks me to sit down and he sits opposite me, with his elbows on his knees, his lively, open face concentrated on mine. I smile at him.

'Are you well, Uncle?'

'Have you enjoyed yourself in this Sennar?' he asks.

I tell him that I have enjoyed myself too much, and so has my sister. We cannot thank him and his family enough for their kindness.

'Can you feel at home among simple people such as us?' he asks.

'More than anywhere,' I say.

He nods. Yes, he says. For a holiday. But could I make my home with them? I don't know what he means, and I say so.

'From the day I met you, Leila, I put it in my mind that you must marry my son, Muiz. He is a good man. And you are a good girl. God willing, everything can go well between you.'

'Uncle,' I stammer. 'I never thought . . .'

'Don't worry,' he says. 'I know you will have to discuss the matter with your family there, in town.'

I back out of the men's quarters and run into the house, pulling the double wooden doors of the bedroom shut behind me. I kick my sandals off and lie down on the satin sheet. From the other side of the wall, in the souk, comes the sound of a saw being pulled through a plank. I have only glimpsed this room before. A vast necklace strung with *hejab* charms – writings from the Koran – in dark leather pouches hangs on the wall. The windows are set low, closed with roughly made shutters through which needles of light slant across the two beds. A glass-fronted cabinet displays Aunt Hawa's china and half a dozen tall glasses. Nearly every piece is cracked or chipped. I hear Uncle Hassan's voice again, shouting for Zulima.

I press the slippery pillow against my face and groan. It has never entered my mind that Muiz might think of marrying me. We have laughed and joked as if he were one of my brothers from the village; did he think I was encouraging him? I think of the way I closed my eyes last night to listen to the music and my face burns. A minute later, the door bursts open and Zulima comes in.

'Well?' she breathes. 'What did you say?'

'Nothing.'

'That was right.' She sits herself down heavily on the end of the bed. 'You can't seem interested, at this stage.'

'What did he say to you?'

'He has selected you for Muiz, and Muiz for you. Muiz is a good man. He doesn't take snuff, or drink. He doesn't smoke. We must tell Father Sayf as soon as we get back. I know he will agree.'

She turns to me, the gold threads in her dress glinting in the gloom.

'How soon do you want to get married?'

*

On the coach back to Khartoum I sit next to Zulima, with Mohamed on my lap. I don't feel the hard seat, the sun on my neck, the roar of the engine. It's not Muiz I think of; it's myself as a married woman, with a family. Muiz's glasses make me think he is serious. But why did he stare at me when he came through the gate? Was it because I'm a city girl, with ribbons in my hair, clothes from Jordan, high-heeled sandals? There is a song about city girls, how the country boys moon after them in their wigs and make-up, how they would sacrifice anything for the promise of a date with a city girl. He seems quiet. He has been to university. Uncle Hassan vouches for him. But he would; it is his son. I think about leaving my work, and everything in me refuses the idea. I have committed myself already, to my brothers and sisters.

Zulima insists on coming to the village with me, even though her children are tired. It's late, but Father Sayf is working in the office. He is busy, he says, looking at me. Most of the workers went away for Eid and his own family have gone to his wife's relatives. He returned early. He seems in a bad mood and I wish Zulima would delay talking to him. But she blurts it out anyway, the minute he closes his mouth.

Father Sayf barely looks up from his papers. He says that we can discuss everything once my uncle comes in person to raise the question with him, but until then it is nothing he can take too seriously. Zulima gapes at him. He sighs, and puts down his pen. He says that marriage to a relative is in general a good idea but that the man has to be considered as an individual. Zulima needs no more encouragement.

'He doesn't drink,' she gushes. 'He doesn't smoke. He goes to the mosque five times a day. He wears glasses.'

Father Sayf folds his papers into his briefcase.

'There is more than that that makes a man,' he says. 'As you must know, Zulima. And we have yet to hear Leila's opinion on the matter.'

Chapter 11

KASSALA HONEYMOON

There is a power cut throughout the village, and by the time I get back to the Blue house I have a headache. Amal fumbles in the cupboard with a torch for aspirin.

'I hope you're comfortable with your new family?' she asks, her back still turned.

'You're my family, you know that.'

I tell her about the simple house, the concert, Uncle Hassan's married daughter, who is expecting a baby; how they ate up Mama Luban's *bousbousa*, and the size of the fish Uncle Hassan caught. Finally, I tell her about the proposal. It is easier in the dark. She is sitting on the edge of her bed; I can hear her legs swinging back and forth.

'You'll be married before I am,' she says. 'He'll be able to afford everything.'

'I want to stay in my job.'

'So you can die an old woman, in a children's village?' she says. 'Impossible. What's he like?'

'Polite. He's got a government job. He taps his foot when he's sitting down.'

'But do you like him?'

'I never thought about him until my uncle spoke to me. Now, I don't know.'

It seems she was right all along, she sighs. All the good fortune goes to Leila.

The electricity stays off; the sound of coughing echoes through the night. Half the children in the village have chest infections. I wake up in the morning and still have the headache, still feel agitated. I go back to work, to try to busy myself with the campaign. I am going to say no, I decide. I didn't go to Jordan for nothing. After taking tea with Alawia, hearing her talk about spending Eid with her family, I change my mind. The answer is yes. I continue like this all week, until on Wednesday a messenger comes from Abu Ali. Zulima and I must come to meet our tribe on Friday. It drives the proposal out of my mind.

Alawia looks on as the messenger delivers the summons. After he's gone, she tells me about a girl she heard of whose family kept her prisoner when she disobeyed them. They locked her in a room, shaved the hair off her head, fed her on dry bread that they passed under the door. 'Be careful,' she says. I don't know what she means but it makes me more nervous. I want these people to think well of me. Zulima agrees to come but says she won't bring her children and she can't stay long. Her husband is getting fed up with this family of hers, calling her away from her duties. His mother is saying he needs another wife, who spends more time at home.

*

We sit in the back of the car, the sun beating through the window. Zulima has powdered her face, wrapped herself in a maroon-coloured *tobe*. I am wearing one of her *tobes* too; I know these people wouldn't consider a long skirt and scarf respectable. I feel hot and not like myself. I pick a newspaper off the back shelf of the car, for a fan. Wagir, my brother from when I first came to the Institute from Mygoma, is accompanying us and Father Sayf has lent us his car.

We cross the bridge to Omdurman and drive off the tarmac towards the district called Umm Badda, along a wide sand road, past donkey carts and buses with dust rising in red clouds behind them. I cling to the door handle, trying to stop my head hitting the roof. Zulima wraps her *tobe* over her nose and mouth. After half an hour, Wagir turns off on to a track between mud-plastered walls; children stare as we pass and a yelping dog chases after the car. We stop outside a wooden gate with all the paint worn off at the bottom.

As Wagir turns off the engine, I hear a commotion rising from behind the high wall. Wagir raps at the gate and pushes it open, and I step through, trying to keep the *tobe* over both my hair and my ankles. Inside is a large, bare yard with an awning strung over the right-hand side. Underneath it are crowds of men dressed in traditional clothes – *jibba* tunics with

loose, calf-length trousers underneath, waistcoats over the top
and turbans on their heads. Several are wearing leopardskin
slippers, like my father did when he came to the village. Some
have spears in their hands. I see the thin face of my Uncle
Hassan, standing apart from the others. As I'm wondering
what he's doing here, the men surge towards us. Zulima's
father Abu Ali looms out from among them, his cheeks covered in silver stubble, a wad of money sticking out of the
pocket of his waistcoat.

'At last,' he roars, pumping our hands, ushering me and
Zulima in under the shade. 'Our lost daughters have
returned,' he announces. 'Thanks be to God.' The others
crowd around, asking how we are, where we have been. Abu
Ali bellows at them to step back, give us room to breathe. He
clamps his hands on our shoulders. 'This is my daughter by
my first wife,' he says, gesturing at Zulima. 'And this is the
girl,' he turns towards me, 'whose future we decide today.' I
keep my eyes on the ground, asking it to swallow me.

'Sir . . .' I begin, but Abu Ali doesn't hear. The family have
decided that the suitable one for me to marry is his nephew, he
booms; he is a businessman and needs a wife. I'm educated
and won't make trouble for him, any fool can see that. They all
agree that this is the match that will be suitable. He yells for
his nephew to step forwards and a large pair of feet appears
on the ground in front of me, inside a pair of leather sandals.
I hear Uncle Hassan's voice remonstrating in the background.

The smell of roasting meat hits me, and with it the fear that
this is a wedding party – that Abu Ali intends to sign the
papers and marry me to his nephew today. Zulima won't be

able to protect me, nor Wagir; they don't count as guardians. Father Sayf could have prevented it, but it's too late. I picture myself locked in one of these small rooms, or chained up near the goat pen. I think of Muiz's face, his cloud of hair. His heel, jiggling up and down.

Abu Ali waves us towards the women's quarters. We brush past a line of drying meat, through a tattered curtain and into a *rakuba*, where ten or more women are stirring pots, setting out dishes on trays. I sit by Zulima on the chairs they drag out for us. I'm shaking all over. The women look at us curiously as they come and shake our hands. Their palms are hard. They are wearing thin, worn *tobes*, and plastic bangles on their arms. One whispers something about government girls, and they all laugh.

I try to smile. These women are our relatives. Some of them must have known our mother well, from when she was a bride. I long to know what they know. I open my mouth to ask after their health, their children, but nothing comes out. Beyond the *rakuba*, the men's voices grow louder. They are quarrelling with my Uncle Hassan, saying he has no right to marry me to a foreigner. I hear Wagir's voice. 'Sirs! You are one family! It's not right!'

The trays are ready, crowded with dishes of lamb stew, fried liver, knuckles of beef in gravy, macaroni, mounds of rice and bread; the women hoist them up and manoeuvre their way out of the kitchen. One puts a tray of food in front of me and Zulima, and another pours water for us to wash our hands. I feel suffocated by the swarming flies, the stifling Omdurman heat, the shouting.

'Eat!' the woman who serves us commands, as I shake the drops off my fingers. 'In the name of God!'

I tear off a piece of bread, dab it in one of the salads. Then I put it down and glance around. The men have fallen silent outside, busy with their food. The women are feeding themselves and their children, gathered around what is left of the meat. It is time to act. I grab Zulima's hand and lurch towards the torn curtain, pulling her behind me. Wagir sees us hurrying along by the wall and kicks the gate open.

Abu Ali raises his head. 'Where do you think you're going?' he shouts, through a mouth full of food. 'Never mind, sir,' I call, tumbling into the street. 'Goodbye.' As Wagir starts the engine, a pair of hands grips the bottom of the open car window. I draw the *tobe* around my face, shrinking into the seat. One nail, on the little finger of the right hand, is very long.

'I want you for my wife,' says a man's voice, low and intimate. 'God willing, I will have you for my wife. I love you.'

*

Uncle Hassan comes at six in the morning, and squats on his haunches by the office wall. He stays there watching the aeroplanes until Father Sayf arrives two hours later. He won't take a seat, or accept a cold drink. He says he wants to make a proposal of marriage on behalf of his son, Muiz. He says he hopes, if it is God's will, I accept the proposal. If not, I will always be welcome in his home in Sennar, as the daughter of his late brother.

At midday Abu Ali turns up, leading his supporters behind him. They march past Alawia and into Father Sayf's office. Abu Ali announces that there are two matters that he wants to sort out. Muiz, he says, is not the true son of my Uncle Hassan. He is the younger brother of Hassan's wife Hawa, and was taken in as a young boy when his mother died. He is therefore a foreigner. He called Hassan to the meeting to show him that the whole family was agreed on this point. The second matter is the marriage. The entire family wishes me to marry his nephew, a businessman working at a trading station in the far north, on the border with Egypt. This man can afford to get married immediately; he can give me a good life and I will be a fool to refuse. If I do, the family wants no more to do with me.

Father Sayf recounts all this to me in the early afternoon, in his office; I have been away from the village all morning, meeting sponsors. He is totally fed up with it, he says. I can smell Abu Ali in the room, the mix of tobacco, sweat and clove oil. Outside, Alawia has stopped typing.

'What is your advice, Father?'

'Do you want to marry?' he asks. 'It will be inconvenient, having to train another assistant. You are starting to be a real help around here.'

'I do want to marry, Father. Of course.'

I don't. But I want what goes with marriage. I want to marry life. And I want to keep on working at the village as well. I want two lives.

'Normally,' Father Sayf says, 'we would say it's right to choose the one who approached you first. Hassan's son, Muiz.

But in this case, it turns out that this Muiz is a foreigner. He is not your real relative. You may be safer with the other fellow. Not that I have much liking for his uncle.'

'Father,' I begin, 'I consider Muiz my cousin. He is like a son to my Uncle Hassan. He has a steady job. He . . .'

Father Sayf stands up and looks out of the office window. There is a gardener outside, squatting among the marigolds; small black and brown birds flutter their feathers in the puddles around his feet.

'Look, Leila . . .' he says. 'You are not a cow, to be bought and sold, as this family of yours seems to think. You must decide for yourself who you will accept as a husband. But please give me plenty of notice if you plan to leave your job.'

Alawia resumes a slow tapping at her keys.

As I walk away from the office, two of the little girls from camp race after me, grabbing my fingers, wanting to sing to me. I shake them off, telling them I'll come and hear them later. I walk around the edge of the football pitch, kicking at the parched ground with the toe of my sandal. The heat is affecting everything: the roses are losing their petals and there are drifts of curled leaves around the roots of the trees. I walk behind the Green house, past Mama Luban's line of washing, her bowls propped against the wall. The green has faded since we first arrived, and the paint has bubbled up in the sun. I picture the pair of feet, the gripping hands. Hear again what he said. I shudder. No one has ever spoken those words to me before. I feel shame, and anger, that they should have been said like that, by a stranger. I can't marry this man. Not in a thousand years. My mind is made up.

Kassala Honeymoon

Two weeks later, Muiz comes from Sennar with gifts of sweets and dates. We have the engagement ceremony at the village in the evening. We sit on Father Sayf's best chairs, in new clothes, in front of everybody. Muiz's heel jiggles up and down. He has jasmine flowers around his neck; he is wearing a cream-coloured suit. He looks like an actor and I feel proud that this man wants me for his wife. The whole village watches as he puts the gold engagement ring on my finger. But only I can hear what he says.

'This is my gift to you and I will never in this life ask you to remove it.'

The words turn out not to be true. But as he says them, I feel as if he is making me a queen like my mother once was. Queen of my own life.

*

'Don't even leave the house until the marriage is complete! A struck match is useless, remember.'

'Never tell him you're tired, when he – you know – wants husband and wife relations . . .'

'Keep him well fed and lazy! Too fat to look for another wife!'

Advice comes from all sides – from Mama Luban and every other mother at the village, from Zulima, from Alawia, from the cleaners at the office, and my future sisters-in-law. All of them have an opinion on how to keep a man, and his money. All of them are more interested in me now than they have ever been before.

Abu Ali and his clan troop up the path to the office from the gate every few weeks. Abu Ali nods at me and heads for Father Sayf; in our tribe, we do not believe in the practice of 'engagement', he informs him. As far as he is concerned, it means nothing. I must obey my stepfather and marry the suitable husband. The other men shake their heads and tap their sticks on the floor and say by God, he speaks the truth. Father Sayf gets so fed up with them, he tells the watchman to say he has gone abroad; for a while, they disappear from our lives.

I continue my work in the office, sending out newsletters and photographs. I show visitors round – from clubs, from the United Nations, from newspapers. There aren't many foreign visitors any more; few white people drive around the city now in their big cars. I get on the phone to business people, ministry officials, professional associations, trying to get them to sponsor us. At the same time I invite them to visit, to see for themselves whether these are bad children. Sometimes, when I put the phone down or wave goodbye to a group, I realize I have forgotten about the time, forgotten about the wedding – forgotten everything except the children, their future. Muiz has agreed that I can carry on with my work; he will look for a new job in Khartoum.

Amal still shares her room with me at the Blue house. We sleep on the same beds as when we were kids; we use the same desk and chair, share her old cupboard from when the village was new. I have bought a small refrigerator out of my salary, so that we can have cold water when we want it. She comes home from the market sometimes with verses from the Koran in calligraphy, in frames that she nails high on the wall.

She puts up one saying that whoever is powerful in this world should remember that there is One more powerful than him. Other than that, the room remains as bare and simple as when we were girls.

After the engagement, Muiz sends 200 dollars for the preparations to begin. I have to have six of everything, all new, and every kind of cosmetic. Mama Luban and Mama Amaani drag me to the souk whenever they can; sometimes Amal comes too. Mama Amaani pounces on the things that are pretty and fashionable, in silky materials and eye-catching colours. Mama Luban fingers the nightdresses, peers at the bright blouses, sniffs. Are they decent? Will they last? Do the colours run?

Gradually, our room begins to look like the People's Market. I have *tobes*, dresses, nightdresses, sandals, knickers, bras, scarves, hair ornaments, hair oils, hair dyes, perfumes for the day, perfumes for the night, nail polish, polish remover, body lotions, hand creams, lipsalve, foundation, face powder, eyebrow pencils, eyeshadows, earrings, necklaces, slippers, slips, soaps, toothpastes, toothbrushes, flannels, loofahs, shampoos, straightening lotions, mousse, hairspray, hair grips, hair bands . . . The cardboard suitcase I brought from Jordan isn't big enough. I fold the dresses and underwear into an old sugar sack that I keep under the bed.

When the shopping is done, Mama Luban dusts off her sewing machine and begins to run up sheets and pillowcases. Amal embroiders flowers around their borders, drawing occasional beads of blood from her finger. When they finish the linen, they embark on a recipe book. Mama Luban dictates the methods for stews with dried meat, dried fish, dried lady's fingers, fresh meat, fresh chicken, fresh fish. . . Amal writes it all down, in a notebook with a picture of tomatoes on the cover. She hoped she would be preparing for her own wedding by now, she says one night. But preparing for mine is the next best thing. I hug her for a long time. I can't say the words. But in my heart I tell her that if it was her wedding we were preparing for, I would be even happier than I am now.

Mama Amaani teaches me the dances I have to do, clapping her hands and singing as I practise the steps in the yard at night, with all the little girls of the village watching and giggling. Mama Luban scolds me for lying on my back on the bed, saying I'll flatten out my best asset. She nags me in her wheezy voice about walking like a man when I move naturally, rather than swaying from side to side. She tries to persuade me to walk with my forearms turned outwards. It thrusts my breasts forwards in what feels to me a very noticeable way. I know, at the back of my mind, that all these preparations are leading up to something, something to do with the marriage. But I can't think what.

*

Two weeks before the wedding, preparations intensify. Mama Luban likes Muiz. Marrying the darker-skinned man, she says, would have been like throwing myself in the garbage. I only ever saw his hands and feet, I tell her; I don't know what he looked like. She sniffs and says everyone in the village has seen his uncle. She is determined to make me as pale as milk before the wedding day. I saw Zulima suffering, at the Institute, in the smoke baths. Now I discover why she moaned and wept, why she couldn't go out in the sun or take off her long socks and gloves.

Every day, when I come back to the house from the office, I find Mama Luban in the Blue house rakuba, filling Mama Amaani's *dukhan* hole with glowing coals with her bare fingers, laying scented woods on top. I have to crouch over the pouring smoke with a blanket around my shoulders. The first time I do it, it feels after a minute as if my blood is boiling in my skin. Mama Luban tells me to put my face down into the smoke, holding the blanket around my ears. I come up choking, with smoke in my nose, my eyes, my throat. I throw off the blanket, grab my old *jellabiya* and cover myself with it.

I want to be a good wife; I want to become a grown-up woman, a normal woman. But I don't see how cooking myself over this fire is going to make me a better wife. The next day isn't much easier. The one after, I manage half an hour. After two weeks, I have built up to an hour. The palms of my hands turn yellow; every pore in my body exudes the scent of sandalwood.

Two days before the wedding, Mama Luban calls me over to the Green house; she sits in the yard with a tin basin of sugar. She squeezes in lime juice, flicking the pips out with the tip of her knife, and puts the mixture over a gas flame in the kitchen. The yard fills with the smell of toffee; small boys appear, sniffing and looking around. When the mixture is dark brown, she takes it off the gas to cool. After lunch, she works it with her fingers, pulling up handfuls until it grows soft and turns the colour of honey. When she is satisfied, we go inside.

I take off my *jellabiya* and pull the sheet over me; she begins on my legs, dragging a handful of the sugar paste downwards over one ankle with her fingertips, then ripping it upwards. I gasp at the first few movements, with shock more than pain. She goes over my legs again and again, until the paste stops sticking to me because there's nothing left – no tiny hairs, not even any dead skin – to come away. Then she turns her attention to the rest of my body. I thank God when she says she's finished; I can't take another moment of this agony. But my skin is soft as a baby's and noticeably lighter. Mama Luban clucks with satisfaction like a chicken.

The night before the wedding, Mama Amaani's sister comes to decorate me with henna. In the morning, the hairdresser arrives. I'm caught up in the excitement; the band is booked and the mothers have been cooking day and night. The children have new clothes. All our sponsors and the friends of the village are invited to my wedding, as well as the families of the mothers. Zulima is coming with her husband and children, along with Nanny Samia, who I loved as a child when she worked at the Institute. She now works at the Ministry for Social Welfare.

Not everyone is coming. The Queen nodded when I told her I was getting married, and closed her eyes; she never leaves her room. The twins and Faisal aren't yet back from the south, although Amal has had a message to say they are coming soon. I have been to the Arab souk where Rashid works and left a message for him with a boy who was minding the shop. I haven't seen Rashid for a long time and it hurts to think about him, because he is my favourite brother. Zulima says he has abandoned us, but I know he hasn't. Zulima's father Abu Ali isn't coming either, although we invited him and his family.

I spend most of the wedding day in our room in the Blue house, with Amal and Mama Luban. In the afternoon, Father Sayf comes to ask for my formal consent to the marriage; he goes to the mosque with Uncle Hassan for the official papers. That evening, for the first time, I put on the gold bangles Muiz has brought for me, and the traditional bride's headdress, with its chain that connects to my nose. I look strange and exotic in the mirror on the back of the old cupboard door. My skin is pale and Mama Amaani has outlined my eyes in kohl and drawn in my eyebrows in fine long lines over the top. My lips are full and shining and the round gold earrings with the crescent moon and single star hang from my ears. The headdress is heavy on my scalp and the bangles glint and clatter on my arm. Amal stands beside me in the mirror, in her new dress, looking over my shoulder. Mama Luban wraps a fine, gauzy *tobe* over me, wiping her eyes as she does it, and – very slowly – we proceed out of the house to where the people are gathered.

Mama Amaani helps me step up on to a wooden stage at one end of the football pitch, and to sit on the empty chair draped in red cloth. In front of me are crowds of people, the women and girls all over on one side. Next to me is a slight man in a pale suit and large glasses, tapping his foot. I don't know him at all. I have met him five or six times, always in the company of other people. And now my life is tied to his.

Every mother of the village ululates as if her life depends upon it and the children dash around under the trees in the darkness.

*

The double bed fills the room; it has a wooden headboard and is spread with a sheet, worn thin in the middle. There are two flat pillows, and small tables on each side with an ashtray on one of them. I stand by the wall, looking at the way the sun beats through the closed orange curtains, as the hotel boy drags our suitcases into the room. He goes into the bathroom and runs a tap, then opens the wardrobe door to display wire hangers. Muiz gives him a coin and he disappears, closing the door behind him.

I suggest going to the hotel restaurant for supper.

'Are you hungry?' he asks.

I'm not hungry. I'm tired out, after two days of wedding celebrations followed by an eight-hour bus journey from Khartoum. I want to kick off the sandals that are rubbing my feet, throw off the *tobe* and lie down.

'Yes,' I say. 'I'd like an omelette.'

We walk down the hotel stairs again. There is no one in the restaurant. The omelette is cold when it comes, and the salt is in a solid lump inside the plastic shaker. I eat as slowly as I can and pretend to be interested in the television in the corner of the room. I admire the plastic flowers on the table, read the brochure about snorkelling in the Red Sea. Muiz drinks glasses of water, one after the other.

Kassala Honeymoon

After two hours, we climb the stairs back to the room. I undress in the bathroom then put on one of the bride's nightdresses, which looked so pretty when Mama Amaani picked them out in the souk. It's shorter than I realized – it doesn't even reach my knees. I sit on the edge of the bath and look at my feet on the tiled floor, the dainty flower patterns running up both sides of my ankles. I run my hands up and down my legs, feeling their soft plumpness. I can hear Muiz through the wall, moving around, clearing his throat.

I wore a short dress when I danced for him on the second day of the wedding. We did it in the Blue house. Mama Amaani put the music on and she and Amal filled the room with incense. All the mothers and girls crowded in to watch. I felt shy when I started dancing, but after a minute I began to enjoy it. The air was warm around me and the floor solid under my bare feet. Muiz stood near me, clicking his fingers, his face mesmerized. When I had done the last dance, I did what the bride has to do – and fell towards the floor, without warning. He caught me. I thought he would miss but he didn't. I felt his arms, the strength of them, for a moment, before he released me again. We were both laughing and my heart was pounding.

I wash off the make-up, clean my teeth and return to the bedroom. Muiz is lying on the bed, dressed only in a pair of loose undertrousers and his glasses. His chest looks smooth and broad. I lie down stiffly on the other side of the bed and he puts out the light. After a minute, his hand feels for mine. When he tells me what has to happen between husband and wife, I don't believe him.

'It will kill me,' I say.

'No,' comes his voice in the darkness. 'It won't kill you.'

*

In the morning we sit opposite each other, with a plate of beans and two glasses of grapefruit juice between us. I am wearing a plain, full-length skirt, a long-sleeved shirt and a blue headscarf, but my elaborate henna and my painted nails and gold bangles give me away as a bride. As the waiter pours tea from the thermos flask, another woman walks into the dining room with intricate patterns all over her hands, gold rings on her fingers. We greet each other as she passes and when breakfast is over she comes and sits at our table with her husband. Like us, the pair has come to Kassala for their honeymoon.

We decide quickly that we will go out together to explore the town. It is a quiet, simple place with the dramatic shape of the mountains always looming in the background. We drink coffee flavoured with ginger, in a café, and talk. As usual, with strangers, when they ask about my family I say that I have a mother and father and too many brothers and sisters to count, thanks be to God. The four of us wander through the market looking at the heaps of guavas and mangos and the women from the Rashaida tribe, with silver bangles on their ankles and rings in their noses. We take a taxi to the tomb of Sayed Hassan under the mountain. The tomb is ruined, its roof gone; the boy who appoints himself our guide says that when rain falls in Kassala it doesn't fall in the tomb, because of the holiness of

Sayed Hassan. The other bride – her name is Muna – wants a blessing from one of the holy men sitting outside.

When we get to the park by the river, Muna and I fall behind the men. The grass scratches my ankles; the trees throw long shadows over the dry ground. I break the silence.

'How long have you been married?'

'Three days,' she says. 'You?'

'Same.'

Silence again.

'Have you?' I begin. 'Are you . . .'

'Not yet,' she says. 'God willing, things will be OK soon.'

'You too! Me neither,' I exclaim.

The men are deep in conversation in front of us. Her married sister warned her, she says, before the wedding. She told her that some husbands cut the wife open themselves with a knife. Some get a midwife to come and do it after the wedding. But her sister told her that the best way is to keep trying.

'It is painful. But with time, the way becomes easier.'

I link arms with her and we wander around in circles in the park until the sun sets, bathing the flat-topped mountains in red, reflected light.

The rest of the honeymoon passes more enjoyably. We spend the days with Muna and Mohamed, her husband, joking, walking, eating, drinking. At night, Muiz is kind and patient. I chose the right husband, I decide. And all the advice-givers were wrong. Marriage is easy.

Chapter 12

HOUSE IN OLD WOMAN

Two weeks later, on a Friday afternoon, the bus from the Arab market brings me and Muiz back to the village. I sit in the women's section, gazing out at a goat that has climbed into the branches of a tree, at closed shops, and at taxi drivers resting on the back seats of their cars, their feet sticking out of the open doors. The city is like a dear friend, a familiar face. I am glad to be home.

I call out to the watchman as I get off the bus. He doesn't answer. He grabs the cases out of Muiz's hands and hurries through the gates in front of us. I have only got a few steps along the path when I see the children, crowded around the Green house. They are still, and quiet. I pick up my *tobe* and run – past the watchman, through the kids, through the front garden full of spinach and the tops of onions – into the house. It takes a moment for my eyes to adjust; Mama Luban is sitting

---

on the floor, surrounded by other women. When she sees me, she raises both arms and lets out a bloodcurdling wail. Amal is next to her. Her hair is rough and her face swollen and dusty.

'What's happened?' I scream.

I know the answer before they tell me. I drop my handbag and run to Amal. The ground underneath me seems to tilt, as if the room, the village, the world, were turning upside down. I tear off my bride's *tobe*, rip my new dress, kick away the sandals, get on the ground with my sister and hold her in my arms. I hear my own voice shrieking too. Then it is lost among all the voices, keening together.

Faisal is dead. He was killed in an ambush, two days before he was due to return home.

We mourn our beloved brother for a week. When the wake is over, we try to resume normal life at the village. The smells of frying garlic and felafel return and with them the shouts from the football pitch, the sound of the girls singing. Muiz returns to Sennar. I go back to the office; Mama Luban turns her attention again to the living, the seven boys and girls now in her care in the Green house.

Amal's grief seems to grow as the weeks pass. Her clothes hang from her shoulders. Her laugh dies. When I speak to her, she doesn't hear. In the night, I hear her praying to God, crying at the same time. I can't help her. I don't know how. I keep quiet most of the time. When I try to cheer her up, to tell her she still has her life in front of her, that she must accept the will of God, she snaps at me.

'What do you know?' she says. 'You, who have known only good fortune.'

It hurts. One evening, she remarks that I am not truly abandoned, since I have met both my mother and my father. I can't hold my tongue any more.

'Was I in Mygoma orphanage for a picnic?' I yell. 'Did I grow up with any family other than this one?'

She apologizes. But after the death of Faisal, a distance begins between us.

Over this time, married life is not very different from single life. I wear a *tobe* to the office now, instead of long skirts and headscarves; Mama Amaani insists that I renew my henna every few weeks. I have learned to do the *helawa*, the sugar treatment, myself. I have a jar of it in the cupboard; as a married woman, it is shameful for me to have any hair on my body. Even if your husband isn't present, says Mama Luban, you need to be ready for death. The young girls at the village pester me to let them try on my sandals, my bangles, but most of the wedding things stay in the flour sack under the bed; there isn't time for hair dyes and creams and scents, and with Faisal passed away I don't feel like dressing up. Amal brings another framed piece of calligraphy home from the market; it says that everything will perish, except His face.

*

This year passes quickly; its end comes suddenly.

'A man doesn't follow a woman. A woman must follow a man.' Muiz can't find a job in Khartoum; he is insisting that I leave the village and go and live in Sennar. Even the President, he says, states that a woman's place is in the home, taking care of her children and her reputation. We have come to Father Sayf for advice, because we can't reach an agreement.

'What have you got to say, Leila?' Father Sayf asks.

'Muiz knew that when he married me, he married the village too. You agreed to everything, Muiz.'

'I've changed my mind.'

I look at this man who is my husband. The big glasses that seemed a sign of his sensitivity look ridiculous. He seems more unknown to me than any stranger could be. And if he doesn't understand that the village is part of me, he doesn't know me at all either.

'You're my wife,' he repeats. 'That's all there is to it.'

'It's a nuisance,' says Father Sayf, distractedly. The office has acquired a computer and he is learning how to use it; I hear him from my office, stabbing at the keys. 'Perhaps you could train someone else, Leila?'

Muiz looks at me with an expression of relief.

'Wait and see,' he says. 'I will do everything to make you happy.'

With the decision made, Muiz is in a hurry. He leaves for Sennar, saying he wants to prepare things for us, and that I should be ready when he returns. While he is gone, I pack the cardboard suitcase once again. I visit Zulima and kiss our mother's hands as a farewell; she still cannot bear to be touched on her face or head. I take a bottle of her favourite scent and a new pair of the round-toed shoes, and put them in her cupboard.

'I'm going with my husband, mother,' I say. 'I'm going to live in another town, far away.'

She doesn't answer but when I get up to leave she raises her head and looks at me, with eyes full of love.

Zulima thanks God that at least her husband didn't try to drag her out of the city. She weeps and says she is losing me for the third time, and then she dries her eyes and promises to try to bring the children to Sennar, for Eid. She asks me to get her a new pestle and mortar, if I see the wooden ones in the marketplace. When Muiz comes again, I say goodbye to Amal, to Mama Amaani and Mama Luban, to Alawia and Father Sayf and to all the children one by one, and we depart, in a taxi, for the coach station with my suitcase and the flour sack on the roof. The refrigerator I bought out of my salary is sticking out of the open boot of the taxi, next to the stool Rashid made for me. In my handbag, I have a small, bent teaspoon, a folded piece of embroidery and a worn-out tape of Sudanese music.

This is the beginning of marriage, I think, looking out of the taxi window at the women begging at the traffic lights with their babies, the small boys selling flannels and kites. But I feel optimistic as I climb on to the coach behind Muiz. It will be the first time since I entered Mygoma orphanage as a baby that I have lived in our society as a normal person.

*

I brought boxes of cakes from Khartoum for the family and on the first night of my new life in Sennar we sit out under the stars, chatting and eating. Muiz's married sister, Bussana, has named her daughter after me. The baby sleeps on my lap. I hold her head gently against my arm; I want them to see that I will be a good mother, when the time comes. Despite the cool weather, the family sleeps outside at night, the men on one side of the yard and the women and children on the other.

The house is poor; Muiz is the only one in the family with a salary. There are three rooms and no brick bathroom. The latrine is fenced with grass, a hole in the ground over a pit; there is no cement around it and the sandy floor is always wet. I enter it with dread, especially at night. This first evening, I go to use the latrine but can't force myself inside. The ground is alive with dark, moving shapes. Two of the small boys come with their rubber slippers, and squash about twenty cockroaches before I can go in.

When I come back, everyone is getting ready to sleep. Aunt Hawa has prepared the best room for us.

'It is a simple home but all we have is yours,' she says, striking a match. The lamp lights up the big necklace of *hejab* charms on the wall, throwing long shadows over the rough plaster. Her glass-fronted cabinet gleams, as do the satin covers on the beds. The sandy floor is soft under my feet and the ceiling low and bowed. It is a humble room but to me it is beautiful; I am with my family.

'Thank you, Auntie. Really, I'm the happiest woman in Sudan, being here with you all.'

Muiz watches but doesn't say anything. We sleep curled up on one small bed, despite the heat in the room.

Even without the village bell, I wake early. Muiz is snoring and when I creep outside the horizon is tinged with pink, the moon still bright overhead. Most of the family are asleep under their blankets but Uncle Hassan's bed is empty; he has gone to the river. I hear stirring in the kitchen. Bussana, wrapped in a shawl, is feeding her baby. The kettle is on and the room is sour with the smell of bottled gas. I feel so happy to be here, doing ordinary things. They can't know what it means to me. I kiss the baby's waving foot and give Bussana the most flowery greeting I know; I wish her a morning of light, roses and jasmine, like my old teacher Mrs Khadija used to do with us sometimes. Bussana looks surprised.

We drink the first cup of tea while cockerels wake up all around us outside. I'm arranging the remains of last night's cake on a plate when I hear angry voices. I hurry outside to see what's happening. The gate is open and a pick-up truck stands in the alley with its engine running. Two men are carrying out the fridge that we brought the day before from Khartoum. Aunt Hawa stands by the gate, twisting the end of her *tobe*. She spins round and for a moment I think she's going to hit me.

'This home was good enough for my brother every day of his life until this one,' she hisses.

'What are you talking about?'

'I am the happiest woman in Sudan, Auntie.' She imitates my Khartoum accent.

'Come, Leila,' Muiz calls from inside the room where we slept. 'Let's go.'

His sisters are staring at me; the baby begins to cry. I push past the girls, into the room. Muiz is kneeling on one of the suitcases.

'I have rented a house just for the two of us,' he says. 'We can live in freedom.'

'Why didn't you tell me?'

He snaps the lock closed and struggles to his feet. 'I wanted it to be a surprise,' he says. 'Just wait until you see it.'

'Muiz, I beg you. Tell Hawa this is not my idea.'

He shrugs. 'I've told her. She doesn't believe it. Leila . . .' He stands in front of me, his eyes shining behind his lenses. 'Today will be the happiest of your life.'

I straighten the sheet, put on my sandals and follow him out of the gate. Not one of the family comes to wish us goodbye.

*

There is a saying in Sudan that even if a thing starts out badly, it doesn't mean it will continue badly. In spite of the poor beginning, this move is the start of the happiest years of my life. Our new house is in the district known as *Ajous*, or Old Woman. Muiz says it's called that because it's neither important nor beautiful.

The first thing that meets my eyes is the lime tree in the middle of the yard. It has slender, spreading branches; its leaves cast a dense shade. The house is even smaller than my Uncle Hassan's; two rooms lead off one veranda on one side of the yard, and on the other side there is a small kitchen, a bathroom and a pit latrine with a clean concrete floor and brick walls. A deep strip of garden runs along the far wall.

I gasp as Muiz leads me from room to room. The walls are freshly painted. New ceiling fans turn overhead and the floors are concrete, covered in patterned linoleum. There is a double bed in the bedroom, with a matching dressing table and a stool. The wardrobe has an inlay of wreaths of flowers, and an oval-shaped mirror. There is a double gas ring in the kitchen, with a metal wand to light it by, and a solid tin trunk for china. The netting on the veranda is taut and new, the yard freshly set with half-bricks. I go back outside and stand under the shade of the lime tree; the leaves whisper over my head, throw dancing patterns over the ground. The heat shimmers and hums. Everyone warned me it would be hotter here.

Muiz drags two beds out from the veranda and arranges them under the tree, and we lie down on the new cotton mattresses to rest. As we lie there, a face appears over the top of the wall behind the strip of garden. Her white hair springs up from her head. Her lips are tattooed blue and she has heavy gold hoops in her ears. Muiz has got it wrong, I think as I hurry over to greet her, stepping through the dry plants, stretching my hand up. This must be the person that the quarter is named after. She introduces herself as Halima, and congratulates me on my recent marriage, her eyes roving past me into the yard.

'Anyone would think you had come from Saudi Arabia,' she says.

She bobs down out of sight on the other side of the wall and I hear her shouting at someone in a less cordial voice. I return to my place in the shade. Soon, the smell of hot oil drifts over the wall. I am relieved when Muiz opens his eyes and announces that he is going to the market for provisions, and will bring back felafel for lunch.

*

When the gate bangs behind Muiz the next morning, I walk from the bedroom to the other room. I pace around the *hosh*, lie down under the tree, get up again. I open the wardrobe, and close it. I sit at the dressing table, look at myself. My hair is still thick and wilful, my eyes bright under shaped eyebrows. I pick up my hairbrush, lay it down again. No bells ring. The air is empty of the cry of children, or the slap of approaching sandals.

A clatter of falling saucepans comes over the wall and I jump up, straighten the bed and pick up Muiz's dirty clothes. I find the grass brush and sweep the bedroom, the veranda, the yard. I wash the linoleum, dragging a heavy cloth backwards over it to pick up the dust that has settled overnight, and throw the waste water over the roots of the tree.

When I have finished, I go into the kitchen and open the refrigerator. I make stuffed tomatoes first, mixing the half-cooked rice with meat, garlic, onion and spices, as the instructions in Amal's neat writing say, then packing the mixture into the hollowed-out tomatoes and putting them back in the pan. I make aubergine salad; the oil pours out faster than I expected from the plastic bag. I make another salad, of yoghurt and sesame paste, then a jug of orange juice mixed with sugar and water, and put them in the fridge to cool.

I have a shower, put on a clean dress, brush my hair. I lie in the shade on one of the beds, listening to the whisper of the leaves, the drifting voices of schoolgirls as they pass the gate. And I wait for Muiz to come home.

He drinks a glass of the cold juice, changes out of his business clothes and sleeps for a while. When he wakes up, he says he is hungry. I go to the kitchen, crowd all the dishes on to the tray and carry it into the veranda. When I set it down on a table in front of him, Muiz begins to laugh. The tomatoes have collapsed a bit and the aubergine salad glistens with oil. The tahini sauce looks sloppy on the plate. I try to hide my disappointment.

'Who helped you do this?' he says.

'No one.'

'Halima must have been here all morning,' he insists.

I feel annoyed, but I don't want to spoil the meal. I bring a bar of soap, its edges still sharp from the packet, and pour water for him to wash his hands. He sits forwards, pulls up the sleeve of his *jellabiya* and begins to eat.

'Mama Luban told me an untruth,' he says, after a while. 'She said you couldn't cook. She said, "Leila knows nothing of this life. You will have to be patient." Those were her exact words, by God.'

'She was wrong. I know a lot. What I don't know, I'll learn.'

*

Sennar is small, with most of the town centred on the market. There are streets of colonial villas, large, comfortable-looking places, owned by big merchants and people from old families.

The pavements are wide, planted with trees that bloom red and yellow and orange after the rains. The town has a sense of space; it's peaceful, with more room for people. It's hotter than Khartoum in the day but the nights can be cool and refreshing. It has an ancient history; Muiz says it is the oldest city in the country. I love it, I quickly decide. I don't care if I never live in Khartoum again.

Halima makes it her job to show me round. She takes me to the most artistic *henana*, shows me the best place to buy fried fish and bakery bread. There are a lot of people here that come from West Africa; they clean houses and knock on the gate asking for work washing sheets.

In these first weeks, I try hard to behave exactly as Mama Luban said I should. I always have food ready for Muiz when he comes home. I get up before him, to make tea and warm water for his bath. I don't ask him for anything, or question what he's doing when he goes out. I take regular smoke baths to keep my skin soft and pale, my body smelling deeply of sandalwood. I keep the house clean and tidy and burn incense every morning to keep bad spirits away. I never sing, even quietly to myself, and I rarely drink coffee.

I listen to Halima's life; I am hungry to know how families live. I grow familiar with the crackle of the radio as her son tunes in to the BBC in the mornings, the sound of him brushing his shoes in sharp short strokes. I hear Halima shouting at her schoolgirl daughter, to get her nose out of her books and come and help. I get to know my neighbour through the smells of roasting coffee beans and frying meat that float over the wall, the sounds of prayer, music, quarrelling. Towards sunset, lying under the lime tree, I look out for her pigeons returning home, their fluttering shadows on the mud wall.

After a while, I begin to relax. Sometimes, going against Mama Luban's orders, I sing as I stand in the kitchen stirring a stew or stripping leaves off a stalk. I make jokes with Muiz. My voice, when I talk to him, starts to sound like the real Leila and my pleasure when he returns home from work is genuine. I realize something none of the other women have told me; a husband can be a friend. And I thank God. Only one thing remains, to make life perfect. I'm beginning to think I might have a problem. My woman's blood comes regularly. Muiz is a progressive man; he even brings sanitary towels home from the pharmacy, to save me the embarrassment of asking for them. But I can see his disappointment in his eyes each month.

Aunt Hawa behaves coolly to me when we visit the old house by the market. She comes once to our house, stays barely long enough to drink a lemonade, and doesn't return. Sometimes, I wonder if she has put a curse on me. There are many holy men and some holy women in Sennar; people go to them about everything, from jobs to marriages and births. Some of them work against the religion, to make bad things happen.

When Halima asks after my family in Khartoum, I say that my father and mother are very well, thanks be to God, and so are my brothers and sisters. 'How many do you have?' she asks.

'So many.' I spread my hands. 'I can't even count them.'
She nods.

'Did your father open many homes?'

She means: how many wives does he have. There are more than fifteen families in the village. But Father Sayf has only one wife.

'No! Yes! He has many homes, my father,' I say, twisting about on my chair.

'Are you the biggest?'

We don't know how old we are, most of us. I'm one of the few who does. I fill the space with a nervous laugh.

'I'm one of the first to marry,' I say.

Halima carries on with her crochet. Soon, she pushes herself up from the bed with both hands and says she'd better be getting back to her house, where her daughter is probably burning the stew. I'm glad when the gate closes behind her.

One by one, or sometimes two or three together, all the neighbours call on me. I bring out the tin of sweets as soon as they sit down, and give them water from the *zir* at a comfortable temperature. They sit on the veranda, or under the tree, and look around with hungry eyes. Some of them giggle when they see the bedroom. The double bed, the framed colour photograph of me and Muiz on the wall – these things are not normal in Old Woman. Some of them stare at me. From Khartoum, educated, and living alone with my husband – I too am unusual in the neighbourhood. Every one of them steals looks at my belly.

Sometimes, I feel dispirited after these visits. I seem to be part of normal society now – and yet, in my heart, I do not feel part of it. I haven't made close friends, or even been accepted by Uncle Hassan's family. I have written twice to Amal but I haven't had an answer. With the village and my brothers and sisters far away, I sometimes feel I don't belong anywhere at all.

*

Halima's face appears over the wall. It's early, and I'm washing Muiz's shirts, sitting on the low stool with the tin bowl on the ground in front of me. We call out greetings, and she stands on her chair and watches me. Am I doing the washing wrong? I scrub at the cotton with more vigour and she clicks her tongue.

'You come to my place,' she says. 'When you're done.'

When I let myself in, Halima calls me into her sitting room. She has three upholstered chairs, a television set that doesn't work, and bunches of pink and red plastic flowers arranged in sprays on the yellow walls. Every surface is covered with bright, crocheted or embroidered mats and covers. It's her best room; we usually sit out in the yard or in her *rakuba*.

'How long have you been married?' she asks. 'More than one year?'

I nod.

'The relations are going all right between you?' She rubs the sides of her forefingers together.

I nod again, embarrassed.

'You enjoy it?'

The blood rushes to my head. I can't even look at her. She sighs.

'He will grow tired of waiting,' she says.

Halima makes coffee and fills the room with incense. On the table, she has a bottle of Girl of Sudan. She unstoppers it and dabs scent inside her ears, in her nostrils, on the tip of her tongue. Then she does the same to me. She motions me to sit in front of her, on the floor, and puts her hands on my shoulders. She closes her eyes and begins to talk as if I am not there, gripping my shoulders with her powerful hands. Her voice has changed; it sounds deeper. The air is thick with scented smoke; the coffee has made my heart race and the taste of the scent is strange in my mouth. She moves herself around in front of me, laying both hands on my stomach and moving them round in one direction, then the other. All the while, she speaks the name Bashir in a strong, deep voice. I have never been to a *zar* ceremony, but I know the name of one of the most famous spirits to possess women.

'Bashir sees all,' she repeats. She opens her eyes and dabs more scent in her mouth; I have seen my mother do the same thing, pressing the neck of the bottle to the tip of her tongue. Halima does all this to me as if neither she nor I are really there. When she has finished, she brings out a packet of Benson and Hedges cigarettes, lights one on the coals and returns to her chair. I stare at her as the smoke curls around her hair. She takes a deep puff and blows the smoke straight out again.

'Bashir has agreed to help you,' she says. 'But he says you must do no heavy washing, you must sing if you feel like it and you must eat anything sour – lemons, white cheese, olives.'

I do not believe in spirits. Father Sayf always ridiculed the idea. But Halima's words seem to act on me. That night, I say casually to Muiz that since the weather is getting so warm, I need help with the washing. I mention that it has been a while since I tasted olives, which I used to love eating when I lived in Jordan. The green ones, I say. They dressed them with oil and lemon juice and sometimes they stuffed them with white cheese.

*

Halima knows before I do. She peers at my eyes, squeezes my breast, and informs me that I will not see woman's blood this month. She sits back in her chair with a look of satisfaction. From the time the doctor confirms that I'm pregnant, I can't wait to be a mother. I no longer get up to make Muiz's tea in the morning; the sweet smell of the powdered milk makes me nauseous. Opening the door of the refrigerator makes me retch; in the mornings, I can only eat dry bread and lumps of the mud that I bought from Khartoum. Muiz calls them my toffees.

Right from the start, I walk with my belly stuck out. I take a new interest in other women's babies. Alone in my bedroom, I slip off my dress and look at my changing body. My breasts are fuller, the nipples enlarged like flowers. My belly blooms beneath them, round and proud. Even my hair seems pregnant; it becomes softer, more tameable, and my skin glows.

Muiz takes me for monthly appointments at the doctor's and pays for iron pills out of his salary. He stops going to the coffee houses with his friends in the evenings and stays at home watching television with me. Every day, when he comes in from work, he brings something home for me; fresh milk, a bottle of shampoo, or a bunch of bananas. Halima, leaning over the wall one afternoon as he opens our gate, calls out greetings to 'the man with two carrier bags'. And so begins his nickname in Old Woman: *keesteyn*, or Two Carrier Bags.

Uncle Hassan's wife Hawa walks into the yard the morning after Muiz has been to tell the family the news. We embrace by the tree, and I feel my heart grow lighter. I never wanted to take Muiz from his family, I explain. I meant it when I said I would have been happy living with them all. Aunt Hawa sits close to me on the bed, blowing her nose and praying for my health.

From that day on, she visits often and is full of advice. I should take ginger tea for sickness, wear a charm against the evil eye, avoid twins. Cats are particularly dangerous – almost certain to bring on a miscarriage if you have the wrong kind of encounter with one. She shudders when she sees the cot Muiz has bought. Her babies never slept anywhere but at her side. That is the best place for them, she says, and Muiz has wasted his money on that contraption.

After three months, the sickness stops.

'Surely now your mother will visit from Khartoum?' Halima enquires one morning. She is sitting on our veranda with a crochet hook balanced between her thumb and forefinger, the skein of wool twitching on the bed beside her.

'Yes, God willing. But she is busy with my brothers and sisters.' I'm ironing a pair of Muiz's trousers. I take a mouthful of water and spray it evenly over the cotton, clamping the hot metal down on to the fabric. When I look up, Halima's sharp eyes are trained on me.

'She has not been well,' I add.

'God willing, she will soon be in good condition,' says Halima. 'What's the matter with her?'

'Oh, you know. Just getting old. Her legs hurt. Her feet. Her arms.'

'No woman is too ancient to come and see her grandchild,' she sniffs. 'What about your father? He'll want to see what sort of mother his daughter makes.'

I shrug. 'They will come if they can. If not, I'll take the baby to Khartoum to visit them,' I say.

Our Book cautions against pride. But I feel proud in these months. The rainy season arrives, and in the garden blue-black baby aubergines droop from strong stalks, tomatoes ripen on the vines and a yellow creeper runs all over the wall I share with Halima. The lime tree comes into blossom, and sends out scores of hard green fruits. I lie underneath it with my hands on my stomach, feeling the sudden movements from inside. I thank God constantly for what He has given me.

Chapter 13

HELPED BY GOD

'You come from strong people! How can you make this noise!'

I have been tricked. All those women who asked how I was, enquired after the baby, whether it moved in the night, made me thirsty . . . none of them told me what it would mean to bring it into this world. The midwife wears a watch pinned to her overall; she feels my stomach with delicate hands. Everything is going well, she says. Aunt Hawa and Bussana, her oldest daughter, stay with me in the delivery room at Sennar's main hospital. My husband Muiz and the rest of the family are waiting outside.

In between contractions, I can hear Uncle Hassan in the corridor, complaining that in the name of God, it is very bad for a woman from our tribe to make a noise during childbirth. The baby will be known forever as the child of a screaming mother, he tells Muiz. These dire warnings can't silence me. The pains when they come are so complete, so inescapable, that screaming is the only relief.

I stay in the room all night; as it begins to get light outside, the midwife says it's time. Aunt Hawa and Bussana hold my knees and she makes the cut; I hardly feel it, the impulse to push is so powerful. Soon afterwards, I deliver a baby. The midwife wraps the baby in a towel and lays it on my chest. While she stitches me up again I stare at this stranger, who I know so well and don't know at all. It has black slicked curls and long eyelashes, fine furry down on its cheeks and fore-head, a full mouth. Aunt Hawa and Bussana thank God that we have another son in the family.

Muiz comes in as soon as the midwife has finished. He is wearing a paper mask over his face, and rubber gloves. He picks up the baby and gazes at him.

'God willing, after this you will deliver a brother for this child. If you have two boys, then you can deliver six girls in a row and no one can say anything to you.'

His voice is muffled by the paper, and I can hear his foot tapping on the cement floor. He is smiling behind the mask.

*

I spend my confinement at the house of Uncle Hassan and Aunt Hawa. For a week, I can't get off the bed; my body feels as if it will never be good for anything again. As the days pass, things become easier. The room is noisy; the souk is just the other side of the wall. But even the sound of hammering doesn't disturb the baby; he is small and as dark as a cardamom seed and spends most of his time asleep.

Amal comes from Khartoum to be with me. When she appears in the doorway, I don't see her face, just her tall figure, her long legs, her braided hair. I shout with joy as she drops her bag and comes and hugs me. She has brought incense from Mama Luban and clothes for the baby from Father Sayf and his wife. Alawia has sent perfume and soap. Zulima sends her greetings and so do the twins. She has seen Rashid; he is well, she says, and asked her to tell his little sister hello, and congratulations on her wedding.

Amal boils up herbs for me to wash myself with. She sleeps on the other bed and wakes at the first whimper in the night. My aunt Hawa makes milk pudding with fenugreek; I eat it cold, from the tip of a teaspoon. It's sweet and gelatinous; the flavour of fenugreek becomes the taste of these first weeks of my life as a mother. Halima, my neighbour in Old Woman, wrings the necks of half a dozen of her pigeons and arrives with them early one morning; pigeon restores the blood of the new mother, she says. When I introduce Amal as my sister, she stares at her as she shakes her hand. Aunt Hawa plucks the birds and pot-roasts them, but when she serves them I can't eat them. Their bodies are so small and delicate, so vulnerable.

*

Amal is shy, here in Sennar. She seems ill at ease with the family, the neighbours, the house itself. She screams if a cat knocks over a tin bowl in the night, or the wind dislodges a lime on to a tin roof. She complains about the cockroaches in the latrine and says she doesn't know how we survive this heat without electricity.

She tells me the news about Father Sayf, Mama Luban, Mama Amaani and all our brothers and sisters. I soon realize that even when she cradles my son in her arms, Amal has her mind on the children at the village. She talks about children who have arrived since I left, and tells me every detail about the way the place is changing and being run. Sometimes, when she asks me a question, I can't answer, or I confuse one child with another. I can't think about anything but the baby – his sweet-smelling head and soft limbs; his strong-sucking mouth and trusting eyes.

'How can you live here?' Amal asks one evening, looking around her at the mud-plastered walls, the strands hanging down from the papyrus ceiling, the hurricane lamp balanced on a rough wooden table. The room is dim and restful; the baby is asleep on a cloth on top of the pink satin cover. Aunt Hawa has put dates on a table and burned incense to protect him; the room is still wreathed in light, fragrant smoke and the necklace of charms on the wall makes me feel comfortable and safe.

'They are good people,' I say.

I don't want to say to Amal that they are my family. She is twenty-seven; since Faisal passed away, she never speaks of marriage. She is my family too. She stands up and takes the baby on to her lap. A fly lands on the corner of his mouth and she waves it away. His hair is damp around his forehead and he snuffles and yawns in his sleep.

'How can you live without your job?' she asks. 'Without working for the children?'

'It wasn't my choice.'

'I never thought you'd become a housewife.'

I reach out and take the baby from her lap. I hold him against my chest.

'This life changes, *ya* Amal,' I say, stiffly. 'And we change with it.'

I'm relieved when Amal returns to Khartoum early, bearing my greetings to everyone there. If we have less in common now than when we were girls, I tell myself, it is not surprising. Our lives have taken different paths. Amal is still abandoned, still on the edge of our society. I am no longer abandoned. With a husband and now a son as well, I can never be abandoned again.

*

When the forty days are over, I return to my own house. The baby grows plump; his skin shines with the oil I smooth on to him after his bath. My body heals, and I forget the discomfort of the early days. I lose myself in the pleasure of being a mother. He is an easy baby, given to watching. He sleeps and eats and soon he smiles, gazing at the leaves over his head while I tidy my tomato plants, water the cucumbers. I keep him near me all the time; I don't even like to put him in the cot. I never want him to feel for a moment that his mother has left him. Halima says I will attract the evil eye. I take no notice. We call him Mansour, which means Helped by God.

Muiz doesn't spend his money on women, drinking or gambling, like some of my friends' husbands. He comes straight home after work and we follow the routine we began when we were first married. He takes off his office clothes and puts on his *jellabiya*, while I fetch him a drink of hibiscus cordial or grapefruit squash from the refrigerator. He lies down to sleep for an hour, until the worst heat of day passes. At about half past three, when he wakes up, I bring all the things for lunch on a tray. I make sure I keep the meals appetizing and varied. We have chicken or liver, or lamb fried in the pan. And fish, in the winter – but not the summer, because it makes you thirsty. I even make dog-will-follow-your-hand stew, because he likes it. I prepare his favourite salads, of aubergine, and tomatoes, and pound up chilli with peanuts like my Aunt Hawa does. After he has eaten, he belches and rinses out his mouth. He jiggles Mansour on his knee and walks him around the yard, pointing out the leaves, the birds, the plants.

My house becomes the centre of Old Woman, with neighbours and family in and out all the time. Now I have a son, my shyness and awkwardness fall away from me. My neighbours invite me to weddings and picnics, send their children to do small jobs for me. I sing all the time, and drink as much coffee as I feel like. Zulima visits me with the children, and not long afterwards Rashid drives all the way down from Khartoum in his dented white car to see us. He is getting a small bald patch on the back of his head, I notice. His fingers are as long and fine as ever, despite the hard work they do. He brings a small rocking chair he has made for Mansour; its back is carved with elephants and crocodiles.

Helped by God

When my son is a year old, I go on a journey. Muiz accompanies me; we pack a bag and we go to the sugar plantation. It's November; they have been burning off the sugarcane, ready to begin cutting. The tall plants stand blackened and smoking in the fields; plumes of steam billow from the chimneys of the processing plant and the air is alive with the shouts of the workers, the rumble of heavy machinery. I had felt lively and talkative on the journey, but when we get off the coach I grow quiet.

We find the restaurant where my father worked; the manager shows us the spot where he is buried, in a small graveyard near some woodland. There are two eucalyptus trees at the head of the grave; their blue leaves dance in the breeze and their red-brown trunks are supple and graceful. I stand at the foot of his grave and ask his forgiveness. As I stand there, holding the baby, I have a vision of Aziz Mohamed Mahmoud before my eyes. He is dressed in a green safari suit and leopardskin slippers. He walks towards me, laughing, with his arms outstretched. I thank God for showing me my father once more.

Before leaving, we visit my half-brother and my father's second wife. I have an immediate understanding with my brother, although he is a secondary-school student. He is outgoing and funny, his delight in his new nephew clear to see. We promise that now we have found each other after this long absence, we will not lose each other again. Muiz and I leave after two days, happy with this new branch of our family.

Back in Sennar, I tell Halima that I have been to my father's grave. She lowers her eyes and asks God to rest his soul. I tell her that he passed away a long time ago, when I was a small girl. Then I remember that I told her my father was alive, and living in Khartoum. I look at the ground in embarrassment. One day, I tell myself, I will explain everything to her.

Not long after we return, I find I am pregnant again. The following year, in the rains when the air is thick as a blanket and the mosquitoes swarm over the town, I give birth. We call our new son Hisham; this time, Aunt Hawa and her daughter Bussana look after me during the confinement. I send a message to the village when the baby is a month old, that Mansour has a brother, thank God. Amal sends shirts and shorts for Mansour and a carrier bag of chips of mud for me, delivered by a relation of Alawia's who is passing through Sennar on his way to the south.

Muiz gets a pay rise at work and buys a small car. On Thursday evenings, before the weekend, he stops at a restaurant and buys *mandi*, the boiled beef joint, with a mound of saffron rice and plastic pots of spiced yoghurt and cucumber salad. Then he drives me, Mansour and the baby out to the banks of the river. We sit under the mango trees and look at the dark water gliding or rushing between the banks according to the season. I love sitting there with my sons and my husband, watching the white ibis birds busy along the edge of the river, eating the strands of dark meat with my right hand, savouring the yellow salty rice.

Sometimes, Muiz tells me jokes. There is one that makes him laugh so much he can barely get through it: 'My friend is coming at six. I'll wait till seven but if he doesn't show up at eight, I'm leaving at nine.' Sometimes, we sit in silence, quite comfortable with each other. I feel at ease in my world, for the first time in my life. The suffering I endured as a child had a purpose, had been leading somewhere. I am making a good family, proving that we can lead good lives. That the things society says about us are just ignorant prejudice.

I look after Muiz and he looks after me and Mansour and the baby. I can see the envy in the eyes of some of my neighbours when they visit, with their barefoot children and their *tobes* that have been reseamed to cover old rips and tears. I share as much with them as I can. But I don't feel any shame about my good fortune. If they knew about my past, they would understand better why God has given me this happiness. I have never told any of them I was once abandoned. At first, it was because I was afraid they would reject me. Now they have accepted me, it's too late. None of them suspect – except perhaps Halima.

*

Everything is perfect. But from the time I brought Mansour home to our house, I have begun to be troubled by a dream. I'm standing in a long, dimly lit room. The room is always different, always the same. Its walls are lined with cots and the air echoes with the sound of children crying. I move from cot to cot, picking up children and comforting them, hugging them. As soon as I manage to soothe one child, another starts crying. It is my responsibility to offer each and every one of these children what it is that they need. They can't name what they want. But I know what it is. And I know more clearly than I can ever know anything in waking life that it is my job to give it to them.

Chapter 14

DREAM OF MYGOMA

The spinach and lamb stew cools in the pot, the salad wilts in its bowl and the loaves harden in the bag. I pray that nothing bad has happened. I stand on a chair and call Halima. God willing, Muiz will be home soon, she says when she hears the situation. Meanwhile, I should get on with looking after my children. She is having her mattresses restuffed; tufts of white cotton lie spread all over the yard and a man sits in the shade, mending the covers. I stand and watch for a few minutes, resting my elbows on the warm top of the wall. I get down from the chair and the children and I eat our lunch, alone.

All through the evening, my ears strain for the sound of his car. It has been raining; the alley is flooded. Mansour always runs to the gate when he hears the car splashing through the puddles, the engine straining over the rutted ground. But this evening, the alley is quiet; for the first time, he falls asleep without seeing his father.

At eleven, music from a distant wedding falls silent. There is a curfew. Shortly afterwards, I hear the car. Muiz walks straight past me, kicks open the veranda door and disappears into the bedroom. The children are asleep outside in the *hosh*; it is a stifling night. For a couple of minutes I don't move. When I go inside, he is lying on the bed facing the wall. The fan squeaks as it turns.

I touch his back. 'Are you ill?' He doesn't answer. He doesn't move.

I sleep outside, curled up with Hisham in the bend of my body. I wake in the dark, to the sight of Muiz's back disappearing out of the gate. He only goes to the mosque at this time of day in Ramadan. I wash sitting on a low stool in the yard, pouring water over my hands and feet, rinsing my mouth. It's hard to reach my toes; the child in my stomach is a hard bump, higher than the previous ones. Halima says it's a girl. Calls from three different mosques echo around the sky as I roll out the worn mat and say my own prayers, asking for strength to face whatever is coming. I wrap my *tobe* around myself and I am waiting for Muiz when he comes back.

I stir sugar and milk powder into his tea and put it down in front of him. He has been dismissed from his job, he says.

'The boss didn't even tell me. He sent his deputy. It's like an axe in the head.'

He is to be replaced by the nephew of an important man. His next salary will be the last. It still isn't light; nothing stirs beyond the walls of the *hosh*.

'I haven't had a chance to say goodbye.' He puts his head in his hands.

I feel fear rising in me but it is mixed with relief. I thought it might be something worse.

'God will provide,' I say. 'You can find another job.'

Later that morning, a neighbour from across the street comes in for ice.

'Is your husband ill?' she asks. 'I see his car guarding the gate like a dog.'

'He is improving, thank God,' I say, turning away from her to knock ice cubes out of their mould and into a china bowl. They slip and burn in my fingers. I wonder how long I will have a fridge for, or even this pearlized china bowl, so much more expensive, so much more fragile, than the tin I grew up with.

*

From the day Muiz tells me the news, I no longer visit the butcher's shop. I feed us with onions and dried okra and buy the cheap tomatoes at the market, the ones that must be cooked that day. This *mullah waka* stew is known as the 'woman with the dishevelled hair'; it is untidy and basic. I make *kisra* instead of buying it: I leave the batter to ferment overnight, cook the thin, spongy sheets on the griddle in the morning. It's hot work; I get small burn lines on my fingers and wrists.

I think of my mother making *kisra* to take to the market, and I begin to understand better how hard her life must have been.

I still have my husband, I tell myself. I am not twice divorced, like she was. I should not feel sorry for myself. If you have a family, you can laugh together, face what comes. These thoughts give me strength. The child inside me stirs and rolls as I crouch by the stove. The delivery will be soon.

I still get up early to make his tea. I light charcoal, if I have any, to heat the iron for his shirt, smooth out the creases on the bed. I give him a squirt of my cologne before he leaves, and wish him God's blessings. Muiz still goes out dressed in his work trousers and shoes. He still carries a briefcase. But now it contains not the sheets of figures he used to work with but his certificates from university; he takes a piece of bread and sets off for another day of looking for work.

When the gate shuts behind him, I pull the stone over to keep it closed. I drink my tea before the children wake, sitting in the shadow of the tree. Mansour is only four years old but he seems to know everything. Hisham is two; his eyes are trained on his older brother. He runs behind him, copying everything he does. He laughs and sings from the moment he wakes up. My dark-faced Mansour seems to have been old from when he was born. My greatest comfort is to feel the children's warm bodies in my arms, to lay my cheek on their heads.

The landlord comes to the gate every few days. I know his knock and I send Mansour to say that his father is not at home. The landlord is forced to go away; he can't insist on coming into a house where only a woman is present. No one can tell any more whether Muiz is there or not because the car is gone, sold to the brother of one of his former colleagues.

One day, two men come to take away my wardrobe. I have folded our clothes into sugar sacks I brought from the plantation. The wardrobe is as good as new, apart from a crack in the mirror. I hope it will bring in enough for two months' rent. I offer the men water, putting off the moment when the neighbours see them drag it out into the street. The children cling to my *tobe* as the men manoeuvre it through the narrow door.

After they have gone, there is a patch of lino where the pattern is darker than the rest. I stand and look at the evidence of all the times I have washed the floor, all the life we have lived in this room over the last six years. Mansour finds a marble that had rolled underneath. 'Look, mother,' he says. 'This is a lucky day.'

The fridge follows the wardrobe out of the gate. Then the double bed. My sewing machine. My wedding gold makes its way to the souk piece by piece in Muiz's briefcase, as do my dresses from Jordan. My Moulinex blender goes, to buy milk for the children. Mansour's knees bulge over his thin calves; his shoulder-blades protrude like wings.

Finally, we are left with a few beds to sleep and sit on, three cooking pots, a roughly made cupboard that was in the house when we came and some low tables that we eat off. The bare minimum of china and glass, and an old black-and-white television. With everything gone, I have a sense of relief. We can manage quite well without all the fancy things. Love is what matters, and family. The child, huge by now and fighting the prison of my belly, stirs inside me, as if this thought has reached it. She is born in my bedroom; the midwife arrives just in time and Halima sends round clean linen, and rice for the boys.

I am glad of the lime tree. It gives its steady shade and

comfort for free, whispering when all else falls silent. Its lux-
uriance gives an air of plenty to the house even when the days
arrive when there is no food, no toothpaste, no milk powder
for tea in the morning, no sugar. The few crumbs of Omo that
I have I save for Muiz's clothes. He continues to go out in the
mornings in a clean shirt; the briefcase is cracked and sagging,
the shoes held together with glue. He still greets the neighbours as if he is in a hurry to get to the office.

*

At first, these circumstances draw us closer. But as time goes
by, Muiz withdraws from me. He begins to stay out late in the
evenings. When he comes back, he isn't in the mood for talking. He doesn't laugh with me any more, or ask me anything
about myself. He still plays with our boys when he's at home,
kisses our daughter on the head. Sometimes I feel bitter, seeing
how the boys look up to him. But I keep quiet. I know what it
means not to have a father. I don't want to destroy their love
for the one they have. I want to support my husband through
this testing time. I try to tell him that I know this situation isn't
his fault, that I don't blame him for our hardships and that
everything will change, God willing, before long. He doesn't
meet my eyes and if he answers at all, he speaks to me angrily.
He still crawls into my bed a couple of times a week.

The time comes when I find I feel relieved when he's out of
the house. I can sit with my prayer beads or a cup of tea, while
the children watch television and the baby sleeps. We have
called her Najat. At night, if it's not too hot inside, I lie on the

bed and stare up at the rafters, at the straight lines of the papyrus-reed ceiling, as if I might see an answer there. I have hardly any visitors now; Muiz's family rarely comes and my neighbours have stopped inviting me to *jebena* coffee sessions and weddings.

If I look in the mirror in the bathroom, I barely know myself. Is this the Leila who laughed and told jokes, who was proud of her smooth skin and pretty clothes, who loved to sing? This sad-eyed woman, her hair wild, her skin grey, who looks back at me from the mirror? I drag a comb through my hair, which is fiercer than ever. I wash my face and rub a little cooking oil around my eyes. I look at the drooping hem of my old housedress and tell myself it's no wonder my husband doesn't want to stay in his home any more.

I think a lot about God, in these days. I have tried since I was a girl to be a good Muslim. When I was young, I didn't really know why. It was to protect my reputation – to show all the people who expected me to behave immorally that I would not, that I was not born bad. But in these days, I develop a new relationship with Allah. I repeat His names, moving the light, hard wooden beads of the *sibha* through my fingers. God the Bountiful, the Watchful, the Responsive. I whisper them right up to the ninety-ninth one: God the Patient. Then I begin again.

*

On Friday afternoons, Muiz and I have always gone to the river. Even after we had to sell the car, we used to get a bus to the edge of the town, buy a few salted beans or a twist of roasted sunflower seeds, cross the bridge by the dam and walk under the mango trees, listen to the movement of the water. Sometimes, I picked my way down the steep bank and put my feet in the cool flow. From my very first visit to Sennar, when I came to find my Uncle Hassan, I have loved everything about the river: the trees, the parched silt exposed in the dry season, the clean, muddy smell of the water and its reliable, tireless movement, which seems like a form of life.

In these days, when I do not want to see another human soul, I still sometimes find the strength to take the children to the river. If I have a few coins, I take cola and a sandwich; if not, a container of water and some bread. At this time of year, early summer, the mangos fall thickly to the ground. Sennar is famous for its mangos; they are small and yellow, but sweet and not fibrous like the ones from the south. The children eat three or four in a row, tearing off the thin skin with their fingers and burying their faces in the flesh, sucking the flat stones dry.

I like to see them in the natural surroundings. Since the troubles that are afflicting me began, I have left them too much in the care of the television. Mansour in particular likes to sit on the floor and gaze at the small screen, as if he wants to block out the life around him and disappear into his cartoons, where the hero always wins and injustice never lasts. It reminds me of the way my sister Zulima used to watch the soap operas from Egypt when she was a schoolgirl.

One Friday, when Muiz is out as usual, we make our way to the river. I have brought a thermos of tea, and after we drink it the children disappear to play while I sit alone on a stone, looking across the water to the far bank, at the trees standing so peacefully. I watch the way the water swirls near the banks, the clumps of hyacinth and the birds that perch on them. The birds are loud. I'm startled by a raucous cry that makes me wonder if what they say is true, that a person can be turned into a bird.

I raise my head and I see Muiz, walking with a woman on the opposite bank. I sit very still. The woman seems to look at me across the water. She is taller than Muiz; her hair is piled up under a yellow *tobe*. We stare at each other for a moment, and she looks away. Muiz is talking, moving his hands. She touches his arm; he turns towards her.

He talks now to others, I realize, with sadness in my heart; this person must be a former colleague from the office, or a friend of his sister's, perhaps. The two of them disappear from view as the children come running from beyond the trees, shouting, holding something up in the air. It is a snakeskin. Light and silvery and empty.

*

One evening, not long after this, there is a soft insistent tapping on the gate. There is a power cut and I am lying on the *angareeb*, looking up at the sky. The stars in Sennar seem closer than they did in Khartoum. It isn't late, but the children are all asleep. I am thinking about my mother. It was my dream, when I was a little girl, to look after her. And although I succeeded in building the room for her at Zulima's house, since my marriage I have rarely seen her. Once, I thought she might come and live with us in Sennar for her final years. Now, that is impossible.

I pull myself off the bed, wind my *tobe* around me and pull back the stone; it's the daughter of my neighbour, Halima.

'Is your mother well?' I ask her, once I have brought her water from the *zir*, and settled it on a table in front of her.

'Thank God. She is strong.'

'Your brother?'

She shrugs. 'Fine.'

I sit and wait for her to say whatever it is she has come to say. I give her an encouraging smile. I want her to know that if I can help her with anything, I will. She looks troubled, but not on her own account. I can see pity in her eyes, I realize.

'The whole neighbourhood is talking of a certain story,' she says, sitting very straight on the bed. 'It concerns you. But no one will sit in front of you and recount that story.' My heart begins to thump. I know what is coming, even before she says the words.

'There is a woman. The two of them walk together in the evenings. He . . . he visits her at her house.'

Everything about Muiz's behaviour falls into place. For a minute, I can't speak. The girl sits, still and quiet. She remarks on the lime tree – lately, it is losing its leaves – and asks after my family in Khartoum. I tell her about my sister Amal, how she is training as a teacher. About the letter I have had from my brother Rashid. I feel the comfort that comes just from speaking their names and I talk some more, about my sister Zulima and her children, Jamila and Habibi and Mohamed and Hoodah. I repeat the names again, just for the sense of safety they give me. When she gets up to leave, the girl hugs me with strong arms.

'They say,' she whispers, 'that he will marry her. Tomorrow.'

Once, when Muiz and I were first married, we were at the cinema. The projectionist put the reel in upside down. The film began playing on screen the wrong way up, with people's feet walking through where the air should be, their heads tipping towards the ground. That is how I feel when the girl leaves, as if I'm falling. I sink to my knees in the *hosh*, pressing my arms and head against the warm ground.

After a while, I go to the bathroom. I run the tap until the bucket overflows and, in the darkness, I try to clean myself. I rub my damp hair, scrape at my skin with the loofah, lather my body with a splinter of soap. I put on a clean *jellabiya*, rinse my mouth out with water. It makes no difference. I am pregnant again; this man is inside me, no matter what I do. I feel as if I will never be clean again.

Chapter 15

RED GOAT, BLUE GOAT

Mornings are the worst time. I wake up in the darkness, heart thudding, hands clutching at the sheet. I grope around in my mind for the reason; as I come to consciousness, I remember. The unfuture has pursued me, stalked me from the shadows. I can never be free of it.

I lie until the sky becomes tinged with pink and I can see the dark shapes of Halima's pigeons huddled on the top of the wall. I drag myself off the bed, clean my teeth, trying to find comfort in the rituals of daily life. I wrap myself in my *tobe*, say my prayers, light the stove, put on the kettle. The day dawns. Soon enough, Halima or another neighbour calls, saying they are waiting for us to share their breakfast. Everyone knows that Muiz has gone. Many of my neighbours stop speaking to me; they think that if a man leaves a woman, she must be a bad wife. But some of them are kind, warmer to

---

me than they were before. We live by Providence. We live by the will of God.

From the day of his second wedding, Muiz does not return to the house at all. I pack his clothes into a sack and ask Halima to keep it in her house. I lie to the children. I say that their father has gone to the city, to look for work. Mansour gives me his intense, sideways glance.

I go to the house of Uncle Hassan and Aunt Hawa. They hug us, make a fuss of the children. Aunt Hawa calls the woman 'the monkey' to make me feel better. She says the monkey has bewitched Muiz, through a *fakir*; she must have done because even his own family weren't invited to the wedding. She says that the woman comes from a rich family and that she paid a lot of money to have spells cast that made him fall for her and forget his responsibilities. While I sit with Aunt Hawa in their *hosh*, I find this talk comforting. I feel strengthened by the idea that it wasn't Muiz's fault, that he didn't choose to abandon his children and humiliate his wife. But when I return to my own home, laden with fried fish wrapped in newspaper, the story falls away. No magic can lure a man away from his wife and family without his consent.

There is a *medan*, a square, at the end of our street, where the neighbourhood children play football. That summer, a burned-out wreck of a car appears there. Free of any glass in its windows, without its tyres or even its wheels, this skeleton vehicle becomes the plaything of every boy in the neighbourhood. They climb up on its roof and fly down to the ground, arms outstretched. They sit in the driver's seat, hands clenched on an imaginary steering wheel, making engine noises and swerving round bends. They return to their homes only to eat. If I do not tell Mansour and Hisham about their father, one of these kids will.

A week after he leaves, I call the boys to sit with me on the veranda. I bring Najat as well, even though she is too young to understand. It's a Friday afternoon; there is no school and the streets of Old Woman are quiet and empty as our neighbours visit the sick in hospital, and their relatives in other parts of town. I take a deep breath and recite the names of all the men I can think of in our neighbourhood who have two wives. Some of them have more; the merchant who owns the big shop on the main road has four. 'And he's got a Japanese pick-up,' says Hisham. I explain to the children that God allows men to have more than one wife. That their father wanted a second wife – and that he has married one.

'My mother,' says Mansour. 'How can he marry a second wife when we have nothing?' He is at school; he knows things I haven't taught him. He knows that the Koran permits men more than one wife only when they can provide equally for them. 'You must ask him yourself,' I say. 'Next time you see him.'

*

'Why don't you go home to your mother? To your family?' Halima's face is long and serious, her eyes fixed on mine. 'Any family will accept their daughter back in circumstances like these.'

I look back into her wise brown eyes. I'm tired. Too tired to

pretend, any longer. What does it matter, now? I dip the soft
bread into the beans she has brought, scoop up a mouthful.
They are delicious, dressed with white cheese and chopped
onion and sesame oil and flavoured with cumin and corian-
der. I try to swallow. Even good food sticks in my throat these
days.

'I have a story to tell you, esteemed Halima. About how I
grew up . . .'

When I have finished talking, I get off the bed. Everything
in me feels looser, more comfortable. The child inside me
lurches, and stills itself. I wash my face, my mouth, trickle
water up my arms and rinse my hands. And I return to where
she sits.

'I guessed something like this,' she says. 'I understood from
the day you came here that you had not lived like everyone
else. Are they not your family, still? Are you too proud to seek
help for your children?'

Even during these hard days, I have the dream of Mygoma.
The dream follows me around some days, clouds my mind. I
know I should be doing something for my brothers and sisters. As I struggle to stay alive with my children, an idea
comes to me. We who are abandoned always remain abandoned. Some of us have the good fortune to grow up in
orphanages or institutes. But once we are adults, we still need
families. And we still don't have them. I get a pen one day and
take one of Mansour's exercise books. I start drawing a picture, of a house that would be big enough for all of us. I draw
a huge house, four storeys tall, with balconies on every floor
to sit out on at night, and a garden full of trees. I imagine

enough room for everyone, for all my brothers and sisters to come back to when they need it.

I sigh and put down the pen. Such a house would cost millions. I tear out the page and screw it up. Then I realize – it isn't a building that we need, it's another kind of structure. In the back of the book I begin to draw up a plan for a self-help society for the abandoned, so that we can be each other's family, continue to help each other all through our lives. By the time I finish, it's dark. But I feel refreshed; for a couple of hours, I have forgotten my own problems.

The following day, I do what my pride has up till now prevented me from doing. I call Father Sayf and tell him that I'm desperate and that my children are on the point of going to live on the street. I apologize for refusing his good advice on which husband to choose. And I beg him to help me.

*

I hear familiar voices in the street outside. I hurry to the gate and see Father Sayf and Amal stepping out of a rickshaw. Amal wears a tightly pinned turquoise headscarf embroidered with red and brown thread; gold sandals peep out from under the hem of her skirt. She looks as smooth and gleaming as an exotic bird. Father Sayf digs in his pocket for money for the rickshaw driver; he greets me as if we parted yesterday. I shout with joy as I throw open the gate and welcome them inside.

I send Mansour for lemonade, hoping the shopkeeper won't refuse. Amal hugs me as we exchange greetings. She has brought sweets and clothes for the children. Father Sayf stands back a little; he seems awkward, looking around the yard. I thank God again for their coming, and ask after Mama Luban, Mama Amaani, my sister Zulima. Rashid. While Amal talks, Father Sayf walks up and down the veranda, blotting his forehead with a white handkerchief. I'm wearing a ragged *jellabiya* and a pair of Muiz's old plastic mules; I have splinters holding open the holes in my ears, and my belly protrudes.

'Why didn't you tell us before?' he asks, lowering himself on to the *angareeb*. 'I could have spoken to Muiz.'

'It wouldn't have made any difference. He is bewitched.'

'Come, Leila. We didn't raise you to believe such foolishness,' he says.

I keep quiet.

'He has already married the woman?'

'So they say.'

'And he stays with her?'

'I haven't seen this happy bridegroom. I don't know where he's living and I don't care.'

Father Sayf frowns.

'He is still your husband,' he says. 'You have to think of the children.'

'Do you suppose I think of anything but the children?' I snap. 'What about him? Did he think of the children?'

Najat begins to cry.

Mansour returns from the shop with two bottles of lemonade. He bangs the lids off on the edge of the old table and puts the bottles in front of our visitors. His feet are rough, the heels spread and cracked, the toes strong. One of his new front teeth is chipped, where he fell on concrete at school.

'What can I do, Father?' I ask, looking at the ground. 'Where can I go? My children will go to the street.'

'Where is the daughter I know?' he replies. 'Where is the Leila who sings? Laughs? Quarrels? You have to be strong, as you have always been.'

I can hear Halima next door, scolding the girl who washes her sheets. I can smell doughnuts frying in another neighbour's yard. Normal life is going on all around me, but I feel separate from it; there is no normal life for me any more.

'Father, I want to come back to Khartoum.'

His face furrows. 'It is not a light matter, to part from a husband.'

'I have no choice. I am abandoned.'

'The village is for children. We are for the orphans.'

'I'm still an orphan.'

I look at my feet. Amal's sandals match her *tobe*; around one slim shin she has a fine gold chain. She picks up her lemonade bottle and puts it down again.

'Father,' she says. 'Leila can stay with . . .'

'Has he divorced you?' Father Sayf asks.

I shake my head.

'Then he has not abandoned you. He is taking his honeymoon.'

Mansour comes to take the bottles back to the shop.

'Young man,' says Father Sayf, in a hearty tone. 'I hope you study well at school.'

He reaches into his pocket and brings out a silver coin. Mansour takes it, his dark eyes wordlessly meeting mine.

Father Sayf has to return to Khartoum the next morning, early.

He leaves me a bundle of notes and says he knows I am still a strong and intelligent woman, who will do the best for my children. When he has gone, Amal folds her pretty clothes into the cupboard and puts on an old *jellabiya*, and for the next three days we live as sisters again. She washes my hair with her shampoo, cuts my nails, and mends my one remaining *tobe*. She goes to the souk and comes back with bags groaning with food. She makes *Umm Ali* pudding, with milk and sugar, and lamb stew. She tells the boys stories about the red goat and the blue goat, she plays with Najat, and at night, when the children sleep, she listens. I talk until there is no more talk left in me. She doesn't argue. She doesn't criticize. She just listens. I feel my strength returning, drop by drop. By the time she leaves, I can stand on my feet again. My heart is beating steadily. My head is lifted.

I stand and wave until the coach disappears from view; then I take a rickshaw back to Old Woman, sitting in the back of the swaying carriage, holding on to the rail, looking at the driver's pin-up pictures of singers batting their eyelids from their postcard photos.

*

The cat stands motionless on the top of the wall, white in the starlight. Lying on the bed in the *hosh*, the sky so low and so black, I feel as if the darkness is my life, all the sadness in it, and the stars, those diamonds scattered over it, are the brief times of happiness I have known. I long to become one with the darkness, to feel it press down on me until I disappear into it. But I know I cannot harbour these thoughts. I have to keep going, to stand between my children and the street. I think of my own mother, being taken to a mental hospital perhaps because of her rage against a man. I too feel rage towards a man, for what he has done to me. But I have to use this anger to make a new life for us.

As I lie there with these thoughts running round my head, the cat jumps down and knocks over the washing bowl. It howls and flees, a streak in the starlight. I look at my daughter, asleep next to me on the single bed, then at the curled forms of my two sons. I make a silent promise to them that I will never leave them. I will stand behind them until the boys become men, and Najat is a grown woman.

The next morning, Halima looks over and sees me on the mat on the ground, groaning. It is two months before the time. She is inside my *hosh* in no time, calling to her daughter to fetch the midwife. I'm lying half in the veranda doorway, half out of it. The waters broke when I got off the bed in the morning and I couldn't even get to the bathroom. I feel the familiar pains gripping my abdomen and I feel no panic, as I had in delivering Mansour. No excitement, as with Hisham. No longing, as with Najat, for a girl. I feel nothing but the pain. Nothing else exists. The labour is long and hard. This baby cannot help me. She is finished with this world before she ever sees it.

*

I hear nothing from Muiz. Then one day, he arrives. He pushes the gate open and walks in as if he still lived with us. The children scream and run to him. I put on my *tobe*, as I would if he were a stranger. I don't look at him as I greet him, or shake his hand. I have Najat on my hip; she looks at him curiously, once he sits down, and he holds his arms out for her.

'I have come to offer my condolences,' he says.

I look past him, at the leafless tree.

'For what?'

'Your child.'

He looks up and for the first time in many months our eyes meet. I see the sorrow in his eyes. For a moment, I recognize the old Muiz. Then my mind substitutes another image – of our late daughter, the tiny curve of her back. I feel the raw agony welling up inside again and I turn away.

'Keep your condolences,' I shout. 'There was nothing good in this world waiting for that child and that is why she died. You killed her.'

I go into the bedroom and lean against the cupboard. I feel shaky and dizzy. Outside, Muiz plays with the children. I hear them talking quietly with him. I lie down on the bed. I must have fallen asleep because the next thing I know he is in the doorway, twisting his hands together. His shoulders are rounded; one arm of his spectacles is held on with sticky tape. It doesn't look as if his new marriage makes him stronger, or happier.

I sit up and feel for the mules with my feet.

'I want a divorce,' I say.

'This family is still the most precious thing to me,' he begins. I interrupt.

'If you won't give it to me, I will go to the courts. The whole town will hear how you abandoned us.'

Normally, a woman cannot divorce her husband. But if he abandons her, and fails to support her and her children, she has the right to divorce. Three days later, a boy knocks on the gate. I take the letter and open it in the bedroom. It says that this isn't what he wants but since I insist, he divorces me. It has a date at the top, clearly written. I fold the letter under my remaining clothes, in the old cupboard. I tell no one about it; it isn't final yet. Three months and ten days later, I take it out of the cupboard. I am divorced.

*

It's four in the morning; a silver half-moon gleams in the sky. I have folded our few spare sheets and clothes into sacks and stored them in the cupboard. I have said goodbye to Halima, paid what I owed at the corner shop for tea and cooking oil and milk powder. There is just enough money left to get us to Khartoum. I haven't told anyone at the village that we are coming. Father Sayf would say there was no place for us. But if there is no place for us there, where in this world is there a place for us?

I wash out of the bucket in the bathroom, shivering from the cold water. I rub my arms and legs with a few drops of glycerine, empty the last of a bottle of *Bint al Sudan* into my palms. The smell takes me back to the rough concrete bench in the grounds of the hospital, the sight of my mother dabbing scent on her tongue. I have one skirt left. I add a green long-sleeved top that Amal gave me when she was here. I have a green headscarf that almost matches. I wrap it tightly around my head and secure the loose end neatly with a pin. I put on a pair of Muiz's socks before putting my sandals on; Amal says you can get whipped in Khartoum if your feet show. Over the top, I put my last *tobe*. I look down at myself, and for a moment I smile. No one would mistake me for a city girl now.

I rouse the boys and pull Hisham into his clothes. Mansour is instantly alert. He rolls up the two cotton mattresses and drags the beds inside. He gives Najat water, holding the tin mug to her lips. When we are ready to go, I shut the veranda door and look over the empty yard, by the grey dawn light. The lime tree is dead, its dried leaves strewn around its roots. The mud walls have crumbled at the top in the rains; they look like sharp teeth. The water pitcher is mildewed and leaking and the glass in the veranda windows is broken. Then I look at my children, standing patiently by the gate, Mansour holding Najat's hand. These have not been wasted years, nor all unhappy.

'Let's go,' I whisper.

As I padlock the gate behind us, the dog down the street begins to howl. Hisham starts to cry. I feel my resolve falter.

'Come on,' I hiss. 'This is not the time for tears. Let's go.'

I hurry in front, carrying Najat in my arms. Mansour walks beside me, dragging the sack along the ground with both hands. Hisham trails behind, with a plastic bag full of school books. The call for dawn prayers begins as we make our way towards the main road. 'Prayer is better than sleep,' intones the muezzin. I hold my breath, thinking someone will appear in front of us, demand to know where we are going. But the streets remain empty, apart from one or two silent figures in white *jellabiyas*, hurrying along with their heads down.

In the souk, I find a lorry – its sides painted with pictures of the flowing rivers and green grass of Paradise – going to Khartoum; the driver wants more money than I have, but when I offer him the notes, he accepts. I pass Najat up into the cab, and pull myself into the high front seat. The driver's assistant hauls the boys up on top of the sugarcane in the back, and we set off, with the sun rising in a luminous pink sea beyond the river.

Chapter 16

A PLACE CALLED PEACE

Najat wriggles on my lap as the driver winds down his window to speak to the soldier at the checkpoint. I whisper to her to keep still, and stare straight ahead. It is forbidden now for a woman to travel without a male guardian. Alawia's niece wasn't allowed to board her plane to go back to college in Cairo, Amal told me. She had to travel the following week, with her father. I'm relieved when the soldier drags the oil drum to one side and waves us out of Sennar.

We move fast along the empty tarmac. The mud houses grow further apart, giving way to acacia trees, their lower branches eaten away by goats. Grasses sway in the early-morning breeze around the lakes that have formed in the rains. Herds of creamy-coloured cattle gather on the edges of the pools, their flanks hollow, their heads dipped to the water.

The driver puts on a cassette of love songs. I concentrate on the stickers across the top of the windscreen that call on God for protection, the string of prayer beads that dangles from the mirror. Any mention of romance, of tender feelings, hurts me now. The cab smells of petrol; the foot pedals are worn smooth as spoons. We pass the wrecks of other trucks, shredded lengths of burst tyres, and animal skeletons, their white ribcages half buried in sand. The boys cling to the side of the truck, their shirts flying behind them, their eyes closed against the dust. Hisham waves to me, excitedly.

After two hours, we stop at a roadside café. The assistant gives out water from the goatskin lashed to the side of the truck. It is cool and sweet. The driver buys breakfast for all of us; there are four others travelling on the back of the lorry, as well as his young assistant and my boys. Under a sacking shade, we rinse our hands and perch on plastic crates, ready to eat.

I put small pieces of soupy bread into Najat's mouth, and encourage the boys to eat. I feel my spirits lifting. I wish we could stay forever in this shady spot, removed from all the problems behind me and those to come. The other passengers buy dried fish and ropes of salty white cheese from boys competing to sell their produce around the parked lorries.

As we stand up to leave, I become aware of the driver staring at me. Passing Najat back up to me in the cab, his hand brushes my breast. I pull myself away; it might have been an accident. Back on the road, he adjusts his rear-view mirror. I glance up to see him leering at me in the glass. I pull Najat closer, and spend the rest of the journey pressed against the door of the cab, praying for our safe arrival.

*

'What are you doing here?' asks Father Sayf after a brief greeting. He glances out of the window and sees the boys coming along the path with our sack of belongings, helped by a dozen other kids. He has a new chair, which swivels and spins and rocks. It creaks in the silence between us.

'We can't help you, Leila. I told you before.'

I expected this. I know he won't turn us away.

'Am I a branch that has been cut from the tree? I'm not asking for much.'

'We are a children's charity.'

The boys arrive in the doorway. Father Sayf takes in their ragged trousers in which the zips are broken, their faded shirts and broken rubber sandals. Mansour and Hisham's faces are drawn and dusty; Najat is asleep on her feet. Father Sayf rubs his eyes with his palms.

'You look tired,' he says. 'Maybe you could stay a night or two.'

Mama Luban hugs me when we walk into the Green house. She exclaims over the children, shaking their hands and pinching their cheeks while they stand silently in front of her. My daughter looks like I did, she rasps; by God, she thinks she is seeing a spirit. She calls all the children from the Green house and introduces them, then moves stiffly towards the kitchen, saying she is going to fetch juice.

I leave the kids there while I go on to the Blue house. Mama Amaani shakes her head, when I tell her what has happened, and says she always thought Muiz was shifty. She thanks God I am home. Men treat women like cigarettes, she says. They kiss them and throw them away. She is divorced now too.

Amal greets me as if she has been expecting me. She throws me a *jellabiya*, puts our things in her cupboard and sends one of the Blue house children to buy more bread. Later, we eat supper in the *hosh*; we talk about hard things – Faisal's death, my miscarriage, Amal's lack of marriage prospects – but I hear the unfamiliar sound of my own laughter. Amal has qualified as a teacher but she hasn't found a job. She is working at the village, helping to look after the older girls. She gives us her room; the boys sleep head to toe on one bed and Najat and I share the other. I wake up in the night, my heart pounding. Hisham is fast asleep, his arms flung over his head. Mansour lies on his side, his dark eyes open.

'What will happen tomorrow, my mother?'

'You will play with your friends here while I sort things out. Go to sleep now. Don't worry about anything.'

*

Zulima's gate creaks when I push it open. I tiptoe round the side of the house to our mother's room. She is inside, asleep on her bed. I stand and take in the familiar scene. The walls have been repainted and lace curtains move in the breeze at the windows. The room smells of incense and the lino is damp from washing. A dish of dates stands on a table by her chair. Her sleeping form is slight, in a flower-patterned housedress, her hair loose over her shoulders. I sit down by her, listening to her breathing. A sense of peace floods into me. I take my mother's hand and kiss it. She opens her eyes.

'Welcome,' she says. 'Welcome, my daughter.'

Zulima is hanging washing round the back of the house; her face is wet with sweat and in the bright light I see threads of silver running through her black hair.

'By God,' she says, 'what has happened to you? You became so thin.'

'I've come back,' I say. 'I'm never leaving again.'

She pulls me into the house, shouting for the children to come and see Auntie Leila, thanking God that we are alive. She makes tea and we have breakfast together. I tell Zulima everything, all my troubles and humiliation. When I describe the miscarriage, tears flow down my cheeks for the first time. I tell her that the husband I loved has died and in his place is a stranger. I show her the divorce letter.

'You did the right thing,' she says, squeezing my hand. 'God will provide.'

She presses me to eat more sugary doughnuts and makes tea with scalded milk, and when I get up to leave she gives me one of her *tobes*. I can't go round offices looking like a country bumpkin, she says; no one these days wears *tobes* like the one I've got on.

Two days after we arrive, Father Sayf and the new Directors of the village hold a meeting about what to do about us.

Afterwards, Father Sayf calls me into his office and offers us a small allowance for the next six months.

'Of course,' he says, 'it won't be enough to support you here in Khartoum. But it will help you get by in Sennar. Just until you resolve things with your husband.'

'Thank you, Father,' I say. 'God bless you.'

I stop to talk to Alawia on my way out. Father Sayf has a new assistant now, a young man. He raises his eyebrows when Alawia tells him I once did the work he does, and informs me that he is a sociology graduate. The sleeves of his shirt are sharply ironed; a gold watch slips up and down his wrist.

If there is no job for me at the village, I will find one somewhere else. Nothing in this world will drag me back to Sennar. Wagir – the brother who helped me and Zulima escape from Abu Ali's place all those years ago – offers to help me find a place to stay. No one will want to rent a room to a woman without a husband or brother with her. Wagir has always been my favourite brother. His shoulders stoop forwards; his shy manner makes me feel protective towards him. When he hears what I can afford, he suggests that we visit a district I've never heard of – 'Peace'. I'll see why it's called that when I get there, he says.

Loaded with people, the bus makes its way out to the edge of the city, beyond rubbish dumps, past a vast open-air market and tracts of building land. It stops at a crossroads, where spoiled fruit and vegetables, cheap clothes, batteries and cooking pots are piled high. All the passengers climb off, including the ones on the roof. I follow Wagir down an alley between high grass walls. The path is worn smooth by feet, too narrow for cars and only just wide enough for the rickshaw that passes us with several women crammed into the back seat and two more squashed in by the driver. The houses I glimpse through open gates are of mud and straw, patched with plastic or flattened zinc. As we go along, Wagir stops people and murmurs that we are looking for a place to rent, with good people, quiet people.

Before long, we are standing behind a man as he unlocks a small, lopsided door. My first impression is that this is a room for animals, not people. The roof is grass, topped with a layer of plastic sacking. The walls inside are unplastered, made of cracked red mud packed between sticks. There is no electricity; three families share the single tap and latrine outside in the compound. As we stand there, a wind gets up; dust blasts into our faces. We haven't passed a single tree since we arrived.

'Yes,' I say to Wagir. 'This will do.'

*

Peace is not a place to bring up children, I quickly realize. There are houses for drinking, houses for visiting women, houses where politics are discussed, and others where stolen goods are bought and sold. There are fights inside the compounds and on the streets. One night, we hear gunfire. The police seem not to know about Peace. Or if they ever did, they have forgotten it.

I have to learn again how to live in the city. A divorced woman is like freshly roasted meat, Mama Amaani warns me.

Everyone wants to help themselves. I wear the headscarf under my *tobe*, pinned round my face so not a single hair can escape. I keep my eyes to the ground outside the house and come home early in the evenings, and when I go to the market I take Mansour with me. Nobody bothers me.

Our room is stifling in the day, with only one small window and the open doorway to catch the breeze. At night, it's cold; we sleep on mats on the ground. Mice run over everything. In the morning, I see their footprints on the pillows. I hang our food from the ceiling, in plastic bags; they eat the soap and the candles. I tell the children we are having an adventure, and soon we will be living in our real house.

My new landlord is from the West African people. His wife goes out before it gets light in the mornings; she works as a cleaner, in a private house in the city. She comes back after dark, carrying bags of vegetables, and charcoal, and begins cooking. The landlord drinks spirits distilled from sorghum, which he pours from a china teapot; he shouts at his children and sometimes when he's drunk he takes off his belt and lashes them. The first time I see it, I challenge him. He staggers on his feet and says: who do I think I am, and what boy raised by a woman ever grew up to be any good? My heart is thudding as I go back into our room. I have to get us out of here.

My brothers and sisters never fail me. Amal comes to visit us on Fridays, and brings stews from Mama Amaani and *bousbousa* semolina cake from Mama Luban. Zulima has the children to stay; she lends me clothes and makes me laugh. Wagir gives me small amounts of money, enough for my bus fares into the city, and takes the boys to the river for lemonade.

I can't rely on their kindness forever. I have to find a way myself. Normally, people in our society find jobs through their relatives. They have an uncle in a bank, who puts in a good word, or a cousin who works in a company where they need someone . . . I have to make the connections myself. I write lists of people to see, people I met through my work, officials I came into contact with when I worked at the village.

Even though I don't sleep well and we don't eat well, I feel full of purpose. Every day, I get up early, fetch water from the tap and sweep the sandy floor. I bath Najat and give the children a breakfast of bread and tea, sometimes with jam or cheese. I tell Mansour to look after the others, and to forbid them to go outside the compound, and I leave. I go into the city, looking for work. I take my certificates from Jordan. I move from office to office, trying to find people who will see me.

Khartoum has changed. Empty land has filled up with new houses, some of them three or four storeys high; apartments stand where goats once roamed. New office blocks have sprung up in the centre, some covered with dark windows. There are supermarkets lit with fluorescent light bulbs and stocked with nappies, frozen meat, cosmetics. New mosques, new roads, new roundabouts, and, everywhere, advertisements – for cigarettes, televisions, bleaching creams. The Arab souk is crowded with southerners, refugees from the war, selling watches, aftershave, shoes. Packs of children live on the street; they have sores on their skin and red-rimmed eyes, and are dressed in rags. Over everything, stiff-winged kites circle on the air currents.

A Place Called Peace

One afternoon, as I return home at the end of a fruitless day waiting outside the offices of important people, a woman walks towards me in the alley. Something about the way she moves makes me raise my head. I see an old woman, her lips painted as red as her ragged dress, one arm of which hangs loose by her side. I drop my handbag and almost faint. It's Quarratulain.

*

We have been back in Khartoum for two months when a boy comes with a message for me. I must hurry to my sister's house. From when I get off the bus, I can hear Zulima wailing. I run down the alley. The gate is open, with women crowding around it. I push past them, around the side of the compound. On the threshold of our mother's room, I hesitate. I ask God to help me face what is coming. Zulima is on her knees in the middle of the room, shrieking and tearing at her clothes while two other women try to restrain her. Our mother is on the bed. She is covered with a sheet, and utterly still.

I have often thought about the moment of my mother's death. From the day I first went to visit her at the hospital, she seemed only half attached to this world. Still, this moment shocks me as much as if I had never imagined that she could pass away. My shouts join Zulima's; I have that sense again of the world tilting, the ground under my feet becoming insubstantial. I hear myself wailing that it can't be true, that I haven't said goodbye to her. Almost immediately, I hear a sharp slapping sound. My hand flies to my face. Zulima's mother-in-law stands in front of me. 'Enough,' she says. 'You have important work to do.'

She clears the room, and brings bowls of water and soap and clean cotton. Zulima is menstruating; she can't help. I wash my mother's body, as if she were my child. Her limbs are light and cool, her face beautiful. I wash her long hair, and gently comb it. By the time we are finished, I am calm. For the first time in my life, I am able to kiss her face. I kiss her forehead; I kiss both soft cheeks. I pray to God to grant her eternal life. I dab her forehead and wrists with her scent, and we wrap her in white cloths. The imam leads prayers for her; then, while the sun remains high and fierce, the men bear away her body for burial. Zulima and I sit close to each other on mats on the ground in her room; crowds of women cry and talk all around us. From beyond the walls of the compound, as the sun sets, the call of the muezzin floats down to us.

La Allah l'il Allah. There is no God but God.

*

After the death of my mother, I resume my search for work. It's hard, putting on a mask of cheerfulness and strength that I don't feel. I worry all the time about leaving the children alone; once the weather gets cooler, I sometimes shut them in the room. Mansour finds it impossible to keep Hisham in the compound and away from his friends on the street. I think often about our mother, how she used to leave me and Zulima locked in a room while she took her bread and spices to the market. Now I understand why she did it.

Back at Peace in the evenings, I continue to puzzle over the lives of the abandoned once we become adults. Does every village girl, if she marries, have to resign herself to dependence on her husband, no matter how he behaves? What happens to her and her children if, like me, they are abandoned again? And what about the boys and the unmarried girls? What happens if they want to study, or travel for work abroad? How can they achieve anything, without a family behind them to encourage them, make introductions, help them when they stumble? Who can any of us turn to, in times of trouble, or need?

Mohamed and Mahmoud, those bright young twin boys who are now men, clean cars by the side of the street for a living. My sister Ekhlas lives on a building site with her husband; he guards the sacks of sand and cement in exchange for their being allowed to raise their babies under a canvas shade in the half-built walls. Another brother, a graduate from the Islamic university, helps behind the counter in a shop selling mobile telephones. Without family, we continue to struggle.

Quarratulain visits. When she recognized me, that evening on the street, she said she expected me to shun her. I invited her to visit us at home and she came the next day, with a thin, dusty girl who she introduced as her daughter. She brought sweets for my children and while they were busy eating them, she told me about her life since I last saw her, ten years ago. She was seduced by the man who worked in the photography shop. He invited her to meet his sisters but when she went to the address, only he was there. He forced himself on her; he said that if she told anyone he would go to the police and accuse her of prostitution. She was fourteen; she didn't know she was pregnant when the mothers at the village realized her condition.

After she was whipped and forced to leave the village, she was taken in by a woman she half knew, who used to sell tea outside her primary school. The woman married her to one of her relatives, an old man. After a few months, the old man divorced her and she was on the streets again, with her baby. She ended up living with a woman who ran a brothel. She is still there now, she says, looking at the ground, her voice flat.

After she has gone, I sit for a long time in the dark compound. I was brought up by Mama Luban to see good and evil as separate things, to see life in black and white. Once, I would have done anything rather than sit with a woman in Quarratulain's situation. I would never have allowed her to kiss my children, or talk with them. Now, things are more complicated. Quarratulain made a mistake; she was foolish. But in her heart, she isn't bad. I decide that the next time Quarratulain comes to our door, I will sit her down. I have something serious to discuss with her.

After a year of searching, I find a job. Not just any job, but a job that might have been made for me. It is with a small charity that helps women who become pregnant before marriage, and their children. The social workers try to arrange marriages between the girls and the fathers of their babies; if that isn't possible, they try to recruit foster carers to look after the babies, so that they grow up in families rather than institutions. They train the foster carers and pay them a small allowance, with money from the government. If possible, they help the women to keep in contact with their children. I work as the receptionist in the office. From this moment onwards, our life improves. My salary is small, but it's enough to make changes.

At about the same time, to general rejoicing, the war between the north and the south ends, with the signing of a peace agreement.

With Wagir's help, I find another place for us to stay, in a more respectable neighbourhood. I rent a room and a veranda; we have our own gas ring inside the room and share the tap and the latrine with just one other family. The floor is concrete and there is electricity; Mansour can study in the evenings. As soon as I am able, I make a trip to Sennar and bring our beds, the fan and the old television to Khartoum, on the back of a truck.

Among these things, I find the notes I made on the idea of a self-help society for the abandoned. It's even clearer to me now that we need something like this: a society to act as a family for abandoned people who are adults, who cannot live like children in orphanages. And at the same time, we need to campaign to make people understand that we are not bad, we are not responsible for the actions of our mothers and fathers, and that if people treat us well – give us a chance – we can live good lives, as good as anyone else.

People at the charity where I work say I should speak out about the abandoned. I shake my head and change the subject. Except with Amal and Wagir, who came with me from those cots, I can't get the name 'Mygoma orphanage' out of my mouth.

I see a great deal of suffering in my job at Hope and Homes for Children. Sex outside marriage is illegal in Sudan. Some of the girls and women who come to us have been flogged, like Quarratulain. But that is not the source of their pain. Almost all of them have been rejected by their families, for giving birth outside marriage. What is the pain of a whip, compared with the agony of being thrown out of your home?

We have quite good success in finding foster homes for the babies. Attitudes are changing, but the stigma is still there; to call someone a 'child of sin' is still one of the worst insults there is. People still believe that the abandoned bring bad luck to a household, and that girls will repeat the behaviour. The prejudice hurts. But I can't fight in the dust any more, like I did with Wifaq all those years ago. I have to find another way to fight. I keep working on the plans for the society. I discuss ideas with Zulima, Amal and the twins, Mohamed and Mahmoud; they all support the idea of a self-help organization that can give advice, support, social help and grants to those in need. One day, the plans are ready. I take them to the Government department that gives permission to set up charities.

When Quarratulain comes again with her daughter, I invite her to live with us. I tell her that if she accepts, she will have to change her behaviour. She will have to live like a good and serious woman, to be a mother to her child, and to do nothing at all that will bring shame or problems for me and my children. She cannot even look at a boy, or a man. Life is too serious for love, I tell her. But if she can do that, she is welcome and we will share with her whatever we have. She walks round in circles in the *hosh* when I've finished. She is thin inside her red dress; her wooden sandals are worn down at the heels and the nail varnish on her hand is chipped. She returns and sits opposite me. It's a still, warm night and the neighbourhood is quiet.

'I don't know,' she says. 'I want to live a good life again, for the sake of my daughter. But I don't know if I can.' Her face gleams in the moonlight; her eyes are soft, troubled. She sleeps with us that night, outside, under the warm blanket of darkness. In the morning, she irons my *tobe* for me before I go to the office and shares our tea and bread, she and her daughter laughing with the children.

When I come home, she is still there. This is how Quarratulain joins us in our new life. She is not the only one who will become part of our family.

Chapter 17

SUNRISE

Another year has passed. My mouth is dry and my hands are clammy. My knees feel as if they will not hold me as I walk up the three wooden steps and on to the stage. It's mid-morning; the university hall is cool, the long windows draped with bright silk curtains. In front of me is a mass of people, men and women, mainly young, all looking at me. I have notes in my hands, but as I steady myself behind the lectern I put them down. I hold on to the lectern with both hands and take a deep breath. There is a microphone, but I keep my voice low and quiet. I greet everybody, wishing for peace to be upon them. I tell them that my name is Leila Aziz. That once I was abandoned. And I begin.

'Most of you here will not have been to a place called Mygoma orphanage. I spent the early part of my life there from the age of about fifteen months until I was three. We lived mainly in our cots. But I was always searching for a face, a voice, a pair of loving arms . . . Some of the carers were kind; some were not. They believed that it was a better fate for us to die than face the life that awaited us.'

Only a few of us survived Mygoma, I tell them, although I didn't fully understand that till later, when I became an adult. 'We died of chest infections, diarrhoea, neglect, doctors would say. I believe we died too of broken hearts.'

My nerves disappear as I begin speaking. I do not pick up my notes. I speak about myself, and my brothers and sisters. I tell them that we are human beings, like anyone else. We are not born with the word 'abandoned' tattooed on our foreheads. We are not responsible for the actions of our parents. All human beings come to this world in one way, I remind them. And if, unfortunately, some babies are born before marriage, they are not the guilty ones. The prejudice against the abandoned comes from our society, not from our religion. Islam encourages us to care for the orphans.

Our parents are people from the society, I tell them. People like the ones in this audience. Ordinary Sudanese people, who made a mistake. We are part of this society. I tell them what it's like to be called a *bint haram*, daughter of sin, when you are a child at school. How much it means when someone accepts you for what you are, invites you to their home like any other child. Treats you as if you are special, and worthwhile.

I remind them that babies are still coming into the world before marriage. Every week, here in our city, more are abandoned – near mosques, or in hospitals, by roadsides, and in rubbish baskets left by mothers too frightened to behave in the right way.

I speak for about twenty minutes. When I finish, I thank them for listening. I ask them to remember me, remember us, when they hear people saying bad things about the abandoned. And to think again about what they say themselves. What they do themselves. What they think in their hearts.

The audience claps and claps. People come to shake my hand and congratulate me. There is a journalist there from one of the newspapers, and people from the United Nations. The last person to shake my hand is a woman with a soft, slim hand. She is wearing a cream headscarf, a matching cream blouse and gold earrings. Her face is intelligent, with almond-shaped eyes behind her glasses. She holds my hand for a long time, then she asks, her voice breaking, whether I remember a girl called Abir?

*

The same subject arises week after week in meetings at work. What can we do about Hala? This girl was brought to Mygoma orphanage by the police as a baby, they say. She was adopted by a man and woman with no children of their own. This couple brought her up, from the age of one, in a small town in eastern Sudan. Then the husband died. The wife, by this time, had two more children. Her family agreed to take her in, but they said she must return Hala to the orphanage. They said that the reason the husband had died was because she had taken in an abandoned child who brought ill fortune with her.

The woman had no choice. She brought Hala back to Mygoma orphanage again. For the first week, the girl didn't speak or eat. Now, a few months have passed and she is wild. She swears, tells lies, wets the bed. Several people have taken pity on her and let her come to their homes, thinking they might adopt her. All of them have brought her back to the orphanage within days, saying that the child is possessed by evil spirits and that no normal family can live with her. She is seven years old. What can we do about Hala? the social workers ask, rubbing their eyes.

I never comment when the subject of Hala is raised. I listen, but I say nothing. One morning, in the meeting, when the question is asked, I raise my hand.

'I would like to take Hala . . .' I say.

'Yes, Leila?' says the Director of Hope and Homes for Children.

'For a picnic.'

The Director looks disappointed.

'Good,' he says. 'Take her.'

The following Friday, I go in a rickshaw to Mygoma. Hala is waiting for me in the office; she is a slim girl, looking younger than her age. She has watchful brown eyes, a wide mouth and small ears flat against her head, with empty holes in them. Her hair is dusty, her dress stained. She gives me a mistrustful look and ignores the hand I stretch out to her.

I take her to a park near the river. It's cool so near to the water, and the eucalyptus and neem trees remind me of Sennar.

We sit down in the shade of a tree and I take out the biscuits I've brought. Hala rips the packet open and crams several into her mouth; she swallows them absentmindedly, staring around. After a few minutes, she runs off to play. There are other children in the park, chasing each other, laughing together, talking. Hala ignores them all. She plays alone, talking to herself. After a while, she comes back and sits down next to me again.

I ask her if she's hungry, and she says she is. We go to a café and she chooses the biggest picture on the menu – a hamburger, with chips. She eats it like a wild animal. Then she grabs a large packet of sweets and begins to throw them into her mouth. My heart is very full as I sit and look at her. I understand where this bad behaviour of Hala's comes from. It comes from the feeling that nobody loves her. Nobody cares about her. She is not special to anyone in this world. I recognize myself in this unhappy child. When she has finished eating, she sits in silence, yawning and biting her nails. She agrees to come home and meet my children.

I have already told Mansour, Hisham and Najat about this girl. When we get back to the house, they are watching television, sitting on the floor, with Quarratulain and her daughter. Hala sits herself down on the end of the row and watches cartoons with them. When they are finished, the children include her in their talk. She doesn't say much. Najat shows her the game she plays, clapping hands and singing. Hala is older than Najat but she fixes her eyes on her and copies what she does. We all eat supper together in the yard before I take her back to Mygoma. She darts through the gate like a cat, slamming it behind her.

Over the next few weeks, I bring Hala home for more visits, and sometimes she stays the night with us. She is troublesome and argumentative; she hates sharing and easily gets angry. She is kind and gentle when she feels safe; she cries when I say it's time for her to go. I talk often with the children about it before I make an appointment to see the Director. When I do, I tell him that all of us understand Hala's situation, and we would like her to join our family.

*

We are seven at home now, in our one room and veranda. Me, my sons Mansour and Hisham, my daughter Najat and my new daughter Hala, plus Quarratulain and her girl, Bibi. It's crowded; in cold weather, we women and girls sleep in the room and the boys sleep on the veranda. On hot nights, we all sleep outside in the *hosh*. Najat shares my bed and Mansour sleeps on a board balanced on a table by the wall of the house. Our yard is always draped with drying clothes, and we have to make whatever beans or vegetables or meat we can afford on my small salary stretch to feed many mouths. But we are happy. We eat together. We sing, laugh, chat.

The children attend school and play and sometimes quarrel. My dark-eyed Mansour remains a serious child, tall and responsible. Hisham is carefree and a joker. He makes everyone laugh. Najat is always on the move, bossier than either of her brothers. My sister Quarratulain has begun to cover her hair. She gets up to pray with me in the early mornings and when our brothers and sisters from the village visit, she is not ashamed. She can hold her head up. She helps me as much as I help her; she watches Najat and Hala while I'm out, helped by her daughter Bibi. She makes the stew for lunch, and washes the children's clothes. She is patient with Hala, and kind in her own rough way.

Hala gets better day by day. She is with younger children at school; I have been to speak to her teachers about what she has endured in her short life but not all of them are understanding. I explain to her that she does not need to take food from the kitchen in secret – that everything in this family belongs to her as much as to the others. I tell her that she had a mother who loved her but had to give her up when she was born. Then she had another mother who loved her as well but wasn't able to do the right thing because of other factors. I tell her that now she has me; I am another mother to her and for as long as I live she will be my daughter. I will never abandon her.

Muiz comes sometimes from Sennar to see the children. We are polite with each other, but distant. I don't ask him about his new wife and he doesn't tell me. He hasn't found a job. The children scream with joy to see their father. I feel sad for them when he leaves; Najat cries, and asks why her father doesn't live with us any more.

'Shut up,' I hear Mansour say fiercely to her. 'Don't be a baby. One day he will come back.'

There is something that I have had in my mind for a long time. One day, when I have time, I get the bus to the central mosque. In the Arab souk, women sit on the ground, selling peanuts, heaps of limes or red chillis, small bags of salt or

black peppercorns, or green sachets of freshly ground corian-
der seeds. I walk through the meat section, where the butchers
hack up the glistening carcasses of goats and sheep. Through
the vegetable market, past gleaming black aubergines and
mountains of tomatoes and sacks of red onions. I walk
through the gold souk, where women cluster at the windows,
pointing at wedding sets, at earrings and bangles. Into the perfume section, where Copts mix oils of sandalwood and musk
and roses. I walk through the other side, to where the car-
penters are gathered.

I see him, bent over a lathe outside the workshop, before he
sees me. His tall figure still looks the same, in a ragged shirt
and trousers, his feet in loose leather sandals. I stand and
watch him for a moment. He turns round and wipes his forehead on his sleeve; the light is behind him, I still can't see his
face. He starts to laugh.

'By God,' he exclaims. 'Little Sister.' He throws down his
tools and pumps my hand in his. His hands are still delicate,
the long fingers fine, despite the strength in them. 'Where
have you been? God willing, you are strong, your children are
all well – and your husband?'

He calls the boy to bring chairs and fetch something cold to
drink, and we sit outside the workshop. The ground is sprink-
led with sawdust and bent nails. A cat sleeps under the lathe,
twitching and lashing its tail on the ground. Rashid's eyes are
bloodshot, I notice, and his hand trembles. For a while I
cannot speak. The understanding between us goes deeper
than words. I bring the cold Pepsi bottle to my lips, feeling its
refreshing sweetness in my mouth.

When I do start talking, I can't stop. I tell him about my life in Sennar, and how it ended. I tell him about my new job, and our family. I tell him all about Zulima, and her five children.

'Is the husband a decent man?' he asks, looking into the distance; the sounds of the souk ring in the air, the cries of boys offering to carry shopping, women haggling, men calling out prices. From all around us, closer by, come the sounds of sawing, hammering, of things being made. The air smells of varnish, and frankincense.

'Thank God,' I say. 'He has not been a bad husband to her, in the end. She is proud of her children.'

As I'm speaking, trying to feel more enthusiasm for Zulima's husband than I really do, I finally see something I have not seen in the last twenty years. Rashid wanted to marry Zulima. And she wanted to marry him. My eyes fill with sudden tears. This keeps happening to me now; my dry-eyed days are gone. I turn and reach for his hand.

'You would have been my brother twice over,' I say. 'If things had been different.'

He nods. 'We were all young, then,' he says, his voice choked with feeling. 'What did we know of life?'

'Life.' I smile, finishing the Pepsi. 'The All-time Deceiver.'

*

With Abir's assistance, we succeed in getting our organization registered with the government. We call it *Sehrish*, or Sunrise, for the light we hope it will shed. Our aim is to help young abandoned people who have nowhere else to turn, and to educate our society, to show them that the abandoned are human beings like any others.

Rashid supports our charity from the little he makes selling his furniture. Zulima's older daughters, Habibi and Jamila, help out in the office. Quarratulain marries a policeman; sometimes she takes in one of the unmarried girls who come to us under cover of dark, desperate and afraid, with illegal babies in their bellies or their arms. Amal is like a mother to all of them. We are again as close as when we were small girls.

My children are healthy and kind. Hala stops wetting the bed and begins to be able to concentrate on her schoolwork, and the dark circles under her eyes lighten. When people from the charity ask me, 'How is Hala?' I ask them: why do you enquire about Hala? I have four children, and Hala is one of them. All are beloved to me.

Muiz continues to come and visit his children; I never try to prevent it. He treats Hala as kindly as the others, sometimes more kindly. He has no children with his second wife. Seven years after we divorce, he begs me to remarry him and allow him to come back to his family. I agree. When you are a young girl, you seek many things from a husband. When you are a woman, you learn to look at what this man brings and over-look the things he does not or cannot offer. I never wanted to bring up children without a father.

My health has suffered from the long years of hardship. I have high blood pressure, and something called goitre. I sit on a chair to say my prayers, like Nanny Souad used to, at the Institute for the Protected. I am at peace with myself.

At the age of almost forty, I leave my job with the charity to

work full-time on setting up our new organization. I give talks
to the radio, to the newspapers, to audiences at clubs, universi-
ties and businesses. Sometimes Amal or Wagir or Quarratulain
come with me and we speak together. I don't shake any more,
or fight for breath, when I stand up in front of people.
Everyone knows I was once abandoned, and that I lived in
Mygoma. I speak from my heart and the talk I give is different
every time, the same every time. I am not ashamed. I understand now that God gave me this loud voice for a reason – to
speak out on behalf of my brothers and sisters, the abandoned.
They are my family. It is among them – and those who cared
for us that I have truly found goodness. Found love.

*

*Sometimes, I visit Mygoma orphanage. I hear the sound of crying from
when I enter the gate from the street. I push open the door to the baby
room, breathing in the smell that I knew so well as a child. Some of the
babies lie listlessly in their cots; some stand up and watch. I go from
cot to cot, picking them up, kissing them. Looking into their eyes,
laughing. I spend as long as I can and I pick up every single baby.*

*All the children long for the same thing that I longed for: for eyes
that see them, a voice that caresses them, arms that do more than
move them from one place to another. They long to see, in the face of
another, that they exist. That they matter.*

*Things are a little better at Mygoma now, thanks be to God. Fewer
babies die. They have more toys, better clothes; better hygiene and
care. But the place still echoes with the sound of children crying. The
air is still thick with grief.*

Sunrise

Beyond the baby rooms, outside in our society, we who survived are breaking the silence. We are trying to bring the unfuture to an end, for our own generation and the generations yet to be born.

God willing, we will succeed.

Glossary

Angareeb – traditional wooden-framed bed, strung with rope

Asida – Arab dish consisting of a cooked lump of dough

Dukhan – perfumed smoke bath, for women

Eid – religious festival

Fakir – a holy man, especially one practising feats of endurance or magic

Henana – woman who applies henna patterns to married women's hands and feet

Hosh – outdoor yard, used for sleeping, eating, cooking and washing

Jellabiya – long, loose, white garment traditionally worn by Sudanese men; also the housedress worn by women at home

Kisra – a thin pancake-like leavened bread made from whole sorghum flour

Rakuba – open-sided structure that gives shelter from the sun

Sheikh – holy man, often a religious leader

Sibha – string of thirty-three Muslim prayer beads, for use in reciting the ninety-nine names of God

---

Glossary

Tobe – the three metres of gauzy material traditionally worn as a head-to-toe wrap over their clothes by married Sudanese women when out in public

Zar – custom originating in Ethiopia, involving possession of an individual (usually female) by a spirit

Zir – clay water pitcher, used for storing and cooling water